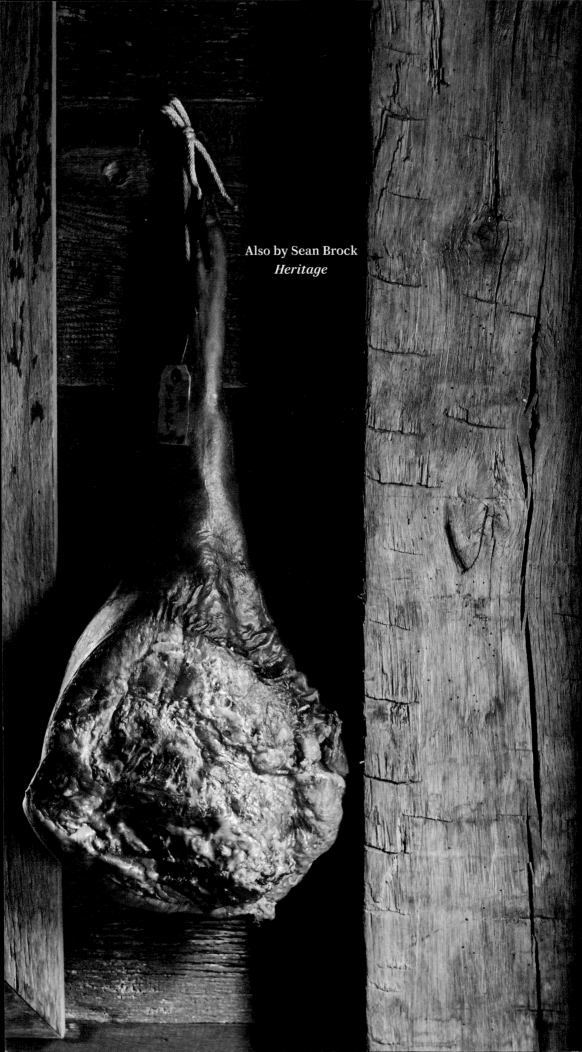

Also by Sean Brock
Heritage

SOUTH

ESSENTIAL RECIPES AND
NEW EXPLORATIONS

SEAN BROCK

With LUCAS WEIR and MARION SULLIVAN
Photographs by PETER FRANK EDWARDS

Artisan | New York

Library of Congress Cataloging-in-Publication Data is on file.
ISBN 978-1-57965-716-1 (hardcover)
ISBN 978-1-57965-967-7 (signed edition)

Cover design and art direction by Michelle Ishay-Cohen
Design by Raphael Geroni and Nina Simoneaux

Artisan books are available at special discounts when purchased in bulk for
premiums and sales promotions as well as for fund-raising or educational use. Special
editions or book excerpts also can be created to specification. For details, contact the
Special Sales Director at the address below, or send an e-mail to specialmarkets@
workman.com.

For speaking engagements, contact speakersbureau@workman.com.

Published by Artisan
A division of Workman Publishing Co., Inc.
225 Varick Street
New York, NY 10014-4381
artisanbooks.com

Artisan is a registered trademark of Workman Publishing Co., Inc.

Published simultaneously in Canada by Thomas Allen & Son, Limited

Printed in China

10 9 8 7 6 5 4 3 2

To Leo

INTRODUCTION

I hope that someday I will be remembered for helping people everywhere understand that Southern food should be considered among the most revered cuisines of the world. Far from the stereotypes of heavy, greasy, and overdone dishes, the food throughout the South is vibrant, diverse, seasonal, and evolving. I don't need to preach this to Southerners. But even if you don't live in the South, the ingredients and cooking techniques that make up the Southern canon ought to be part of your pantry. These heirloom ingredients and culinary traditions are part of *American* history, not just the history of the South. The traditions have stood the test of time because the food is both insanely delicious and nutritious. As human beings, we are hardwired to crave food that is good for our bodies and good for our souls. Southern food satisfies those needs for me, and I think you'll agree when you try these recipes. It is an honor to share my favorite classic Southern recipes and my more modern creations, too, for you to cook for the people around your table.

I feel lucky to be able to cook Southern food for a living; it is a gift I am grateful for every day. Feeding people is a privilege, and I have spent my life observing how food nurtures and connects us. Food is medicine, after all—it can heal the soul, help mend a broken heart, or calm a busy mind. The craft of cooking, specifically cooking a cuisine that is so rich with tradition, has allowed me to see this in action all over the world and experience how deeply food contributes to our culture. Cuisine is our common thread, and it allows us to speak the same language even when we don't. But what is cuisine? I define it as a combination of three important factors: the people cooking the food and the cultural experiences and history they bring to the table; the physical geography of the place where the food is cooked; and the plants and animals that grow there.

When I think about where American Southern food fits in the scheme of the world's cuisines, I am filled with pride. I enjoy discovering the links between different cultures that prove we all crave the same kinds of comfort. For example, almost every culture has a beloved porridge or soup or slow-roasted meat dish that is at heart the same as our favorites in the South, only differing in the ingredients that are unique to each particular place. For example, Italy's *tortellini en brodo*, the chicken and dumplings of the American South, and Korea's *dak kalguksu* are all dishes based primarily on water, chicken, and flour. And all these dishes have two things in common: simplicity and comfort. These traditional dishes have stood the test of time and show how we are all more similar than we are different.

This book is filled with recipes for the foods of my South, but if you dig a little deeper, you just might discover that the foundations of Southern cooking can inspire your own dishes, no matter where you call home. Soul food is soul food wherever you are. Cooking doesn't require complex recipes to leave a lasting memory. I truly believe that if food is made mindfully, that's really all that matters. We are all chasing the same sensations or emotions.

THE BEGINNING

I was born and raised in the southern Appalachian Mountains of Virginia, and I moved to Charleston, South Carolina, to attend cooking school while still in my teens. That move was my first culinary culture shock, and I fell head over heels in love with the city and its food. After stints in Richmond, Virginia, and Nashville, Tennessee, I returned to Charleston to take the executive chef position at McCrady's. It was there that I first started to define my relationship with Lowcountry cuisine and, more broadly, Southern cuisine. In the beginning, around 2006, McCrady's was a restaurant where food was not only sustenance but also entertainment, where experimentation was a significant impetus for creativity. This was also a time when I realized that I needed to get back to the dirt to find true inspiration. So I tried farming for the first time on my own, without the guidance of my grandmother Audrey, experimenting with new plants and vegetable varietals we could serve at the restaurant. I had gardened growing up, but with my team at McCrady's, I took it to another level. Working with the soil reinforced for me just how difficult it can be to grow truly delicious foods and get them out of the field and onto the plate.

Some of the ingredients that we have incorporated into our culinary vocabulary and even take for granted—think Sea Island red peas, Jimmy Red corn, and Carolina Gold rice—were barely in our collective consciousness ten years ago, but now you can go online and order these Southern heritage ingredients with one click. This is extraordinary considering how closely I used to guard the handfuls of seeds given to me by people like Glenn Roberts of Anson Mills and Bill Best, a professor, farmer, and seed saver in Kentucky. It proves that we can actually contribute to our cuisine one seed at a time and really make a difference.

Later, during my years at Husk, I cooked the traditional dishes that showcased the importance of ingredients that scholar-revivalists like Dr. David Shields and Glenn Roberts have worked so painstakingly to revive. These were the iconic grains, legumes, and seeds that formed the foundation of the Carolina Rice Kitchen, the historic food-ways that underpin Lowcountry cuisine as we know it today. You may have eaten hoppin' John or a bowl of grits, but until you try dishes like these made with the original, heritage ingredients, you have no idea how good they can be.

Cooking a cuisine using these heritage ingredients demanded a certain simplicity and needed to be presented in a context that made sense. Husk became my worship house for classic Southern dishes. And it not only filled a void in Charleston (and subsequently in Nashville; Greenville, South Carolina; and Savannah, Georgia) but also told the story of Southern cuisine—and explored its future too. Reconnecting with, understanding, and respecting these culinary traditions set the stage for innovation.

Keep in mind that Southern cuisine is relatively young. As we recognize it today, it is at best a little more than 250 years old. In contrast to the culinary traditions of France, Italy, Japan, China, and many other nations and regions, Southern food is still in its infancy. Southern cuisine has had to deal with some setbacks too. In the years following the Great Depression, World War II, and the subsequent population boom and increased urbanization of the region, many rural culinary traditions and ingredients were lost. Agricultural development favored efficiency and yield over flavor and nutrition. It all created a situation where traditional recipes made with the available local ingredients were no longer hitting the mark.

It's no wonder that more flavorful ingredients like sugar began to be added to Southern classics like cornbread. The natural sugars in the dried corn were no longer there, so cooks did what they could to make cornbread taste the way it ought to. The flavors of rice, beans, and even livestock were similarly affected by the changing agricultural practices. But in the years since I began cooking in the Lowcountry, the vast majority of the heritage ingredients that once filled the region's pantry have been restored. I'm proud to have played some part in that, and I now want to turn my efforts toward doing the same for my home region of Appalachia and, hopefully, for the South as a whole. I'll spend the rest of my life trying to restore our traditions and figuring out where the cuisine can go next.

MICROREGIONS OF THE SOUTH

The American South has a geographical area roughly equal to that of continental Europe. How many distinct cuisines can you name in continental Europe? I'd venture that almost every state in the South has just as many. My home state of Virginia is a perfect example of this. There is no such as thing as "Virginian cuisine"; most people just call the cooking there Southern. Yet the cornbread and soup beans I grew up eating in southwest Virginia are a world away from the crab cakes and sugar toads eaten along the estuary of the Chesapeake Bay. The food in the parts of Virginia that border Kentucky is different from that found in the region that borders Tennessee. As you delve deeper and deeper, it becomes clear that the monolith of the American South is, in reality, a collection of many microregions, bound by certain cultural connections but differing wildly in terms of cuisine.

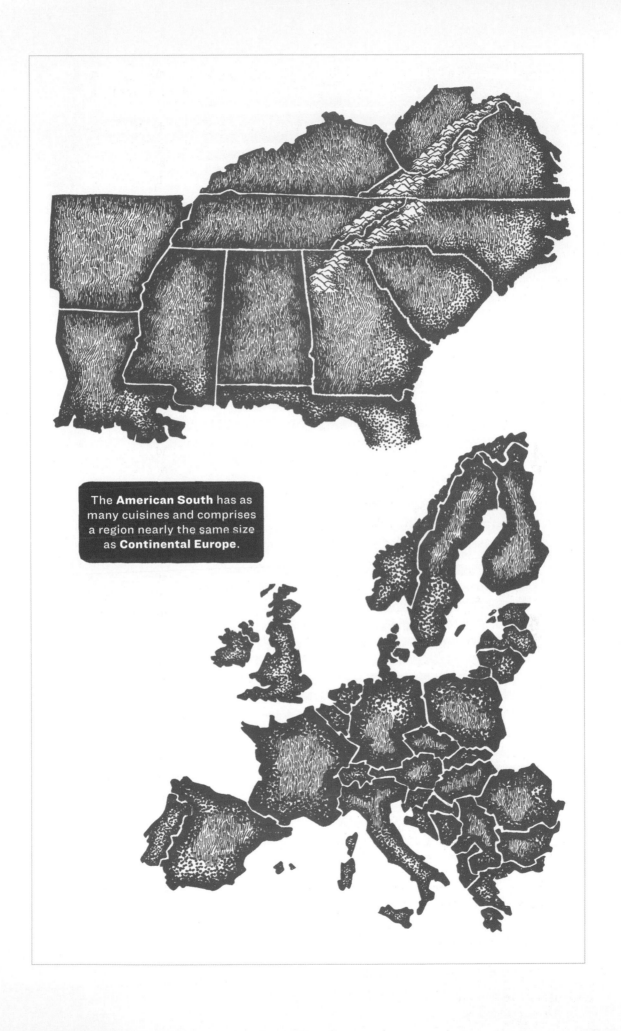

The **American South** has as many cuisines and comprises a region nearly the same size as **Continental Europe**.

South Carolina illustrates this fact particularly well. The state has three distinct geographical regions as you travel from the northwestern corner down to the coast. The cuisine of Upstate, which encompasses towns such as Greenville and Spartanburg, contrasts with that of the Midlands, and it actually has far more in common with the food of the Smoky Mountains of Tennessee than with the food of Charleston and the Lowcountry. But it would be a mistake to suggest that the Lowcountry is itself a homogenous region. The distance separating the two coastal cities of Charleston and Savannah is pretty negligible in terms of modern travel. And in a superficial way, the two places have the same natural feel. But the dishes you'll find on the tables of these cities tell a tale of two divergent cuisines. The pantries are quite similar, but they are funneled through the different cultural, economic, and historical experiences of each locale. In a variety of ways, Savannah's founding and its first few decades of development are in sharp contrast to the path Charleston went down. Savannah didn't start its life under direct colonial rule. Charleston was named after King Charles II. Savannah's early years had a remarkably egalitarian bent. Charleston was a full-blown capitalist port city.

These social differences can be pretty succinctly summed up by one particular ingredient plentiful in both cities: whiting, *Merlangius merlangus*. In Charleston, whiting is considered poverty food, something to eat when you can't catch or afford something else. It's most certainly looked down upon by fine dining restaurants there. Just down the coast, though, still in the Lowcountry, Savannah fell in love with whiting, which is plentiful and delicious, before any sort of social stigma had a chance to stick. To me, it is *the* fish of Savannah. That's what you cook there, and that's what you eat, no matter who you are or what side of the tracks you hail from. A similar story is played out countless times with countless ingredients all across the American South.

Shrimp and Grits

Shrimp and grits is the perfect dish to use in illustrating how different the food of the microregions of the South can be, even when made with the same base ingredients.

Corn speaks of terroir. The corn grown around Nashville, where I live, tastes completely different from the corn grown in the Lowcountry, because of the different varieties from different cultures, and different time periods, grown in different soils and in different climates. But it's not just agricultural differences: The preparation of the corn differs in each microregion. In Charleston, for example, grits tend to be creamy and luxurious—decadent, even—often with the addition of cream and cheese. The grits in Nashville offer up a very simple, straightforward corn flavor, with little or no dairy added.

The shrimp is a good indicator of location too. Order shrimp and grits in Nashville, and you'll likely get giant Georgia Royal Reds. They're flash-frozen while still on the boat somewhere off the coast of Georgia and then shipped to landlocked locations. In the Lowcountry, you'll find great fresh brown or white shrimp from the local waters.

Finally, the bowl of shrimp and grits is often finished with the soulful flavors representing each microregion's cuisine. I'm referring to ingredients and tastes that give each place its distinct feel—whether it's andouille sausage in New Orleans, Louisiana, or fresh ramps in the Smoky Mountains. When you lay out all these factors, you get a sort of shrimp and grits "flavor matrix" that shows how Southern cuisines can differ from one region to the next.

Use these examples as a jumping-off point for your own bowl of shrimp and grits. There are as many ways to customize a bowl as you can imagine. But in this book, you'll find two of my favorite ways to serve shrimp and grits (see pages 61 and 62). One is a

	SHRIMP	GRITS	LOCAL SOUL/UMAMI
LOWCOUNTRY	Fresh white or brown shrimp	Creamy and rich	Tomatoes, bacon
APPALACHIA	Boat-frozen Royal Reds	No-nonsense, straight-forward corn flavor	Ramps, morels, salt pork
GULF COAST	Fresh white or brown shrimp	Cheesy	Okra, andouille sausage

super-simple preparation that is an ode to a Southern cooking hero and would be in contention for my number one choice for a last meal. The deliciousness, simplicity, and thoughtfulness of the dish rock me to the core. I have also included the very first iteration of shrimp and grits that I created for the opening Husk menu. Aside from its being a sentimental favorite, it's an example of daily "off-the-cuff" cooking. Shrimp and grits is a perfect template for cooking by the seasons—you can push yourself to create something new each time.

Cornbread

Cornbread is another great example of a beloved food that shows the regional diversity of the American South. When I started opening restaurants in different parts of the South, I spent a good deal of time interviewing locals and old-timers. I was blown away by the various perspectives on cornbread held by the people in various places. No matter where you are, cornbread reflects the cravings and flavors that people associate with home.

Cornbread at its most basic is quite simple: dried field corn milled and mixed into a batter with some type of leavening. But the theory of cornbread relativity is more complicated than it might appear on the surface. The regional differences and the factors that affect them can be examined at grandparents' tables, soul food restaurants, meat-and-threes, and barbecue joints throughout the South. Sometimes these variations are inspired by the local agriculture—for example, the day-old rice that is folded into cornbread batter in parts of the Lowcountry (see page 217). Oftentimes sugar makes its way into the batter when the cornbread will be served alongside a spicy dish, as in the cornbread served with the amazing barbecue from Rodney Scott in South Carolina.

In Nashville, I discovered "hot-water" cornbread (see page 219). It's essentially like seared polenta, a skillet-fried cornmeal porridge without any chemical leaveners, relying on the steam trapped inside for the rise as it is quickly cooked. You know your hot-water cornbread is legit when you can see the fingerprints of the cook in the top of it; it is very much a sign of traditional cookery. In the Appalachian Mountains, the local palate tends to crave the fermented foods and flavors introduced by German immigrants, and these find their way into the cornbread there (see page 217).

The accompaniments for cornbread also change as you move throughout the South. I grew up eating my cornbread with sorghum syrup on the side. And I know more than a few families in the Appalachians that would rather have Country Crock spread on their cornbread than butter. In Louisiana, cornbread might be eaten with cane syrup and a healthy slathering of butter. I like to serve mine with a combination of lard, honey, and butter that has the ability to make people lose their minds.

Although the cuisines of the microregions of the South inspire me as a chef and culinary researcher, and I've used these examples to help you understand how different the regions of the South can be, I also want them to inspire you to take a deep dive into your own microregion. There are always stories waiting to be discovered and, more important, delicious ingredients and dishes waiting to be reinvigorated and devoured.

MADE IN THE SOUTH

In my restaurants, I always ask myself, "What does it taste like, feel like, smell like, and sound like to eat in this place on this day, at this time?" Eating in the moment was the way we ate when I was growing up in the mountains of Southern Appalachia, although we were doing so because it was natural and made sense. This concept continues to be my guiding light when creating and cooking food for my guests. And it doesn't stop with my professional life. Every time I turn on the range or fire up the grill at home, it seems like a snapshot of the moment but also of the progress I, along with many others, have made exploring the traditions, possibilities, and diversity of Southern food. I constantly look back at the culinary history of the South, finding and collecting for myself the forgotten plant and animal breeds that were left behind by industrial agriculture and paying homage to the cultures that contributed them. All this is also done with an eye toward the future. I want to ensure that our cuisine not only persists but also continues to grow and progress. And I want everyone to feel like he or she can be a part of this progression. A big part of keeping a cooking culture alive is making these traditional dishes at home, which means that every person can make a difference.

As I study and obsess over the cuisines and microregions of the South, that idea encompasses Southern culture too. I had always wanted Husk, through all its iterations, to be a gallery for the South's farmers and artisans. I wanted it to be a place where their stories could be told and their hard work could be celebrated. I wanted guests to look at the producers as if they were rock stars—the gods of our cuisine. And I wanted my guests to leave feeling like they wanted to seek out those producers and ingredients and bring them into their own homes. I knew that pursuing these goals would fill me with Southern pride.

While I continue to define what Southern cuisine is to me, the simple truth is that the only way to truly taste the South on any particular day is to be hyperseasonal and hyperlocal. I'm sure you're thinking, "Big deal. Anyone can do that. That's how everyone is cooking these days." But think about it: When you focus on the hyperlocal and remove things like balsamic vinegar and olive oil from your cooking, what do you replace them with? The case can be made that those ingredients are part of Southern food in some way. After all, historical import registries show that ingredients like these once flowed into the ports of Charleston, Savannah, and New Orleans. But that line of thinking misses the mark for me; it's too easy. Including these ingredients in a plate of Southern food is a distraction and steers the dialogue in the wrong direction. I encourage you to cook the way people historically have in the rural South and other regions, without access to imported ingredients. If you eat only vegetables that you or your neighbors have grown or fill your pantry with grains, oils or other fats, and dried herbs and spices produced in your own community, your relationship with food and cooking will change pretty quickly. And that is the only way to re-create what a day tastes like in the South, or in your region, in a very pure sense.

As exciting a prospect as deciding to do this is, it can also be a scary one. A lot of your favorite ingredients will be off the table. But I eventually realized that such a strict discipline didn't limit my cooking but instead created a catalyst for discovering the hidden products of the South and, eventually, for innovation. I couldn't buy balsamic, so I made it. No more California olive oil? I found someone growing olives nearby. If you approach this challenge the right way, you can not only celebrate the local ingredients of your own region but also help the farmers and other producers in your area.

Learning to cook with the seasons—and to control my cravings until an ingredient is at its peak—was a pivotal act for me. It has connected me to the land and the water and my community in a way that I hadn't been before. This desire to eat my way through my own piece of the world forever changed my view on food and cooking. I'm happier making shrimp and grits with just four ingredients and focusing on the purity and authenticity of those ingredients than I am starting a dish by thinking about how I can creatively tamper with it. Sharing my increasing respect for local ingredients, treating them simply, and giving them the spotlight has become my obsession.

WITHIN ARM'S REACH

No matter where you live, you can find people growing and producing amazing food. Who's raising beef nearby? Pork? Chicken? Eggs? Who's harvesting or raising fish and shellfish? Who's growing specialty vegetables, and who's growing bulk produce? Who's growing organic and who's not? How often does a particular farmer harvest? What does he or she have at any given time? Finding the answers to these questions will provide you with a massive amount of information about your own regional foodways as well as eventually culminate in a complete pantry of local foods for you to cook with.

The relationships you may develop as a result of this process can be invaluable. Meeting the producers, getting to know them, and connecting on a level deeper than the typical seller-buyer relationship will also come through when you cook their ingredients. If most of your produce comes from a big chain grocery store, it's easy to be cut off from the reality of how it all came to be. A sad-looking industrially grown carrot at the supermarket can't evoke the same emotions as a vibrant carrot just plucked from the soil and handed to you by a hardworking farmer at the market. You will look at the hand-grown carrot with a different kind of respect and therefore a different sense of responsibility.

When you walk through the fields with a farmer, you're likely to discover things that don't normally make their way to the supermarket or even the farmers' market. It might be an herb he thinks nobody would want, something that's about to get turned under to make way for the next crop. But these plants can be among the most delicious, and buying and cooking with them will result in less waste and increased profitability for a small farmer. Oftentimes the farmer thinks I'm crazy for wanting some of these things, but then he catches on, and soon enough, you're paying fifty dollars for a haul of coriander berries.

Because of the relationships I've formed with them, some of these farmers also grow plants specifically for me. I might pick out a vegetable from a seed catalog or show up at the farm with an armful of random seeds that I've collected in tiny bags for the purpose of saving. I can't describe how exciting it is to be able to share the seeds of my grandma's greasy beans, the ones I grew up eating, with my farmer friends and then get some of their harvest in return.

All the time you spend on discovery and on getting to know the people growing your food funnels into the finished dish. When a farmer's ingredient finally lands on the plate, I see it almost like an ode to that particular producer. It inspires me, and in turn I want my food to say, "I appreciate what you do, respect what you do, and am grateful." It's my way of sharing the hard work and passion of these Southern producers with my guests, whether in a restaurant or my dining room at home. Contributing to the South's economy, telling the region's story, and learning from its past through food are at the core of my ethos as a chef and a human being. It's a mindful way of cooking and immeasurably rewarding.

HOW TO USE THIS BOOK

The recurring feature of all my favorite cookbooks is that they make me feel like I need to get up and cook. The photographs, recipes, and stories come together in a way I can almost taste. With this book, I provide recipes for all the key Southern foods and tell a little of the ever-evolving story of the South's cuisine. I wrote it with the hope that I will inspire you to head to your market and then into your kitchen to cook delicious and fulfilling dishes to share with your own family and friends.

A FEW THINGS TO KEEP IN MIND WHEN COOKING FROM THIS BOOK

- You owe it yourself to eat with the seasons. Waiting another month or two until an ingredient is at its peak will always be worth it.

- Shop first and pick a recipe second. Buy what looks delicious and inspiring at the market and go from there.

- Be sure to read Grilling (page 96). Many of these recipes feature an ingredient that gets some grill time.

- Read all the way through the recipe before you start cooking. There's nothing worse than getting halfway into a dish and realizing you don't have a certain ingredient or enough time to get it done.

- These recipes shouldn't be treated like gospel. See an ingredient you don't like? Leave it out or replace it with something you do. Don't let one ingredient keep you from trying the whole dish. You're the chef in your kitchen! Unless, of course, your mom or grandma is around. . . .

- Use the times provided as guidelines. Every oven is a little different and every stove is too.

In these pages, you will find my versions of the recipes that form the backbone of the Southern kitchen, from fried chicken (see page 127) to biscuits (see page 223) to cornbread five different ways (see pages 216–219). These recipes are the building blocks of my cooking and the recipes I've made a hundred times at home and will continue to cook forevermore. You'll also find a whole range of recipes that might not strike you as Southern in the traditional sense but that make use of the best Southern ingredients—from a quick and easy chilled summer squash soup flavored with buttermilk (see page 66) to an impressive lamb roast glazed with sorghum syrup and finished with rhubarb butter (see page 148). Although some of the recipes can be time-consuming or complicated, there is an equal number of easy and accessible recipes.

What I cook at home—and in my restaurants, for that matter—is dictated by the products I find in the markets or in the fields. A beautiful, irresistible head of cauliflower or a succulent rack of pork can spark my imagination and provide the perfect jumping-off point for a great dinner. With that ingredient in hand, I file through my flavor memories and my notebooks and search through my collection of cookbooks to find a delicious and interesting preparation. I hope that's exactly how you use this book. Consider it a field guide to the components of my Southern cuisine. These recipes are foundational but also interchangeable. Many of the recipes include Goes Well With suggestions, so you can see which recipes go best with others and the pairings I'm partial to. Use these suggestions as a guide, but I want you to put these dishes together in the way that makes your own mouth water.

All the recipes in this book have been tested and retested in a home kitchen, and if you follow the instructions to a T, they'll turn out great. But it's important to remember that any ingredient grown in a different place, and at a different time of year, is going to taste a little different and maybe even cook a little differently. I urge you to cook with your senses. Taste your food at every step along the way and season it to your own liking. Use your sense of smell too. If a vegetable you're cooking starts to smell burnt but the recipe says to cook it for a minute more, go with your gut and take it off the heat.

Eating my way through the foods of other cultures and across other continents has only reinforced how grateful I am for what I have at home. The flavors are incredible and the culture is rich, and Southern cuisine is experiencing a period of revitalization and growth that I think is just getting started. (It sure has come a long way for me since I planted my first Jimmy Red corn seeds over a decade ago.) There's no limit to what Southern food can become, because the roots of Southern cooking are driven by something that I believe we share with all cultures: the joy and happiness we feel when we gather around a table with our families and our communities.

SNACKS AND **DISHES** TO SHARE

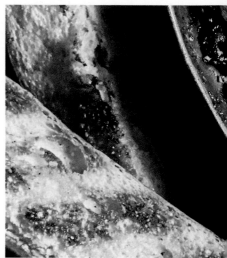

BOILED PEANUTS

MAKES 4 CUPS

2½ pounds green peanuts
　　(see Resources, page 369)

One 2-ounce piece slab bacon,
　　preferably Benton's (see
　　Resources, page 368)

2½ Charleston Hots or cayenne
　　peppers, seeded and sliced into
　　thin rounds

¼ cup kosher salt

2 tablespoons chili powder

2¼ teaspoons light brown sugar

2¼ teaspoons onion powder

1½ teaspoons ground cumin

1 teaspoon dried oregano

¾ teaspoon Bourbon Barrel
　　Bourbon Smoked Paprika
　　(see Resources, page 368)

¾ teaspoon garlic powder

¼ teaspoon cayenne pepper

⅛ teaspoon mustard powder

EQUIPMENT

Slow cooker

Boiled peanuts are one of the first things that come to mind when I think about the South. I didn't eat them growing up in Appalachia, but I fell in love with them when I went to Charleston for culinary school. Boiled peanut stands dot the roadsides, and everyone has his or her favorite. The most important thing about this recipe is the peanuts. You have to use green peanuts in the shell—fresh peanuts that have not been cooked or dried. The recipe won't work any other way.

NOTES: The peanuts must be refrigerated in the brine overnight before serving. You can save the "potlikker" and use it to cook a pot of collard greens.

In the slow cooker, combine the peanuts, bacon, chili peppers, salt, chili powder, brown sugar, onion powder, cumin, oregano, paprika, garlic powder, cayenne, and mustard powder and add water to cover. Cook for about 8 hours on high, replenishing the water as needed to keep the ingredients covered; the peanuts will float to the top when they are done and should be very tender on the inside.

Pour the peanuts and brine into a heatproof container and cool to room temperature, about 30 minutes.

Remove the bacon from the peanuts, shred it, and return it to the peanuts. Cover the peanuts and brine and refrigerate overnight. *(Tightly covered, the peanuts will keep in the brine for up to 2 days in the refrigerator.)*

Reheat the peanuts in the brine in a medium saucepan over low heat. Remove them from the brine with a strainer or slotted spoon and serve warm.

DEVILED EGGS

MAKES 12 DEVILED EGGS

6 large eggs

1 tablespoon mayonnaise, preferably Duke's (see Resources, page 369)

1 tablespoon yellow mustard

2½ tablespoons small dice Bread-and-Butter Pickles (page 243), plus 1½ teaspoons of their brine

2½ tablespoons small dice Pickled Ramps (page 251)

Hot Sauce (page 260) or Red Clay Original Hot Sauce (see Resources, page 369)

Bourbon Barrel Bourbon Smoked Paprika (see Resources, page 368)

EQUIPMENT

Pastry bag fitted with a star tip (optional)

Deviled eggs are my go-to snack when I'm having friends over or need to take something to a potluck. They're portable and pretty darn resilient, and I don't know too many people who won't line up to try one. Every cook in the South has his or her own way of making them, from complex and exotic to simple and classic. Mine fall somewhere in between.

A long time ago, my friend Tyler Brown, chef of Southall Farms in Franklin, Tennessee, taught me his secret: seasoning the yolks with pickle brine. I have made deviled eggs the same way ever since.

Using a sewing needle or pushpin, pierce a hole in the shell at the wide end of each egg. Put the eggs in a large saucepan and cover them with room-temperature water. Bring the water to a boil over medium-high heat and boil the eggs for 2 minutes. Remove the saucepan from the stove, cover it, and let the eggs remain in the water for 10 minutes.

Carefully drain the eggs in a colander in the sink, then peel them under cold running water.

Cut the eggs lengthwise in half. Remove the yolks and put them in a bowl; set the whites aside. Add the mayonnaise and mustard to the bowl and mash the yolks well. Add the bread-and-butter pickles, their brine, and the pickled ramps and stir to combine. Add hot sauce to taste. Transfer the mixture to the pastry bag or to a zip-top plastic bag (seal the bag and snip off one bottom corner).

Cut a small slice off the bottom of each egg white so they will stand upright, and arrange them on a serving dish.

Pipe the yolk mixture into the whites. Garnish with a sprinkling of paprika and serve.

NOTE: The deviled eggs can be made up to a day ahead: After you remove the yolks from the whites, place the whites upside down on a tray lined with paper towels, cover with plastic wrap, and refrigerate. Make the filling, cover, and refrigerate. Thirty minutes before you are ready to serve, pipe the filling into the egg whites and let the deviled eggs come to room temperature. Garnish with paprika just before serving.

RICE-AND-SHRIMP CROQUETTES

with Tomato Chili Sauce

SERVES 6 AS A SNACK

TOMATO CHILI SAUCE

½ cup diced sweet onion

1 garlic clove, chopped

1 cayenne pepper, chopped
(with seeds)

1½ teaspoons kosher salt

1 tablespoon peanut oil

1 cup Tomato Jam (page 281)

2 tablespoons thinly sliced scallion
greens

1 tablespoon minced tarragon

RICE

1 cup Anson Mills Carolina Gold
Rice (see Resources, page 368)

1 teaspoon extra-virgin olive oil

1½ teaspoons kosher salt

1½ cups water

CROQUETTES

Canola oil for deep-frying

2 tablespoons unsalted butter

¾ cup small dice sweet onion

½ cup small dice celery

¼ cup small dice green bell pepper

1 pound 21–25-count shrimp,
peeled, deveined, and cut into
¼-inch pieces

2 teaspoons kosher salt

1 teaspoon Espelette pepper

½ teaspoon freshly ground white
pepper

Chef BJ Dennis has dedicated his life to preserving the Gullah Geechee cuisine of his ancestors. I first made these croquettes with him. You simply drop spoonfuls of the rice batter into hot oil; no need to bread the croquettes, as you would in Italian cuisine. Dicing the shrimp into small but not *too* small pieces is the key to the croquettes. The bits of shrimp cook through as they fry but still retain some of their texture.

The tomato chili sauce was inspired by my first trip to West Africa, where I tasted black-eyed-pea fritters with a dipping sauce made from a fragrant, flavorful Senegalese tomato paste, a recurring note in that cuisine. This version is based on a tomato jam I've been cooking for years.

FOR THE SAUCE: Combine the onion, garlic, cayenne, and salt in a mortar and crush with the pestle until the mixture becomes a wet paste.

Heat the peanut oil in a small saucepan over high heat until it shimmers. Add the onion mixture and cook, stirring constantly, until most of the liquid has evaporated, about 1 minute. Stir in the tomato jam, reduce the heat to medium-low, and simmer for 5 minutes to develop the flavors. Transfer the sauce to a blender and blend on high until completely smooth, about 1 minute. Transfer to a heatproof container and cool to room temperature.

Stir the scallion greens and tarragon into the sauce, cover, and refrigerate. (*Tightly covered, the sauce will keep for up to 5 days in the refrigerator.*)

FOR THE RICE: Combine the rice, olive oil, and salt in a medium heavy-bottomed saucepan and stir to coat the rice with the oil. Add the water and bring to a boil over high heat. Reduce the heat to low, cover, and simmer until the rice is tender and all the water has been absorbed, about 12 minutes. Remove from the stove and let stand, covered, for 3 minutes.

Fluff the rice gently with a fork, then spread it out on a rimmed baking sheet and cool to room temperature. Transfer the rice to a large bowl and set aside.

FOR THE CROQUETTES: Fill a deep fryer with canola oil according to the manufacturer's directions and heat the oil to 325°F. Alternatively, fill a deep heavy pot half full with canola oil and heat the oil over medium heat to 325°F. Preheat the oven to 200°F. Line one rimmed baking sheet with parchment paper and another with paper towels.

Meanwhile, melt the butter in a medium skillet over medium-high heat. Add the onion, celery, and bell pepper and cook, stirring, until the vegetables are translucent, about 5 minutes. Spread the vegetables out on a plate and cool to room temperature.

Add the cooled vegetables, shrimp, salt, Espelette pepper, and white pepper to the rice and stir to combine. The mixture will be very tacky to the touch and should hold together when rolled into a ball. Form the croquette mixture into balls about 1 inch in diameter and place them on the parchment-lined baking sheet.

Working in batches and taking care not to overcrowd the fryer, fry the croquettes until deep golden brown and cooked through, about 4 minutes. Transfer the croquettes to the paper towel–lined baking sheet and keep warm in the oven while you fry the remaining croquettes.

TO SERVE: Pile the croquettes on a platter and offer the tomato chili sauce alongside.

CHILLED OYSTERS

with Buttermilk, Apple, and Caviar

MAKES 12 OYSTERS

¼ cup full-fat buttermilk (see Note)

½ teaspoon fresh lemon juice

12 fresh oysters

1 tablespoon very finely diced apple, preferably Granny Smith

1 ounce caviar, preferably Kelley's Katch Paddlefish Caviar (see Resources, page 369)

1 tablespoon finely chopped chives

2 cups crushed ice

Briny, pearlescent black caviar usually conjures up images of classic French cuisine, but Tennessee paddlefish brings it to the South. I discovered Kelley's Katch Tennessee paddlefish caviar in 2003 when I was the executive chef at the Hermitage Hotel in Nashville. Here I use the caviar for a Southern spin on the classic pairing of oysters, crème fraîche, and caviar. Instead of crème fraîche, I use buttermilk (I like the one from Cruze Farm in Knoxville, Tennessee, cultured from the milk of their pastured Jersey cows). The diced apple gives the oysters a pop of texture and sweetness that rounds the dish out nicely.

NOTE: The resulting taste makes it worth the effort to seek out a cultured, full-fat buttermilk, but any buttermilk will work in this recipe.

Combine the buttermilk and lemon juice in a small bowl. Cover and refrigerate while you shuck the oysters.

Lay a dish towel on a cutting board and put an oyster, flat side up, on one edge of the towel. Fold the towel over the oyster, covering the curved lip of the shell and leaving the tapered hinge end exposed. Carefully pry the shell open by inserting an oyster knife into the hinge and twisting the knife to pop the shell. Run the blade of the knife flat against the top shell, releasing the oyster from the shell, and discard the top shell. Carefully release the oyster from the bottom shell by gently running the oyster knife under it, leaving the oyster and its liquor in the shell. Remove any shell debris or sand from the oyster, then transfer it to a shallow baking dish lined with a kitchen towel. Repeat with the remaining oysters. *(The shucked oysters can be refrigerated for up to an hour.)*

Spoon some buttermilk onto each oyster. Sprinkle the oysters with the apple, divide the caviar among them, and sprinkle with the chives. Line a platter with crushed ice and transfer the oysters to the platter.

GRILLED OYSTERS with Green Garlic Butter

MAKES 24 OYSTERS

GREEN GARLIC BUTTER

4 whole green garlic stalks
(about 6 ounces)

Kosher salt

9 tablespoons unsalted butter,
at room temperature

¼ cup dry white wine

2 teaspoons grated lemon zest

1 teaspoon fresh lemon juice

½ teaspoon Aleppo pepper
(see Resources, page 369)

OYSTERS

24 fresh oysters

3 cups ice cream salt

1 tablespoon grated Crab Roe
Bottarga (page 295; casing
removed, grated with a
Microplane)

2 teaspoons very finely diced
Preserved Lemon peel
(see page 257)

2 teaspoons very thinly sliced
lovage leaves

EQUIPMENT

Round 15-inch open-top fine-mesh
wire grill basket

As an extension of my waste-not-want-not philosophy, I use the embers from my fireplace to cook these oysters. They are quickly warmed in the hot embers and pick up a hint of that wood-fire magic. But you don't need to light a fireplace to enjoy them at home. Oysters are just as good cooked on the grill. Be sure to use hardwood lump charcoal, which will impart its own subtle smokiness.

The green garlic butter adds richness to the dish, and the lovage gives it that fresh celery pop. Look for green garlic in the springtime at your local farmers' market. It's often one of the first crops of the season. I like to use my crab roe bottarga for a burst of briny ocean flavor, but you could substitute a good mullet bottarga (see Resources, page 368).

FOR THE GREEN GARLIC BUTTER: Separate the white and green parts of the garlic. Wash and dry them both. Thinly slice the whites and chop the greens, keeping them separate.

Bring a large pot of salted water to a boil over high heat. Make an ice bath with equal parts ice and water in a large bowl. Put the chopped green garlic parts in a fine-mesh sieve and submerge them in the boiling water until tender and a vibrant green color, 1 to 2 minutes. Leaving them in the sieve, transfer to the ice bath and submerge until cold.

Remove the blanched garlic greens from the ice bath and transfer to a blender. Add ¼ cup of the ice water and blend on high until very smooth, about 1 minute, scraping down the sides as necessary. Transfer the puree to a bowl and set aside.

Heat 1 tablespoon of the butter in a small saucepan over medium heat until foamy. Add the white parts of the garlic and cook, stirring frequently, until translucent, about 5 minutes. Add the wine and cook, stirring, until the wine has almost completely evaporated, about 2 minutes. Remove the mixture from the stove and cool to room temperature.

Stir the remaining 8 tablespoons butter into the green garlic puree, then add the cooked garlic whites, the lemon zest, lemon juice, ½ teaspoon salt, and the Aleppo pepper and stir to mix well. Set aside at room temperature. (*The garlic butter can be made ahead. Tightly covered, it will keep for up to 3 days in the refrigerator. Remove from the refrigerator 30 minutes before using.*)

FOR THE OYSTERS: Prepare a hot fire in a charcoal grill (see page 96), removing the grill rack and distributing the hot coals in an even layer in the bottom of the grill.

While the charcoal is heating, shuck the oysters: Lay a dish towel on a cutting board and put an oyster, flat side up, on one edge of the towel. Fold the towel over the oyster, covering the curved lip of the shell and leaving the tapered hinge end exposed. Carefully pry the oyster shell open by inserting an oyster knife into the hinge and twisting the knife to pop the shell. Run the blade of the knife flat against the top shell, releasing the oyster from the top shell; discard the top shell. Carefully release the oyster from the bottom shell by gently running the oyster knife under it, leaving the oyster and its liquor in the shell. Remove any shell debris or sand from the oyster and transfer it to a shallow baking dish lined with a kitchen towel. Repeat with the remaining oysters. (*The shucked oysters can be refrigerated for up to an hour.*)

Spread 2 cups of the ice cream salt out on a platter. Put the remaining cup of ice cream salt in the grill basket and spread it out in an even layer. Arrange half the shucked oysters in the grill basket and top each with 2 teaspoons of the green garlic butter. Place the grill basket directly on the coals and cover it with a pizza pan or cookie sheet. Grill the oysters for 1 minute, or until the butter has completely melted and the oysters are bubbling. Transfer the oysters to the prepared platter and cover lightly with foil to keep warm while you grill the remaining oysters.

Sprinkle the oysters with the bottarga, preserved lemon peel, and lovage leaves.

FIREPLACE COOKERY

Wood-fire cookery is absolutely central to my cooking style and philosophy. The aromas of the burning hardwood and the food cooking are intoxicating. My first real, professional foray into cooking this way began in Charleston, when I developed some recipes to use with a wood-fired oven. As I became more and more comfortable with it, that oven became an indispensable part of my restaurant's kitchen. It changed the way I thought about food and cooking and led to my viewing almost every ingredient with an eye toward the fire. When I moved to Nashville, I incorporated a hearth in one of my restaurants for the first time and continued to refine my approach.

That said, all the grilling recipes in this book were developed and tested keeping in mind that most home cooks will be using a simple kettle-style charcoal grill. For the enthusiast or anyone lucky enough to have the space for a more involved outdoor cooking setup, or the adventurous reader ready to start cooking in his or her fireplace, the techniques described below provide an overview of the ever-changing ways of and tools for using fire to cook Southern cuisine.

- **Cooking Directly on the Coals.** Some ingredients do really well placed right on top of the hot coals. You can use this technique with everything from red peppers, winter squash, beets, and leeks to giant rib-eye steaks—in short, any ingredient where a nice, deep char is desired. And the intense heat helps lock in and concentrate the flavorful juices.

- **Cooking in a Mesh Grill Basket on the Embers.** Imagine that the basket is your sauté pan and the bed of embers is your stovetop burner, but one that adds an incredible depth of flavor, with just the right amount of smoke and char. Using this technique, you can introduce the flavor of the hearth to almost any ingredient you can think of: squid, mushrooms, even fresh peas.

- **Braising in a Dutch Oven Hung over the Fire.** I remember making a blackberry cobbler in a Dutch oven at Boy Scout camp and being fascinated that you could put the pot right into the fire. To open the lid and see that perfection, the high-heat cooking transformation that occurs when you surround something completely with hot coals, was just amazing. This is a great way to cook large cuts of meat and to braise tougher ones. By experimenting and moving the Dutch oven closer to or farther from the fire, you can find the sweet spot for everything from cooking beans and grains to keeping things warm.

- **Covered Cowboy Grill.** You can use this piece of equipment to emulate how barbecue pitmasters capture the smoke of the embers: The meat is suspended over glowing embers in a large pit and covered, leaving enough space to allow the light ember smoke to circulate. You can do the same thing on a smaller scale in your hearth. A cowboy grill is basically a square four-legged grill that has a box-shaped lid. With one, you are essentially mimicking cooking in a covered kettle grill but with the versatility and more controlled heat of the hearth. You can also infuse foods with an ephemeral wisp of smoke by sprinkling the coals with a little bit of hardwood sawdust. That light smoke quickly enshrouds the food and adds a layer of flavor right before it hits the plate.

- **Four-Legged Grill.** With this simple contraption, the food is elevated over the embers, and more embers can easily be added to maintain an even cooking temperature. One version has a coiled metal handle that makes it super easy to move the grill to the different heat zones of the hearth.

- **Cast-Iron Spider.** A traditional piece of equipment, a cast-iron spider sits over the fire on three feet. Like a Dutch oven, it has a tightly fitting lid, and like a chicken fryer, it has one long, sturdy handle. Because it is shallower than a typical Dutch oven, it's the perfect choice for making cornbread in the hearth. You can scoop some coals right on top of the lid, surrounding the cornbread with radiant heat and yielding an exceedingly crispy exterior and moist interior.

- **Cooking on Racks Suspended Above the Hearth.** Metal resting racks that sit a few feet above the coals are one of the most important features of my hearth. Depending on the heat of the fire, this zone of the hearth can be used for everything from tempering meats and fish before cooking to imparting a subtle hot smoke to resting meats and vegetables after they've spent time in the intense heat of a grill. The temperature variance the racks allow is extremely important when cooking a big piece of meat like a rib-eye or a rack of pork. Carefully alternating periods of searing high heat and relaxing ambient heat is the key to achieving the perfect balance of crispy, savory crust and even, melting doneness inside.

- **Hearth Drying.** You can use the ambient heat of a wood-fired hearth to dehydrate everything from shiitake mushrooms and lemon slices to beef jerky and oysters. The subtle, clean smokiness of the wood fire slowly lends its flavor in the dehydrating process, yielding incredibly delicious results. It's also the best place to make leather britches, the Appalachian staple of pole beans strung up and dried for the winter.

- **Japanese Handled Grill Grates.** On a trip to Japan, I came across some small circular grill grates with handles. These are generally placed directly on the coals or set over a very thin layer of embers. I like to put a tender piece of braised meat or a delicate fish fillet on one of these grates and snug it up next to the fire, but not directly over the coals. It's a great way to gently warm food or to imbue it with the scent of the embers while avoiding intense direct heat. The handle and the grate's small size make it easy to move the grate around the hearth in search of that "just right" temperature zone.

- **Poaching and Confiting.** Poaching and confiting in butter or another tasty fat are simple but luxurious ways to infuse flavor into ingredients that require delicate cooking. Think tender scallops or plump lobster tails. Put your ingredient and butter or oil in a sturdy pot, like a cast-iron Dutch oven, cover, and set the pot near the fire. The radiant heat of the coals makes it possible to do a really gentle poach. I also like to rest a nice piece of grilled meat in some of its own fat this way. The steak or chop comes off the hot direct heat of the coals into the warm fat, where it can rest to doneness.

- **Slow-Roasting.** The hearth is also the place to mimic the open-pit *asador* cooking typical of South America. You can hang everything from a lamb shoulder to aged duck or quail above the coals and slowly cook it, glazing and basting it with a flavorful vinaigrette, until it is done to perfection.

- **Hearth-Dried Seafood.** On my first trip to Senegal, I saw a preservation technique that I've since applied to tons of different ingredients. Senegalese cooks salt shellfish or fish and cook it over a fire just long enough to ensure that the outside isn't raw. Then the seafood is slowly dried over the fire until it is shrunken and shriveled and ready to be stored. This process concentrates the natural glutamic acid (one of the primary umami elements in foods) in the seafood and ferments it very slightly. The dried seafood is used to flavor soups, stews, and broths, just as we would use a smoky ham hock or turkey neck in the South.

- **Metal Skewers.** Long, thin metal skewers are fantastic for cooking anything from whole fish to vegetables. They're razor sharp and pierce the ingredient cleanly without tearing, which is important when you're dealing with something as delicate as fish. And because metal transfers heat so well, the ingredient cooks gently from the inside as the outside sears over the hot coals.

- **Whole Fish Basket.** Essentially a metal cage with a long handle that locks it closed, a fish basket makes it possible to move what would otherwise be an unwieldy whole fish around the hearth with ease.

- **Foil Packets.** I've carried one of my favorite wood-fire cooking techniques with me since childhood. My father and I would wrap some new potatoes and onions tightly in foil packets and throw them right into the morning's fire before heading out to (hopefully) catch a fish or two. When we got back to camp, the vegetables would be cooked, so we only needed to quickly clean and grill our catch. The moist, smoky environment of the foil packet makes it a natural choice for cooking anything from root vegetables to poultry or seafood.

- **Ash Salt Dough.** I first read about ash cookery in a book on Appalachian cuisine. The original recipe instructed you to bury sweet potatoes in the ashes and cinders of the evening's fire so that come morning, the residual heat had cooked them and you'd have something hearty all ready to eat for breakfast. In a restaurant setting, because I couldn't consistently rely on the results, I developed an ash-infused salt-dough crust that imparts that subtle ash flavor while ensuring even cooking every time. I've found it to be a particularly good way to cook celery root and whole fish.

- **Cooking Adjacent to the Coals.** Sometimes you'll want to use the intense, searing heat of the fire without necessarily picking up its smoky flavors. Putting whatever you're cooking right up against the side of the fire, not over it, allows the food to get some char and color from the radiant heat.

- **Ember Burner.** For a makeshift burner, build a little fort out of fire bricks, fill it with glowing embers, and top it with a cast-iron skillet. This is a great way to sear a fillet of fish or pan-roast a chicken breast. As you cook and baste it in the skillet, your food picks up all the wonderful flavors and aromas of the hearth.

- **Cast-Iron Griddle.** Set level on a bed of hot embers, a cast-iron griddle becomes an amazing cooking surface, with the added bonus of that smoky ember flavor. Pancakes cooked this way are the best.

- **Infusing with Embers.** What happens when you throw a glowing-hot ember into some freshly rendered lard? It goes nuts, sizzling, hissing, and smoking like crazy. As the action subsides and the lard cools, the fat takes on all those delicious smoky flavors. You can try this with different cooking fats: olive oil, chicken fat—you name it. My initial experiments eventually resulted in Hickory-Smoked Ice Cream (page 339).

- **Salt-and-Ember Crust.** Roasting vegetables in a salt-and-egg-white crust is nothing new. To adapt this technique to the hearth, though, spread a layer of the crust mixture (sometimes adding a little bit of ash) in the bottom of a big cast-iron skillet, add your ingredient (my favorite is first-crop baby potatoes), and cover with another layer of the crust mixture. Set the skillet on the hot embers and then cover the top with embers, placing them right on the salt crust. The crust creates a very even, moist, and flavorful cooking environment.

SOUTHERN CLAMS CASINO

SERVES 4 AS A SNACK

CORNBREAD CRUMBLE

¼ recipe Basic Cornbread (page 216), made a day ahead

½ ounce Asiago cheese, preferably Kenny's Farmhouse Dry Fork Reserve (see Resources, page 369), grated

½ teaspoon kosher salt

¼ teaspoon freshly ground black pepper

2 tablespoons Rendered Bacon Fat (page 342), melted

2 tablespoons Pork Stock (page 346), at room temperature

CLAMS

32 littleneck clams, scrubbed under cold running water (see Note)

2 ounces Tuscan kale

1 recipe Tomato Gravy (see page 110)

¼ cup small dice sweet onion

½ teaspoon canola oil

Kosher salt and freshly ground black pepper

1 cup ice cream salt

1 tablespoon Hot Sauce (page 260) or Red Clay Original Hot Sauce (see Resources, page 369)

EQUIPMENT

Large pot with a steamer insert

Round 15-inch open-top fine-mesh wire grill basket

Clams Casino—broiled clams topped with bacon and bread crumbs—was a mainstay appetizer in the 1970s and '80s. My recipe starts with beautiful clams (I'm partial to the ones harvested by Dave Belanger in Charleston, but ask your local fishmonger for his freshest littlenecks), which are topped with a tomato gravy and disks of cornbread crumble. The combination of cornbread crumbs, bacon fat, and preserved tomatoes turns this version of the classic decidedly Southern.

NOTE: The hard clams commonly found, grown, and harvested along the Eastern shore of the United States go by many names: round clam, hard-shell clam, or quahog depending on where you're eating them. They all refer to the same species, *Mercenaria mercenaria*. There are different size grades, with littleneck being the smallest commonly harvested, usually about 1½ inches across, and the most tender.

FOR THE CORNBREAD CRUMBLE: Line a rimmed baking sheet with parchment paper.

Crumble the cornbread into a large bowl. Add the cheese, salt, and pepper and drizzle in the bacon fat, then slowly stir in the pork stock just until the mixture will stick to your fingers and hold its shape when pressed together; you may not need all the stock. Divide the cornbread mixture into 4 equal parts, then divide each one into 8 pieces and shape each piece into a small ball. Place the balls on the prepared baking sheet, cover, and refrigerate for 15 minutes.

Pat each chilled ball out into a thin disk the size of a clamshell, return to the baking sheet, cover, and refrigerate until ready to use.

FOR THE CLAMS: Bring 3 cups water to a gentle boil in the large pot with a steamer insert. Put the clams in the steamer insert in a single layer (work in batches if necessary). Carefully set the insert in the pot, cover, and steam the clams until they just open, about 6 minutes. Transfer the clams to a rimmed baking sheet and cool to room temperature.

Pry open each clamshell with your fingers and twist to separate the two halves. Discard the top shells. Release the clams from the bottom shells by gently running an oyster knife or small spoon under each one and transfer the clams to a small bowl. Rinse the bottom shells under cool running water and arrange them on the same baking sheet. Place a clam in each shell, cover, and refrigerate.

Prepare a hot fire in a charcoal grill (see page 96), removing the grill rack and distributing the hot coals in an even layer in the bottom of the grill.

Meanwhile, remove the stems and ribs from the kale leaves. Make stacks of the leaves, roll them lengthwise into cylinders, and cut into very thin ribbons. Wash the kale in a large bowl of cold water, changing the water several times, to remove any sand. Drain and dry with paper towels.

Preheat the oven to 200°F. Warm the tomato gravy in a medium saucepan over medium-low heat.

Combine the kale, onion, and canola oil in a bowl, season lightly with kosher salt and pepper, and toss. Transfer the mixture to the grill basket and place the basket directly on the coals. Grill the kale and onion, stirring with long-handled tongs so they cook evenly, until the kale is wilted and the onion is lightly charred, about 1 minute. Add the kale and onion to the saucepan of tomato gravy and stir to combine.

Cover the grill to maintain the heat for cooking the clams; add a few more pieces of charcoal if necessary.

Spoon some tomato gravy onto each clam, making sure it doesn't spill over the edges. Lay the cornbread disks on the clams and lightly press them down.

Place the grill rack as close to the coals as possible. Put the ice cream salt in the grill basket and spread it out in an even layer. Lay half the clams out in a single layer in the basket and set the basket on the grill rack. Cover the grill and grill the clams until the cornbread disks are lightly browned, about 3 minutes. Using tongs, transfer the clams to a rimmed baking sheet and keep them warm in the oven while you grill the remaining clams.

Place the clams on a platter and drizzle each with a few drops of hot sauce.

CLAMS with Sausage, Braised Peppers, and Grilled Bread

SERVES 4 AS A SNACK

BRAISED PEPPERS

2 tablespoons extra-virgin olive oil

2 garlic cloves, sliced paper-thin

½ cup thinly sliced sweet onion

3 red bell peppers (about 6 ounces each), cored and thinly sliced

3 yellow bell peppers (about 6 ounces each), cored and thinly sliced

¼ cup apple cider vinegar

1 tablespoon light brown sugar

1 cup Chicken Stock (page 344)

2 teaspoons kosher salt

½ teaspoon freshly ground black pepper

GRILLED BREAD

One 12-inch piece of baguette

2 tablespoons extra-virgin olive oil

Kosher salt and freshly ground black pepper

CLAMS

8 ounces smoked breakfast sausage, preferably Jakes Brothers (see Resources, page 368)

1 cup Preserved Tomatoes (page 278) or canned whole tomatoes, roughly chopped, with their juices

¼ cup heavy cream

¼ cup dry white wine

1 fresh bay leaf

32 littleneck clams, scrubbed under cold running water

1 tablespoon fresh lemon juice

1 tablespoon Hot Sauce (page 260) or Red Clay Original Hot Sauce (see Resources, page 369)

1 tablespoon Fines Herbes (page 356)

When I make this dish, I use my backyard wood-burning oven (see Fireplace Cookery, page 30) to cook the clams and impart an incredible smoky flavor to the sauce. You can easily re-create it at home on a grill. The combination of sausage and braised peppers is delicious, and when the clams open and give up their juices, it goes to the next level. Serve the clams with grilled bread to sop up all that sauce, because—trust me—you aren't going to want to leave a drop behind.

FOR THE BRAISED PEPPERS: Heat the olive oil in a large skillet over medium-high heat until it shimmers. Add the garlic and onion and cook, stirring frequently, until translucent and softened, about 3 minutes. Add the bell peppers and cook, stirring frequently, until they begin to soften, about 4 minutes. Stir in the vinegar and brown sugar and cook, stirring occasionally, until the vinegar has almost completely evaporated, about 10 minutes. Add the chicken stock and cook, stirring occasionally, until the stock has reduced to about ¼ cup and the peppers are very soft, about 30 minutes. Season with the salt and black pepper, remove from the stove, and set aside. (*The peppers can be made ahead. Tightly covered, they will keep for up to 2 days in the refrigerator. Remove from the refrigerator 30 minutes before using.*)

FOR THE GRILLED BREAD: Prepare a hot fire in a charcoal grill (see page 96), removing the grill rack and distributing the hot coals in an even layer in the bottom of the grill. Place the grill rack at its normal height.

Cut the baguette crosswise in half. Cut each piece lengthwise in half and then lengthwise in half again, producing eight 6-inch-long pieces of bread. Lightly brush the wedges of bread with the olive oil and season lightly with salt and pepper. Grill the bread cut side down until lightly charred and toasted, about 4 minutes. Remove from the grill and set aside.

FOR THE CLAMS: Cook the sausage in a large cast-iron skillet set on top of the grill rack, stirring frequently, until browned and broken up into small pieces. Add the tomatoes, braised peppers, cream, wine, and bay leaf and cook until the mixture has slightly reduced and thickened, about 10 minutes. Add the clams, put the lid on the grill, and cook until the clams have opened, about 5 minutes. Remove and discard the bay leaf.

CONTINUED

TO SERVE: Divide the clams, peppers, and sausage among four warm rimmed soup plates. Drizzle each portion with the lemon juice and hot sauce, sprinkle with the fines herbes, and place 2 pieces of grilled bread on the rim of each soup plate.

DEVILED CRAB

SERVES 4 TO 6 AS AN APPETIZER

2 cups water

3 teaspoons kosher salt

⅜ teaspoon freshly ground white pepper

1 fresh bay leaf

¼ cup Anson Mills Carolina Gold Rice (see resources, page 368)

1¼ cups panko bread crumbs

1 large egg

½ cup ketchup, preferably Heinz

½ cup mayonnaise, preferably Duke's (see Resources, page 369)

1 tablespoon Hot Sauce (page 260) or Red Clay Original Hot Sauce (see Resources, page 369)

1 tablespoon Hominy Miso (page 264)

1 tablespoon fresh lemon juice

1 teaspoon Dijon mustard

1½ teaspoons cayenne pepper

½ cup small dice celery

½ cup small dice green bell pepper

3 tablespoons thinly sliced scallion greens

1 tablespoon minced seeded jalapeño pepper

1 tablespoon Fines Herbes (page 356)

1 pound fresh lump blue crab meat, carefully picked over for shells and cartilage

2 teaspoons Bourbon Barrel Bourbon Smoked Paprika (see Resources, page 368)

3 tablespoons unsalted butter, at room temperature

EQUIPMENT

12 crab tins (see Resources, page 369) or 4-ounce ramekins

Deviled crab is one of the great traditions of the Lowcountry. Unfortunately, due to the many more-bread-crumb-than-crab, freezer-burned versions out there, most people turn their noses up when they think of it. I can't really blame them. Bad deviled crab is really bad. But man, truly good deviled crab is damn tasty. To make vibrant, fresh, moist deviled crab, use delicious Carolina Gold rice to help bind the filling. I like to serve deviled crab in little silver crab tins for a cool retro presentation, but if you're getting fresh whole blue crabs, by all means, use the shells themselves.

Combine the water, 1 teaspoon of the salt, ⅛ teaspoon of the white pepper, and the bay leaf in a small saucepan, bring to a boil over medium-high heat, and stir to be sure the salt has dissolved completely. Reduce the heat to medium, add the rice, stir once, and bring to a simmer. Simmer gently, uncovered, stirring occasionally, until the rice is just al dente, about 10 minutes. Drain the rice, spread on a rimmed baking sheet, discarding the bay leaf, and cool to room temperature.

Preheat the oven to 400°F. Line a rimmed baking sheet with parchment paper.

Put the panko in a food processor and process until finely ground. You need 1 cup; discard any excess.

Put the egg in a large bowl and beat it lightly. Add the ketchup, mayonnaise, hot sauce, miso, lemon juice, mustard, remaining 2 teaspoons salt, remaining ¼ teaspoon white pepper, and ½ teaspoon of the cayenne and mix well. Stir in the cooked rice, the celery, bell pepper, scallions, jalapeño, and fines herbes and combine thoroughly. Fold in the ground panko, then gently fold in the crab.

Divide the crab mixture among the crab tins or ramekins, patting the tops lightly to smooth. Combine the paprika and the remaining teaspoon of cayenne in a small bowl. Divide the softened butter among the prepared crab and sprinkle with the paprika mixture.

Place the crab tins or ramekins on the prepared baking sheet and bake for 15 minutes, or until hot throughout. Turn on the broiler and broil the crab mixture for about 1 minute, until golden brown on top. Transfer to a platter and serve.

CRISPY PIG'S EARS with Pimento Ranch

SERVES 6 AS A SNACK

7 fresh pig's ears

3 cups Pork Stock (page 346) or
    Chicken Stock (page 344)

Canola oil for deep-frying

1 cup rice flour

Kosher salt

About 2 cups Pimento Ranch
    (recipe follows)

EQUIPMENT

Electric pressure cooker (see Note)

Somehow I've become known as the crispy-pig-ear guy; I can't tell you how many times I've been stopped in airports to talk pig's ears. I was scared to put pig's ears on the menu at Husk when we first opened in Charleston. They were simply not an ingredient a lot of diners had tasted or felt comfortable with. Nowadays I don't think I could have a restaurant without offering pig's ears. I'm always trying to come up with new ways to serve them, from the lettuce wraps I started with to this gem. You can dip the fried strips of ears in the pimento ranch like you would French fries, or just douse them in the sauce for a Southern version of poutine.

NOTE: I like electric pressure cookers much more than the traditional stovetop ones. They are very easy to set, allowing you to cook your ingredients at a specific pressure for a precise amount of time, with no worries of overpressurization or an explosion from an unattended cooker on the stove. All the recipes in this book that call for pressure cookers were tested using an electric cooker.

Combine the ears and pork stock in the pressure cooker, lock on the lid, bring the cooker up to high pressure, and cook for 90 minutes.

Line a rimmed baking sheet with parchment paper. Carefully release the steam from the pressure cooker. The ears will be very soft; you should be able to pierce one easily with no resistance. Using a slotted spatula, carefully remove the ears and place them in a single layer on the prepared baking sheet. Refrigerate until cold. Strain the stock and freeze for another use, if desired.

When the ears are cold, cut them into ¼-inch-wide strips. (*The ears can be prepared to this point up to 1 day ahead. Put the strips in a container, cover, and refrigerate. Bring to room temperature before frying.*)

Fill a deep fryer with canola oil according to the manufacturer's directions and heat the oil to 350°F. Alternatively, fill a deep heavy pot half full with canola oil and heat the oil over medium heat to 350°F. The oil will splatter when the strips hit it, so have a splatter guard or a lid at hand. Line two wire racks with paper towels.

CONTINUED

Put the rice flour in a shallow bowl. Working in batches, dredge the ears in the flour, shaking off the excess, and fry until golden brown and crisp, 1½ to 2 minutes. Transfer the strips to wire racks to drain, season liberally with salt, and let stand for 1 minute.

Pile the pig's ears on a platter and serve with the pimento ranch alongside.

PIMENTO RANCH

MAKES ABOUT 3½ CUPS

1 cup Pimento Cheese (page 361), at room temperature

1½ cups full-fat buttermilk (see Note, page 27)

⅔ cup sour cream

1 teaspoon minced Pickled Ramps (page 251), plus 8 teaspoons of their pickling liquid

2 tablespoons minced jarred pimento peppers

1 tablespoon finely chopped chives

2 teaspoons Hot Sauce (page 260) or Red Clay Original Hot Sauce (see Resources, page 369)

2 teaspoons orange cheddar powder (see Resources, page 369)

2 teaspoons white cheddar powder (see Resources, page 369)

¼ teaspoon garlic powder

¼ teaspoon onion powder

¼ teaspoon Espelette pepper

⅛ teaspoon Bourbon Barrel Bourbon Smoked Paprika (see Resources, page 368)

Pinch of cayenne pepper

Leftover ranch makes an excellent dressing for iceberg wedge salads, with a little bacon.

Combine all the ingredients in a bowl and mix well. Transfer to a container, cover, and refrigerate. Tightly covered, the pimento ranch will keep for up to 1 week in the refrigerator.

SMOKED TROUT DIP

SERVES 6 AS A SNACK

SMOKED TROUT

4 cups water

½ cup loose black tea, or 8 regular black tea bags, preferably Bigelow's Charleston Tea Plantation American Classic Tea (see Resources, page 368)

¼ cup kosher salt

¼ cup sugar

12 ounces skin-on fresh trout fillets (about 2 fillets)

DIP

4 ounces cream cheese, at room temperature

½ cup sour cream

3 tablespoons prepared horseradish

2 teaspoons kosher salt

½ teaspoon Espelette pepper

1 tablespoon fresh lemon juice

1 tablespoon finely chopped Fines Herbes (page 356)

1 recipe Sorghum Seed Crackers (page 232), for serving

EQUIPMENT

Smoker

GOES WELL WITH:

*Sorghum Seed Crackers
   (page 232)*
Pickled Ramps (page 251)
Pickled Okra (page 242)
*Hominy and Pokeweed Griddle
   Cakes (page 211)*

This trout dip uses all parts of the fish, including the delicious fatty belly. I serve it with freshly baked sorghum seed crackers, but you can use whatever cracker, bread, or toasts you like.

You'll need to fire up the smoker to make this recipe. With that in mind, you might want to smoke more trout than you need for the dip. Tightly wrapped, smoked trout will keep for up to 2 months in the freezer.

NOTE: You'll need to start this recipe a day ahead of time to brine the trout.

FOR THE SMOKED TROUT: Put the water in a medium saucepan and bring to a boil over high heat. Remove from the stove, add the tea, and steep for 8 minutes.

Strain the tea into a nonreactive heatproof container large enough to hold the trout comfortably. Add the salt and sugar and stir until they have completely dissolved. Let cool to room temperature, then refrigerate the brine until completely cold.

Place the trout in the brine, cover, and refrigerate for 12 hours.

TO SMOKE THE TROUT: Line a wire rack with paper towels. Remove the trout from the brine, rinse under cold running water, and place on the rack. Let air-dry at room temperature for 1 hour.

While the trout is drying, prepare the smoker with hardwood charcoal and apple wood (see page 57); maintain the temperature at between 150°F and 160°F.

Smoke the trout for about 1 hour, until the flesh just starts to flake when lifted with a spatula. Transfer to a rimmed baking sheet and let cool to room temperature.

When the trout is cool, peel away the skin and discard. Gently flake the trout into approximately ½-inch pieces.

FOR THE DIP: Combine the cream cheese, sour cream, and horseradish in a medium bowl and mix until smooth. Add the salt, Espelette pepper, and lemon juice and mix well. Gently fold in the smoked trout and fines herbes. *(The dip can be made ahead. Tightly covered, it will keep for up to 2 days in the refrigerator. Remove from the refrigerator 20 minutes before serving.)*

TO SERVE: Offer the dip with crackers on the side.

GRILLED CHICKEN WINGS

with West African BBQ Sauce

MAKES 12 PIECES

WINGS

8 cups water

¼ cup kosher salt

1 tablespoon sorghum syrup, preferably Muddy Pond (see Resources, page 369)

6 chicken wings, separated into flats and drumettes, tips discarded or reserved for stock

3 tablespoons canola oil

½ teaspoon freshly ground black pepper

WEST AFRICAN BBQ SAUCE

1 jalapeño pepper

½ small sweet onion (about 4 ounces)

One 1-inch piece fresh ginger

1 tablespoon peanut oil

½ teaspoon Bourbon Barrel Bourbon Smoked Paprika (see Resources, page 368)

½ teaspoon coriander seeds

¼ teaspoon ground turmeric

¼ teaspoon black peppercorns

¼ teaspoon brown mustard seeds

1 black cardamom pod (see Resources, page 369)

1 dried bay leaf

One 1-inch piece cinnamon stick

½ star anise pod

¼ cup sorghum syrup, preferably Muddy Pond (see Resources, page 369)

1 cup BBQ Sauce (page 352)

1 tablespoon Boiled Peanut Miso (page 268)

¼ teaspoon kosher salt

It seems like I never reach my limit when eating chicken wings. (I've got a lot of research to do on the topic!) Here the spicy barbecue sauce combines my tried-and-true base recipe with some of the flavors I enjoyed on my trips to West Africa to study the region's wood-fire cooking traditions and their culinary connections with the South. I've yet to try it on something I didn't like. If you have any left over, serve it alongside a piece of simply seared fish.

NOTE: You'll need to plan ahead to brine the wings.

TO BRINE THE WINGS: Put the water in a pot and bring to a boil over high heat. Remove from the stove, add the salt and sorghum syrup, and stir until they have completely dissolved. Pour the brine into a nonreactive heatproof container large enough to hold the wings and cool to room temperature, then refrigerate until thoroughly cold.

Place the wings in the cold brine, cover, and refrigerate for at least 8 hours or up to overnight.

FOR THE SAUCE: Prepare a hot fire in a charcoal grill (see page 96), removing the grill rack and distributing the hot coals in an even layer in the bottom of the grill.

Put the jalapeño, onion, and ginger in the grill basket, place it on the coals, and grill, shaking the basket occasionally, until they are charred and the onion is starting to soften, 6 to 8 minutes. Transfer them to a cutting board and let cool slightly. Cover the grill to maintain the temperature to cook the wings; add a few more pieces of charcoal if necessary.

Peel the jalapeño and ginger. Cut the jalapeño in half and seed it. Roughly chop the jalapeño, onion, and ginger.

Heat the peanut oil in a large skillet over medium-high heat until it shimmers. Add the jalapeño, onion, and ginger and cook, stirring frequently, until lightly browned, about 8 minutes. Add the paprika, coriander seeds, turmeric, peppercorns, mustard seeds, cardamom pod, bay leaf, cinnamon stick, and star anise and cook, stirring constantly, to toast the spices, about 1 minute. Add the sorghum syrup and BBQ sauce and bring to a simmer, then reduce the heat to low and cook, stirring occasionally, for 5 minutes to develop the flavors. Remove from the stove and cool slightly.

EQUIPMENT

Round 15-inch open-top fine-mesh
   wire grill basket

GOES WELL WITH:

Pickled Peaches (page 250)
Pickled Chilies (page 248)

Transfer the sauce to a blender, add the miso and salt, and blend on high until completely smooth, about 1 minute. Transfer to a serving bowl and cool to room temperature. (*The sauce can be made ahead. Tightly covered, it will keep for up to 3 days in the refrigerator. Remove from the refrigerator 30 minutes before serving.*)

TO GRILL THE WINGS: Drain the wings and discard the brine. Dry the wings with paper towels and place them in a large bowl. Add the canola oil and toss to coat, then add ¼ teaspoon of the black pepper and toss again. Place the wings in a single layer in the grill basket and put the basket directly on the coals. Grill, turning the wings often with long-handled tongs, until deeply charred on all sides and cooked through, about 15 minutes. Transfer the wings to a bowl and toss with the remaining ¼ teaspoon black pepper.

TO SERVE: Pile the wings on a platter and offer the sauce alongside.

SEA ISLAND RED PEA SPREAD

with Cucumber-Tomato Salad

SERVES 4 AS A SNACK

RED PEAS

⅔ cup Anson Mills Sea Island Red
Peas (see Resources, page 368),
soaked in water to cover in the
refrigerator overnight

5 cups water

⅛ teaspoon baking soda

Kosher salt

SPREAD

2 tablespoons Vegetable Stock
(page 348)

1 garlic clove, grated or minced

1½ teaspoons grated lemon zest

2 tablespoons fresh lemon juice

2 tablespoons Benne Tahini (page
357)

1 teaspoon kosher salt

1 tablespoon extra-virgin olive oil

CUCUMBER-TOMATO SALAD

¾ cup small dice heirloom
tomatoes

¾ cup small dice English cucumber

1 tablespoon distilled white vinegar

1 teaspoon sugar

1 teaspoon ground sumac
(see Resources, page 369)

½ teaspoon kosher salt

1 tablespoon finely chopped mint

1 tablespoon extra-virgin olive oil

¼ teaspoon Bourbon Barrel
Bourbon Smoked Paprika
(see Resources, page 368)

1 recipe Appalachian Fry Bread
(page 231)

What would hummus look like if it came from the South? Like this beautiful spread made from Anson Mills dried red peas. The peas take the place of the traditional chickpeas, and they are blended with a tahini made from benne seeds. For a Southern analogue of the traditional pita, I make an Appalachian pone bread or fry bread. The cucumber-tomato salad adds crisp texture and cuts through the richness of the spread.

NOTE: You'll need to start this recipe a day ahead of time to soak the red peas.

FOR THE RED PEAS: Drain the peas. Transfer to a large saucepan, add the water and baking soda, stir well, and bring to a boil over high heat. Reduce the heat to low, cover, and cook, stirring occasionally, until the peas are completely soft and offer no resistance to a knife tip, about 45 minutes. Drain the peas, spread out on a rimmed baking sheet, season lightly with salt, and cool to room temperature, then transfer to a container and set aside. *(The peas can be cooked ahead. Tightly covered, they will keep for up to 1 day in the refrigerator.)*

FOR THE SPREAD: Combine 2 cups of the peas and the vegetable stock in a food processor and process until completely smooth. Add the garlic, lemon zest, lemon juice, benne tahini, and salt and process, slowly adding the olive oil, until smooth. Transfer to a container, cover, and refrigerate until thoroughly chilled. *(Tightly covered, the spread will keep for up to 3 days in the refrigerator.)*

FOR THE SALAD: Combine all the ingredients in a bowl and stir gently to mix well. *(The salad can be made ahead. Tightly covered, it will keep for up to 1 day in the refrigerator.)*

TO SERVE: Transfer the spread to a serving dish, drizzle with the olive oil, and sprinkle with the paprika. Offer the cucumber-tomato salad and fry bread alongside.

FRIED GREEN TOMATOES

SERVES 6 AS A SNACK OR APPETIZER

1½ cups full-fat buttermilk (see Note, page 27)

1 teaspoon Hot Sauce (page 260) or Red Clay Original Hot Sauce (see Resources, page 369)

1 tablespoon plus 1 teaspoon kosher salt, plus more for seasoning

1½ pounds medium green tomatoes, cored and cut into ½-inch-thick slices

1½ cups fine yellow cornmeal, preferably Anson Mills (see Resources, page 368)

½ cup all-purpose flour

½ teaspoon freshly ground black pepper

½ cup canola oil

¼ cup Rendered Fresh Lard (page 343)

1 cup Sour Corn Chowchow (page 274)

There are a hundred different ways to make fried green tomatoes, and some are more successful than others. The problem with most bad fried green tomatoes is overbreading, which can muffle the character and flavor of the tomatoes. I soak the sliced tomatoes in seasoned buttermilk and give them a dredge in cornmeal, but the most important part of the recipe is letting the breaded tomatoes rest in the refrigerator before you fry them. That rest eliminates the need for additional flour and a messy egg wash, and the tomatoes can be breaded up to 2 hours ahead of time, which is convenient when you're entertaining. When it's time to serve them, just pull them out and fry away. Chowchow—the quintessential Southern relish—is my go-to condiment for fried green tomatoes.

Combine the buttermilk, hot sauce, and 1 teaspoon of the salt in a large bowl. Add the green tomato slices and toss to coat. Let marinate at room temperature for 30 minutes, occasionally turning the tomatoes to ensure even coating.

Line a rimmed baking sheet with parchment paper. Combine the cornmeal, flour, the remaining tablespoon of salt, and the pepper in a shallow baking dish. Working with one slice at a time, shake off any excess buttermilk from the tomatoes, dredge in the cornmeal mixture, shake off any excess, and transfer to the prepared baking sheet. Transfer the baking sheet to the refrigerator and let the slices rest for at least 30 minutes and up to 2 hours.

Fifteen minutes before frying, remove the tomatoes from the refrigerator. Preheat the oven to 200°F. Line a rimmed baking sheet with paper towels.

Combine the canola oil and lard in a large deep cast-iron skillet and heat over medium heat to 350°F.

Working in batches, without crowding the pan, fry the tomatoes until crispy and golden brown on both sides, about 4 minutes; using a fork, carefully turn the tomatoes over halfway through frying to ensure that they cook evenly. As they are done, transfer the tomatoes to the prepared baking sheet, season lightly with salt, and keep warm in the oven while you fry the remaining slices.

Arrange the fried green tomatoes on a serving plate and accompany with a bowl of the chowchow.

FRIED BOLOGNA with Pickled Peach Mustard

MAKES 12 SLICES

PICKLED PEACH MUSTARD

½ cup Dijon mustard

½ cup chopped drained Pickled
  Peaches (page 250), plus
  1 teaspoon of their pickling juice

¾ teaspoon kosher salt

BOLOGNA

½ recipe Bologna (page 290),
  cut into ½-inch-thick slices, or
  1½ pounds high-quality store-
  bought bologna, cut into 12 slices

2 tablespoons unsalted butter

Like many kids in the South, I grew up eating fried bologna. It was one of the first things I was trusted to cook by myself. I loved getting out my mom's cast-iron skillet and cutting four slits in the edges of the bologna slice so it wouldn't curl up. The smell of it frying up always reminds me how lucky I am to have been raised in the Appalachian Mountains. The pickled peach mustard marries my childhood favorite with my more grown-up palate, with a nod to the summer flavors in my pantry.

FOR THE MUSTARD: Combine the mustard, pickled peaches, pickling juice, and salt in a blender and blend on high until completely smooth, about 1 minute. Transfer to a small serving dish. *(The mustard can be made ahead. Tightly covered, it will keep for up to 2 weeks in the refrigerator.)*

FOR THE BOLOGNA: Line a baking sheet with paper towels. Using a paring knife, notch each slice of bologna four times evenly around its circumference, cutting about ½ inch into the bologna.

Heat 1 tablespoon of the butter in a large cast-iron skillet over medium-high heat until foamy. Add half the bologna slices in a single layer and cook until deep brown on the first side, about 1½ minutes. Flip the slices and cook until the other side is deep brown, about 1 minute more. Transfer the fried bologna to the prepared baking sheet. Wipe out the skillet, add the remaining tablespoon of butter, and cook the remaining bologna slices.

TO SERVE: Arrange the bologna slices on a platter with the pickled peach mustard.

SMOKED BABY BACK RIBS

with Benne BBQ Sauce

SERVES 4 AS A SNACK

RIBS

1 rack baby back pork ribs (about 2 pounds), white membrane removed

⅓ cup BBQ Rub (page 363)

2 tablespoons Anson Mills Antebellum Benne Seeds (see Resources, page 368)

BENNE BBQ SAUCE

1 cup BBQ Sauce (page 352)

¼ cup Benne Tahini (page 357)

1 teaspoon sorghum syrup, preferably Muddy Pond (see Resources, page 369)

1 teaspoon benne oil (see Resources, page 369)

½ teaspoon kosher salt

2 tablespoons thinly sliced scallion greens

8 pieces Pork Rinds (page 355)

EQUIPMENT

Smoker

Pork ribs are one of those iconic Southern offerings that every cook has his or her own method for. For a long time, I've been obsessed with perfecting the process of making them, and I've eaten a lot of ribs over the years, with countless sauces and condiments alongside them. This technique is the one I keep coming back to. The earthy nuttiness of benne seeds adds an unexpected depth of flavor to the barbecue sauce.

Take your time and enjoy the experience of hanging out by the smoker while slow-cooking the pork. Some of the best lies I've ever heard have been served up in a cloud of rib smoke.

FOR THE RIBS: Prepare the smoker with hardwood charcoal and hickory (see page 57); maintain the temperature at between 240°F and 250°F.

Liberally rub the ribs with the BBQ rub, making sure to cover every surface. Put the ribs in the smoker and smoke them until a bone comes away easily when pulled, 4 to 5 hours.

While the ribs are smoking, heat a large skillet over medium heat. Add the benne seeds and cook, stirring constantly, for 2 to 3 minutes, until the seeds start to smell a little nutty. Transfer to a plate and cool to room temperature.

FOR THE SAUCE: About 30 minutes before the ribs come out of the smoker, combine the BBQ sauce, benne tahini, sorghum syrup, benne oil, and salt in a blender and blend until smooth.

About 10 minutes before the ribs are done, baste them with the sauce, using about half. When the ribs are ready, transfer them to a cutting board and let rest for 5 minutes.

TO SERVE: Cut the ribs into 2-bone pieces and put them in a large bowl. Add the remaining sauce and the benne seeds and toss to coat the ribs. Pile the ribs on a platter and sprinkle with the scallion greens and pork rinds.

SMOKING

Smoking as a method of food preparation and preservation is almost as old as cooking itself. Our ancestors noticed that food exposed to wood fire and smoke not only kept longer but tasted better too. It's a technique that is found in Southern cooking and practically every other cuisine across the globe.

The chemical makeup of wood smoke is incredibly complex, with hundreds of compounds released in combustion. Every wood produces its own cocktail of these volatile chemicals, and they differ further depending on temperature and how dry (or cured) the wood is. All these factors combine to give any hardwood its unique flavor and aroma characteristics. I use apple or hickory for the recipes in this book, but you should use whatever cured hardwood you like.

By nature, the smoking process is a social thing. Doing it properly takes not only time but also fairly regular attention to make sure the temperature and smoke levels are just right. It's a great opportunity to sit around with a group of friends and family, whiling away the time with good stories, all punctuated with that enticing wood smoke aroma. Lawn chairs, cold drinks, and good music are crucial ingredients of any smoking recipe.

You don't need an expensive setup to make delicious smoked foods at home. Whether you have a charcoal smoker or one fueled by propane or electricity, there are three elements involved in successful smoking: wood, temperature, and cooking time. Getting these right will result in a finished product that you and your guests won't be able to get enough of. Here are a few things to keep in mind while manning the smoker.

- **Before starting, scan a range of recipes for whatever ingredient you're smoking.** Taking an average of the times and temperatures you find will give you a good estimate of what to aim for.

- **Keep a notebook where you jot down the results each time you fire up the smoker.** Tracking the differences in cooking time, temperature, and wood choice each time you smoke the same item will help you zero in on the formula that's just right for your equipment and conditions.

- **Keep the temperature in your smoker 30 to 40 degrees higher than the target internal temperature for whatever you're smoking.** For Pit-Cooked-Chicken Sandwiches (page 130), for example, the barbecue-rubbed whole chickens need to cook until an instant-read thermometer registers 165°F, so you will need to keep the temperature in your smoker hovering at just around 200°F.

- **Cook your meat until it's really ready.** I know that might sound like a silly thing to say, but doneness doesn't mean the time is up. For meat with bones, you ought to be able to pull the bone away cleanly, with little to no resistance. For a boneless cut like brisket, you should be able to easily pull away a big hunk of meat. If you're following a recipe or method from a cookbook or online source and the meat is still tough after the recommended time, keep smoking!

- **Relax and enjoy yourself.** Have fun taking part in a cooking tradition that reaches back to prehistory.

OL' FUSKIE CRAB RICE

SERVES 6 AS AN APPETIZER

BASE

¼ cup small dice slab bacon, preferably Benton's (see Resources, page 368)

⅓ cup dried shrimp (see Resources, page 369)

1¼ cups very finely diced sweet onion

1 cup very finely diced celery

1 cup very finely diced red bell pepper

2 teaspoons minced garlic

1 tablespoon kosher salt

RICE

4 cups water

1 tablespoon kosher salt

¼ teaspoon freshly ground white pepper

1 fresh bay leaf

1¼ cups Anson Mills Carolina Gold Rice (see Resources, page 368)

4 tablespoons unsalted butter, diced

CRAB

3 tablespoons unsalted butter

1 pound fresh lump blue crab meat, carefully picked over for shells and cartilage

1 tablespoon fresh lemon juice

2 tablespoons Tomato Jam (page 281)

2 tablespoons finely chopped chives

2 tablespoons grated Crab Roe Bottarga (page 295; casing removed, grated with a Microplane)

There are two key things to know when cooking a good plate of crab rice: The first is to cook the rice separately, really focusing on it so it keeps its unique flavor and character. The second is to cook the crab with the attention it requires. The trick is to spread the crabmeat mixture in a thin, even layer in the skillet and then not disturb it until it's browned on the bottom. It takes a lot of patience, courage, trust, and confidence in yourself, but once you make crab rice a couple of times, it will all seem natural.

Use all your senses when cooking this dish. Smell the crab as it starts to brown; it has a very distinct, delicious aroma. Listen for the popping and crackling that will start when the pan is almost dry. Once you hear that, take a little peek underneath to see if the crab is getting some light brown color. When you smell that aroma, hear that sizzle, and see that color, take the pan off the stove and gently fold in the lemon juice. There are few things better than crab cooked just right.

FOR THE BASE: Put the bacon in a large skillet and cook over medium heat until it starts to soften and the fat begins to render, about 1 minute. Add the dried shrimp and cook, stirring, for 1 minute. Add the onion, celery, bell pepper, garlic, and salt and cook, stirring occasionally, until the vegetables are softened, about 6 minutes. Remove from the stove and set aside.

FOR THE RICE: Combine the water, salt, white pepper, and bay leaf in a medium saucepan, bring to a boil over medium-high heat, and stir to be sure the salt has dissolved completely. Reduce the heat to medium, add the rice, stir once, and bring to a simmer. Simmer gently, uncovered, stirring occasionally, until the rice is al dente, about 10 minutes. Drain. Transfer to another medium saucepan, discarding the bay leaf. Stir in the butter and cover to keep warm.

FOR THE CRAB: Heat the butter in a large skillet over high heat until foamy. Add the base mixture and the crab, spread it into a thin, even layer, reduce the heat to medium, and cook, undisturbed, until the crab begins to brown on the bottom, 3 to 4 minutes. Remove from the heat and gently fold in the lemon juice.

TO SERVE: Put a dollop of tomato jam in the center of each of six warm plates. Divide the rice among the plates, placing it on top of the jam, and sprinkle with the chives. Spoon the crab on top and sprinkle with the bottarga.

TRADITIONAL SHRIMP AND GRITS

**SERVES 6 AS AN APPETIZER,
4 AS A MAIN COURSE**

½ cup all-purpose flour

1 tablespoon kosher salt, plus more
for seasoning

½ teaspoon freshly ground black
pepper, plus more for seasoning

1 teaspoon canola oil

2 ounces country ham, preferably
Bob Wood's (see Resources, page
368), cut into ¼-inch dice

1 pound 21–25-count shrimp,
preferably local, peeled and
deveined

4 ounces small button mushrooms,
washed, dried, and quartered

¼ cup thinly sliced scallions

½ cup Vegetable Stock (page 348)

2 tablespoons unsalted butter,
diced

1 tablespoon fresh lemon juice

1 recipe Stovetop Grits (page 220),
just cooked and still warm

This is shrimp and grits at its simplest. It's a quick, easy, one-pan dish, and it is the only way I cook shrimp and grits at home. The recipe is a tribute to the late chef Bill Neal, of Crook's Corner in Chapel Hill, North Carolina. He was one of the first chefs to celebrate the dish and elevate it into the realm of the restaurant. Bill's vision made it possible for chefs, including me, to serve shrimp and grits in restaurants all over the South. Making this dish is my chance to pay back that debt.

Combine the flour, salt, and pepper in a shallow bowl, mix well, and set aside.

Heat the canola oil in a large skillet over medium heat, add the ham, and cook, stirring frequently, until the fat has rendered and the ham is crisp, about 3 minutes.

Lightly dredge the shrimp in the seasoned flour, shaking off any excess, and carefully add them to the hot skillet. Cook until lightly browned on the first side, 1 to 2 minutes. Turn the shrimp, add the mushrooms and scallions, and cook until the other side of the shrimp is lightly browned and the mushrooms and scallions begin to soften, about 2 minutes. Add the vegetable stock, bring to a simmer, and cook until it has reduced by half and the shrimp are just cooked through, about 2 minutes. Stir in the butter and lemon juice and season lightly with salt and pepper.

Give the grits a good stir, then divide them among warmed bowls. Spoon the shrimp and mushrooms, with their broth, on top.

SHRIMP AND GRITS

with Roasted Tomatoes, Fennel, and Sausage

**SERVES 6 AS AN APPETIZER,
4 AS A MAIN COURSE**

8 ounces smoked breakfast
   sausage, preferably Jakes
   Brothers (see Resources, page
   368)

1 recipe Oven-Roasted Tomatoes
   (page 198)

1 recipe Braised Fennel (page 194),
   with the cooking liquid

⅓ cup heavy cream

Forty 26–30-count shrimp,
   preferably local, peeled and
   deveined

1 tablespoon fresh lemon juice

1 teaspoon Hot Sauce (page 260)
   or Red Clay Original Hot Sauce
   (see Resources, page 369)

2 teaspoons kosher salt

1 tablespoon Fines Herbes
   (page 356)

1 recipe Pressure-Cooker Grits
   (page 221), just cooked and still
   warm

½ recipe Crispy Pig's Ears (page
   43; optional)

Fennel fronds and flowers for
   garnish (optional)

The shrimp and grits recipe on the preceding page represents tradition; this one explores what shrimp and grits can be. It blends the food of the coastal South with one of the great ingredients of the Appalachian Mountains: sack sausage. Sack sausage is a version of traditional pork breakfast sausage. Stuffed into a linen sack, bag, or (in the worst-case scenario) even a sock, it's left to ferment and then cold-smoked for days and days. The sausage adds a depth and soul to the dish that you don't always find in the traditional recipes. But because sack sausage can be hard to come by, this recipe calls for good breakfast sausage, which works well here. The roasted tomatoes and braised fennel brighten up the whole dish and give it the freshness it needs.

Oftentimes I finish the dish with some crispy fried pig's ears, but don't skip this recipe because you don't want to go through all the effort of cooking pig's ears. Leave them out, and it's still delicious.

Cook the sausage in a large skillet over medium-high heat, stirring frequently, until browned and broken up into small pieces. Add the roasted tomatoes, fennel wedges, fennel cooking liquid, and cream and cook until the liquid has slightly reduced and thickened, about 10 minutes.

Add the shrimp and simmer, stirring gently, until they are pink and just beginning to curl, about 4 minutes. Stir in the lemon juice, hot sauce, salt, and fines herbes.

Give the grits a good stir, then divide them among warm bowls. Spoon the shrimp and vegetables, with their broth, on top. Divide the pig's ears, if using, among the bowls. Garnish with fennel fronds and fennel flowers, if desired.

SOUPS and SALADS

CHILLED SUMMER SQUASH SOUP

with Buttermilk and Sunflower Seeds

SERVES 4

BUTTERMILK CURDS

2 cups full-fat buttermilk (see Note, page 27)

1 tablespoon fresh lemon juice

¼ teaspoon kosher salt

⅛ teaspoon freshly ground white pepper

SQUASH SOUP

4 cups thinly sliced yellow summer squash (from about 1 pound squash)

½ cup small dice English cucumber

¼ cup plus 2 tablespoons small dice sweet onion

1½ cups Vegetable Stock (page 348)

1 cup sunflower oil (see Resources, page 369), plus more for drizzling

2 teaspoons kosher salt

½ teaspoon freshly ground black pepper

1 tablespoon fresh lemon juice

SUNFLOWER SEEDS

½ cup raw hulled sunflower seeds

1 teaspoon sunflower oil (see Resources, page 369)

¼ teaspoon Espelette pepper

¼ teaspoon kosher salt

4 baby cucumbers with blossoms attached for garnish (optional)

This simple soup pairs the clean flavor of fresh yellow squash with buttermilk, sunflower, and cucumber. It's not uncommon to find the three plants growing side by side in a summer garden, so putting them together makes for a natural fit. The tart buttermilk curds and the sunflower oil give the soup a hint of richness, and, because you'll have leftovers, the toasted sunflower seeds double as a crunchy garnish and an addictive snack. Make this during the balmy summer months.

NOTE: You'll need to start this recipe a day ahead of time to allow the buttermilk curds to drain overnight.

FOR THE BUTTERMILK CURDS: Line a strainer with a double layer of cheesecloth and place it over a bowl. Heat the buttermilk in a small nonreactive saucepan over medium heat, stirring frequently, until the temperature reaches 170°F (use an instant-read thermometer to check). Stir in the lemon juice, salt, and white pepper and keep the mixture at 170°F for 2 minutes; curds should form. Pour the mixture into the strainer, place the bowl and strainer in the refrigerator, and refrigerate overnight.

The next day, transfer the buttermilk curds to a container, cover, and refrigerate until ready to use. (*Tightly covered, the curds will keep for up to 3 days in the refrigerator.*)

Measure out ¼ cup of the whey that drained into the bowl for the squash soup and refrigerate. Reserve the rest of the whey for another use, if desired. (*Tightly covered, the whey can be kept for up to 3 days in the refrigerator or up to 3 months in the freezer. It can be used in baking or a buttermilk dressing, or to season a potato puree.*)

FOR THE SOUP: Combine the squash, cucumber, onion, vegetable stock, and the reserved ¼ cup whey in a blender and blend on high until completely smooth, about 2 minutes. With the motor running on low speed, slowly drizzle in the sunflower oil and blend until emulsified. Blend in the salt, black pepper, and lemon juice. Strain the soup through a fine-mesh sieve into a container, cover, and refrigerate until chilled. (*Tightly covered, the soup will keep for up to 2 days in the refrigerator.*)

CONTINUED

FOR THE SUNFLOWER SEEDS: Preheat the oven to 325°F. Line a rimmed baking sheet with parchment paper.

Spread the seeds out in a single layer on the prepared baking sheet and toast them in the oven for 25 to 30 minutes, stirring occasionally, until golden brown and crisp.

Transfer the seeds to a small bowl, drizzle in the sunflower oil, and toss. Add the Espelette pepper and salt and toss again. Return the seeds to the baking sheet, spread them out in an even layer, and cool to room temperature, then transfer to an airtight container and set aside at room temperature until ready to serve. *(You need only about ¼ cup of the seeds to garnish the soup; the rest are great for snacking. Tightly covered, the seeds will keep for up to 1 month at room temperature.)*

TO SERVE: Divide the soup among four bowls. Spoon some of the buttermilk curds into the center of each bowl and sprinkle with about 1 tablespoon of the sunflower seeds. Drizzle each portion with sunflower oil and garnish each with a baby cucumber, if desired.

GROUNDNUT SOUP

SERVES 4

2½ tablespoons unsalted butter

½ cup fine dice sweet onion

¼ cup fine dice celery

1 teaspoon minced garlic

2½ tablespoons all-purpose flour

4 cups Chicken Stock (page 344)

1 fresh bay leaf

¼ cup plus 1 tablespoon Boiled
   Peanut Miso (page 268) or
   creamy peanut butter

1 tablespoon Frangelico liqueur

½ teaspoon kosher salt

¼ teaspoon freshly ground white
   pepper

¼ cup shelled green peanuts
   (about 4 ounces in the shell; see
   Resources, page 369), finely
   chopped

2 tablespoons peanut oil, preferably
   Oliver Farm Green Peanut Oil (see
   Resources, page 369)

4 tablespoons chervil leaves for
   garnish

I'd never heard of groundnut soup before I moved to Richmond in my early twenties to work at Lemaire in the Jefferson Hotel. But the soup is very, very popular in that town, so I quickly learned how to make it from chef Walter Bundy. When I started collecting classic old Southern cookbooks, I saw the recipe in nearly all of them. Not surprisingly, none of those recipes includes boiled peanut miso, but I think it's worth making. The miso adds a unique umami boost and texture to the soup, but in a pinch, you can substitute creamy peanut butter; just be sure to season the soup with a little extra salt.

NOTE: Green peanuts are available from summer into fall throughout the South and are sold in many grocery stores—or see Resources (page 369).

Heat the butter in a medium saucepan over medium heat until foamy. Add the onion and celery and cook, stirring often, until translucent, about 5 minutes. Add the garlic and cook, stirring frequently, for 2 minutes. Reduce the heat to medium-low, stir in the flour, and cook, stirring constantly, for 2 minutes to make a light roux.

Slowly add the chicken stock, stirring constantly to prevent lumps. Add the bay leaf, increase the heat to medium, and simmer, stirring frequently, until the soup begins to thicken, about 5 minutes. Reduce the heat to low and simmer for 15 minutes more to develop the flavors. Remove from the stove and cool slightly; remove and discard the bay leaf.

Working in batches if necessary, transfer the soup to a blender, add the miso, and blend on high until completely smooth, about 2 minutes. Blend in the Frangelico, salt, and white pepper. Strain the soup through a fine-mesh sieve into a clean saucepan. (*The soup can be made ahead. Tightly covered once cooled, it will keep for up to 3 days in the refrigerator.*)

Gently reheat the soup over medium heat if necessary, stirring often. Divide the soup among four warm bowls. Sprinkle with the green peanuts and drizzle with the peanut oil. Garnish each bowl with about 1 tablespoon of the chervil leaves and serve.

CREAM OF MOREL SOUP

SERVES 4

1½ cups plus ½ teaspoon kosher salt

8 ounces fresh morels

2 tablespoons unsalted butter

2 tablespoons small dice sweet onion

1 teaspoon minced garlic

2 tablespoons all-purpose flour

3 cups Mushroom Stock (page 349), at room temperature

1½ cups heavy cream

½ teaspoon freshly ground white pepper

In the mountains where I grew up, the old-timers called morels "dry-land fish" and usually ate them fried in a beer batter. But fresh morels are a luxury, and I like to let them shine in the most luxurious cream of mushroom soup you can imagine.

Fill a large deep bowl or container with 2½ gallons warm water, add ½ cup of the salt, and stir until it has dissolved. Add the morels and let them soak for 1 hour.

Using a wire rack, push the morels down a little in the brine and, with your other hand, skim any leaves and debris from the top with a fine-mesh sieve. Remove the rack and gently lift out the morels, trying not to disturb the debris that has settled at the bottom of the bowl. Repeat the soaking procedure twice, using ½ cup salt each time, then lay the morels out on the rack and let them air-dry at room temperature until completely dry, 30 minutes to 1 hour.

Roughly chop the morels.

Heat the butter in a medium saucepan over medium heat until foamy. Add the onion and morels and cook, stirring often, until the onion is translucent and the morels are softened, about 10 minutes. Add the garlic and cook, stirring frequently, for 2 minutes. Reduce the heat to medium-low, stir in the flour, and cook, stirring constantly, for 2 minutes to make a light roux.

Slowly add the mushroom stock, stirring constantly to prevent lumps, then bring to a simmer and cook, stirring frequently, until the soup begins to thicken, about 5 minutes. Add the cream, reduce the heat to low, and simmer the soup for 15 minutes to develop the flavors. Remove from the stove and cool slightly.

Working in batches if necessary, transfer the soup to a blender and blend on high until completely smooth, about 3 minutes. Blend in the remaining ½ teaspoon salt and the white pepper. (*The soup can be made ahead. Tightly covered, it will keep for up to 3 days in the refrigerator.*)

Reheat the soup gently over medium-low heat, if necessary. Divide among four warm bowls and serve.

SHE-CRAB SOUP

SERVES 4

Three 6- to 8-ounce live blue crabs (see Note), or one 8-ounce container fresh blue crab meat, carefully picked over for shells and cartilage

3 cups whole milk

1½ cups heavy cream

4 tablespoons unsalted butter, diced

¾ cup small dice sweet onion

3 tablespoons all-purpose flour

1½ teaspoons Worcestershire sauce, preferably Bourbon Barrel (see Resources, page 368)

¼ teaspoon ground mace

2 teaspoons kosher salt

½ teaspoon freshly ground white pepper

¼ cup finely chopped tarragon

¼ cup dry vermouth

1 tablespoon fresh lemon juice

4 tablespoons grated Crab Roe Bottarga (page 295; casing removed, grated with a Microplane)

She-crab soup has several origin stories, but there seems to be a consensus that it came to the Lowcountry via Scottish immigrants, who brought with them a recipe for *partan bree*, or crab soup. The dish as we would recognize it now was probably served for the first time in the early 1900s. One bit of lore has it that Charleston's then mayor, Robert Goodwyn Rhett, instructed his butler, William Deas, to spruce up traditional crab soup to impress President Taft during his visit to the city. Deas added the bright orange roe of Charleston's blue crabs, and a classic was born. When the soup is prepared well, you realize that it is famous for a reason. Make it during crab season when you can get beautiful live fresh blue crabs. I cure the crab roe much like bottarga and finish the soup with a generous grating of it right before it hits the table.

NOTE: Ask your fishmonger for male crabs. They generally have a higher ratio of meat to shell. If you don't want to cook fresh crabs or can't get them, you can substitute a container of fresh blue crab meat.

To humanely kill the crabs, chill them in the refrigerator for at least 2 hours to gradually reduce their body temperature; this will slow their metabolism and make them easier and safer to handle. Then, one at a time, remove the crabs from the refrigerator, place on a cutting board, and insert the sharp point of a sturdy knife through the shell directly behind the eyes.

Combine the crabs, milk, and cream in a medium pot and bring to a simmer over medium heat, stirring occasionally to prevent scorching. Reduce the heat to low and simmer, uncovered, for 30 minutes to cook the crabs through and develop the flavor. Remove the crabs with tongs, quickly rinse them under cool running water, place on a rimmed baking sheet, and cool to room temperature.

Strain the milk mixture through a fine-mesh sieve into a container and cool to room temperature.

When the crabs are cool, pick the meat (see the box on the following page) and discard the shells. Transfer the crabmeat to a container, cover, and refrigerate until ready to use.

CONTINUED

Heat the butter in a medium saucepan over medium-high heat until foamy. Add the onion and cook, stirring often, until translucent, about 4 minutes. Stir in the flour and cook, stirring constantly, for about 1 minute to make a very light roux.

Slowly add the milk mixture, stirring constantly to prevent lumps. Add the Worcestershire sauce, mace, salt, and white pepper, reduce the heat to low, and simmer, partially covered, for 10 minutes to develop the flavors.

Fold in the crab and heat through. Fold in the tarragon, vermouth, and lemon juice.

Divide the soup among four warm bowls and sprinkle each with about 1 tablespoon of the bottarga.

HOW TO PICK A COOKED BLUE CRAB

Using your hands, break off the two large front claws and set aside. Hold the crab in one hand and carefully pry off the top shell with your other hand. If you have female crabs and find bright orange, sweet roe when you open the shell, remove it and reserve it as an additional garnish for the soup. Give the inside of the crab a quick rinse under cold running water to wash away the internal organs and any fat. Using kitchen shears, cut away the triangular gills from both sides of the crab and discard. Turn the crab over and remove the apron—the tab-like feature—and discard. Cut the crab lengthwise in half. Using the kitchen shears or a large chef's knife, make a cut between each leg through the body of the crab. Using your fingers, carefully pick the crabmeat from the cartilaginous membranes where the legs meet the body. Using the back of a large chef's knife or a small wooden mallet, crack open the claw and leg joints to reveal more crabmeat; remove it. Discard all the shells. Pick over the crabmeat for any shell fragments or cartilage. Transfer to a container, cover, and refrigerate. Tightly covered, the crabmeat will keep for up to 3 days in the refrigerator.

KILLED LETTUCES

CORNBREAD CRUMBS

12 ounces slab bacon, preferably Benton's (see Resources, page 368), cut into ¼-inch dice

¼ recipe Basic Cornbread (page 216), made a day ahead, crumbled

½ teaspoon kosher salt

¼ teaspoon freshly ground black pepper

VINAIGRETTE

¼ cup apple cider vinegar

2½ teaspoons sorghum syrup, preferably Muddy Pond (see Resources, page 369)

¼ teaspoon kosher salt

¼ teaspoon freshly ground black pepper

TO COMPLETE

1 red spring onion (with a 1-inch bulb), green top removed and reserved for another use

1 white spring onion (with a 1-inch bulb), green top removed and reserved for another use

1½ pounds baby lettuces, such as Black Seeded Simpson, Lolla Rosa, and red oak leaf, washed and dried

3 tablespoons onion flowers (optional)

GOES WELL WITH:

Pickled Eggs (page 253)

"Killed lettuces"—also known as "kilt lettuces"—at its simplest is nothing more than fresh lettuces and hot fat, usually bacon grease (it's the original hot bacon dressing). You can serve the lettuce simply with some sliced red onion to give it a kick. To take it to another level, as I do here, add seasoned cornbread crumbs, delicate slices of spring onions along with their flowers, and a hot vinaigrette enhanced with sweet sorghum syrup.

FOR THE CORNBREAD CRUMBS: Preheat the oven to 350°F.

Put the bacon in a large cast-iron skillet and cook over medium heat, stirring frequently, until the fat has rendered and the bacon is crisp. Remove the bacon with a slotted spoon and drain it on paper towels. You will need approximately ½ cup of the rendered bacon fat; if there is more, remove it from the skillet, cool to room temperature, cover, and refrigerate. *(Tightly covered, the bacon fat will keep for up to 3 weeks in the refrigerator.)* Move the skillet to the back of the stove to keep the reserved ½ cup bacon fat warm.

Combine the cornbread crumbs, 1½ teaspoons of the reserved rendered fat, the salt, and the pepper in a large bowl and gently stir to mix well. Transfer the mixture to a rimmed baking sheet, spread it out in a thin, even layer, and bake for 10 to 12 minutes, until the crumbs are dried and crispy. Remove from the oven and cool to room temperature.

Combine the crumbs and half the crispy bacon pieces in a container. Cover and set aside at room temperature. Reserve the remaining bacon for another use, or snack on it.

FOR THE VINAIGRETTE: Whisk the vinegar, sorghum syrup, salt, and pepper into the bacon fat remaining in the skillet.

TO COMPLETE: Thinly slice the onion bulbs and separate them into individual rings. Divide the lettuces and onions among six salad bowls.

Heat the vinaigrette over medium heat, whisking, until it begins to bubble. Sprinkle each salad with cornbread crumbs and some onion flowers, if desired. Pour the hot vinaigrette over the salads and serve immediately.

HEIRLOOM TOMATO AND WATERMELON SALAD

SERVES 6

PECANS
....

1 cup raw pecan pieces
(about 3 ounces)

2 teaspoons pecan oil, preferably
Oliver Farms (see Resources,
page 369)

½ teaspoon kosher salt

VINAIGRETTE
....

¼ cup Watermelon Molasses
(page 284)

2 teaspoons fish sauce

2 tablespoons fresh lime juice

2 tablespoons extra-virgin olive oil

2 tablespoons pecan oil, preferably
Oliver Farms (see Resources,
page 369)

SALAD
....

3 pounds heirloom tomatoes, cut
into ¾-inch dice

½ ripe 8- to 10-pound watermelon,
rind removed, seeded, and cut
into ¾-inch dice

2 banana peppers, seeded and
sliced into very thin rings, or to
taste (see Note)

Kosher salt and freshly ground
black pepper

Small basil leaves for garnish

GOES WELL WITH:

Cottage Cheese (page 360)
Fresh Cheese (page 362)

At one time in the nineteenth century, the Bradford watermelon was among the most coveted varieties in the South, so much so that it even resulted in the killings of some unlucky would-be pillagers. Farmers protected their crops by poisoning unmarked melons in the field or even electrifying their melon patches to give unsuspecting thieves an often deadly jolt. The Bradford watermelon would have been lost to us forever if it weren't for the passion, foresight, and hard work of just a few people. The current Bradford responsible for continuing the line is Nat, the sixth great-grandson of the melon's developer, Nathaniel Bradford.

When I get my hands on one of these prize melons for the first time each year, it's hard not to eat the whole thing as it is, but this salad accentuates the melon's natural sweetness and refreshing texture—or that of any good ripe watermelon. Dress the salad with molasses made from watermelon and accompany it with field-ripe tomatoes and spicy banana peppers.

NOTE: Banana peppers vary in heat. Taste a small slice of yours first to see how much you want to add.

FOR THE PECANS: Preheat the oven to 325°F. Line a rimmed baking sheet with parchment paper.

Spread the pecan pieces out in a single layer on the prepared baking sheet and toast them in the oven for 10 to 15 minutes, until aromatic and slightly crisp. Transfer the pecans to a small bowl, drizzle in the pecan oil, add the salt, and toss to coat. Return the pecans to the baking sheet, spread them out, and cool to room temperature.

Roughly chop the pecans, transfer to an airtight container, and set aside. (*Tightly covered, the pecans will keep for up to 1 week at room temperature.*)

FOR THE VINAIGRETTE: Combine the molasses, fish sauce, and lime juice in a small bowl. Combine the olive oil and pecan oil in a separate small bowl. Whisking constantly, slowly drizzle the oils into the molasses mixture and whisk until emulsified. (*The vinaigrette can be made ahead. Tightly covered, it will keep for up to 2 days in the refrigerator. Whisk before using to re-emulsify.*)

FOR THE SALAD: Combine the tomatoes, watermelon, pepper rings, and pecans in a bowl, add the vinaigrette, season with salt and black pepper, toss to coat, and sprinkle with basil leaves.

BABY COLLARDS

with Benne Caesar Dressing and Cornbread Croutons

SERVES 6

PICKLED ONIONS

1 cup red wine vinegar

1 cup water

¼ cup sugar

¼ teaspoon kosher salt

1 small red onion (about 8 ounces), shaved paper-thin

BENNE CAESAR DRESSING

¼ cup Anson Mills Antebellum Benne Seeds (see Resources, page 368)

⅓ cup red wine vinegar

¼ cup benne oil (see Resources, page 369)

¼ teaspoon grated or minced garlic

¾ teaspoon grated lemon zest

3 tablespoons fresh lemon juice

¾ teaspoon grated bottarga, preferably Cortez Bottarga mullet bottarga (see Resources, page 368; casing removed, grated with a Microplane)

¾ teaspoon mustard powder

½ teaspoon minced Preserved Lemon peel (see page 257)

1 tablespoon agave nectar

½ teaspoon freshly ground black pepper, preferably Bourbon Barrel Smoked Black Pepper (see Resources, page 368)

¼ cup plus 2 tablespoons mayonnaise, preferably Duke's (see Resources, page 369)

¼ cup plus 2 tablespoons grated Manchego cheese (about 1½ ounces)

1 large egg yolk

I eat a *lot* of Caesar salads, and I know I'm not alone in my love of a good Caesar. I'd always wanted to do a Southern riff on one but could never really make it work because there aren't many options for anchovies produced in the South. Finally I found the solution in Florida-based Cortez Bottarga's mullet bottarga. I use it in the dressing for this Southern Caesar, which also includes cornbread croutons and benne seeds.

FOR THE PICKLED ONIONS: Combine the vinegar, water, sugar, and salt in a small nonreactive saucepan and bring to a boil over high heat, stirring to dissolve the sugar and salt. Put the onions in a nonreactive heatproof container and pour the hot pickling liquid over them. Cool to room temperature, cover, and refrigerate for at least 4 hours. (Tightly covered, the onions will keep for up to 1 week in the refrigerator.)

Preheat the oven to 350°F.

FOR THE DRESSING: Heat a large skillet over medium heat. Add the benne seeds and cook, stirring constantly, for 2 to 3 minutes, until they start to smell a little nutty. Transfer to a plate and cool to room temperature.

Combine the benne seeds, vinegar, benne oil, garlic, lemon zest, lemon juice, bottarga, mustard powder, preserved lemon peel, agave nectar, and pepper in a blender and blend on high until completely smooth, about 1 minute. Add the mayonnaise, cheese, egg yolk, Worcestershire sauce, garlic powder, onion powder, and olive oil and blend on low until just combined. Transfer to a container, cover, and refrigerate until ready to serve. (Tightly covered, the dressing will keep for up to 2 days in the refrigerator.)

TO COMPLETE: Combine the collards and dressing in a large bowl and toss well. Divide among six individual salad bowls. Divide the pickled onions and cornbread croutons among the salads and top with the bottarga, cheese, and benne seeds.

1 tablespoon Worcestershire sauce, preferably Bourbon Barrel (see Resources, page 368)

½ teaspoon garlic powder

¼ teaspoon onion powder

¾ teaspoon extra-virgin olive oil

TO COMPLETE

10 ounces baby collard greens, cut crosswise into 1-inch-wide strips, washed in several changes of water, and dried

1 cup Cornbread Croutons (358)

2 tablespoons grated bottarga, preferably Cortez Bottarga mullet bottarga (see Resources, page 368; casing removed, grated with a Microplane)

¼ cup grated Manchego cheese (about 2 ounces)

1 teaspoon Anson Mills Antebellum Benne Seeds (see Resources, page 368)

GOES WELL WITH:

Strip Steak with Worcestershire (page 142)

Grilled Swordfish with Green Gumbo (page 101)

COUNTRY HAM ROAD MAP

Geography class would've been so much more fun with this map. Dotted across the Southern states are amazing examples of one of my all-time favorite foods: the cured country ham. Here's my top-nine list of the best country hams—these are some of my favorites. Variations in microclimate, smokiness, saltiness, and sweetness make for an entire world to explore.

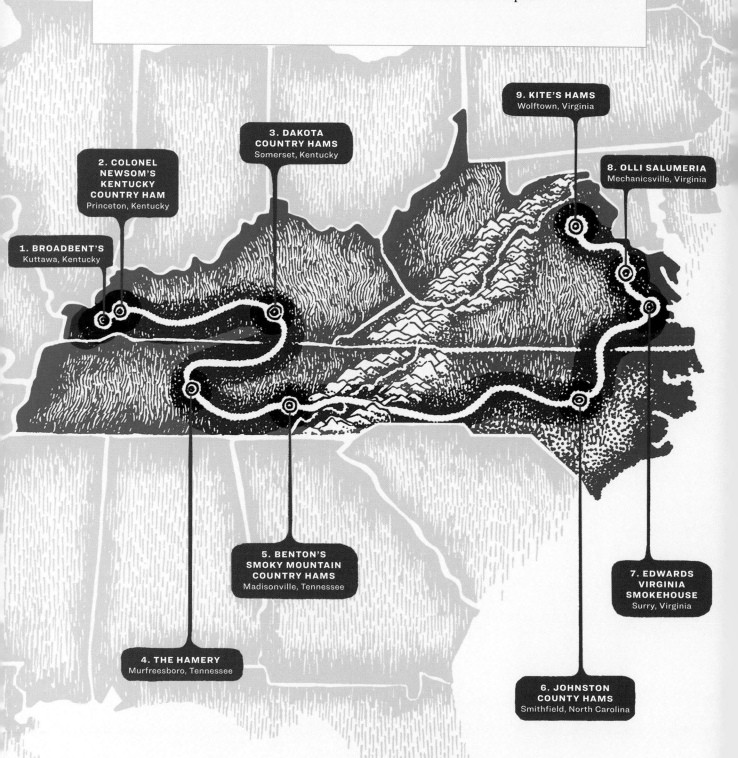

9. KITE'S HAMS
Wolftown, Virginia

3. DAKOTA COUNTRY HAMS
Somerset, Kentucky

8. OLLI SALUMERIA
Mechanicsville, Virginia

2. COLONEL NEWSOM'S KENTUCKY COUNTRY HAM
Princeton, Kentucky

1. BROADBENT'S
Kuttawa, Kentucky

5. BENTON'S SMOKY MOUNTAIN COUNTRY HAMS
Madisonville, Tennessee

7. EDWARDS VIRGINIA SMOKEHOUSE
Surry, Virginia

4. THE HAMERY
Murfreesboro, Tennessee

6. JOHNSTON COUNTY HAMS
Smithfield, North Carolina

A. Curemaster · B. Type of cure · C. Wood used for smoking (if smoked) · D. Time aged · E. Biographical info

1. BROADBENT'S (BROADBENTHAMS.COM)

A. Ronny Drennan
B. Salt and sugar
C. Hickory
D. 6 to 9 months
E. Broadbent has been curing hams and smoking bacon and sausage for more than a hundred years. For the last fifty, they've operated a mail-order business, shipping their hams across the country. They've been winning tasting prizes for about as long as that.

2. COLONEL NEWSOM'S KENTUCKY COUNTRY HAM (NEWSOMSCOUNTRYHAM.COM)

A. Nancy Newsom
B. Salt and brown sugar
C. Hickory
D. 12-plus months
E. The family behind Colonel Newsom's has been in the food business for a hundred years and curing hams for about as long. The simply cured hams rely on the changing seasons to give them a depth of flavor that makes them one of my favorites.

3. DAKOTA COUNTRY HAMS

A. Dwight Muse
B. Salt, sugar, and black pepper
C. Unsmoked
D. 14 to 36 months, depending on the weather and the ham
E. Dwight Muse's maternal great-grandmother Dakota Simpson Brock (no relation) is the namesake of this operation, and she passed down the know-how and the cure recipe used for generations in this family. Dwight has been regularly curing and aging the hams and shoulders of pastured hogs for more than twenty-five years. The hams are suspended in pillowcases and hung in the open air of an old warehouse, and Mother Nature decides how long they stay.

4. THE HAMERY (THEHAMERY.COM)

A. Bob Woods
B. Salt and sugar
C. Apple and hickory
D. 9 to 12 months or 18-plus months
E. Bob Woods is the second-generation proprietor of the Hamery. The curing operation was opened by his father, Dr. Sam Woods, almost fifty years ago to provide their small town with a ham to be proud of. The hams are still cured using the recipe passed down from Bob's grandfather Old Doc.

5. BENTON'S SMOKY MOUNTAIN COUNTRY HAMS (BENTONSCOUNTRYHAMS2.COM)

A. Delmer Benton
B. Salt, brown sugar, and crushed red pepper flakes
C. Hickory (some hams are unsmoked)
D. 9 to 12 months
E. The old block building that houses Allan Benton's operation has been the site of smoking and aging country hams and bacon for seventy years. Started after World War II by Albert Hicks, the smokehouse and its current and longtime caretaker, Allan Benton, deserve a lot of recognition for bringing cured and smoked country hams out of the homes of the South and into the wider culinary world.

6. JOHNSTON COUNTY HAMS (COUNTRYCUREDHAMS.COM)

A. Rufus Brown
B. Salt and sugar
C. Hickory
D. 3 to 6 months
E. The operation started in 1946 but truly found its footing in 1967 with the addition of curemaster Jesse Brown to the staff. In the more than fifty years since, starting with Jesse and continuing with his son Rufus, Johnston County has produced some of the finest hams in the country.

7. EDWARDS VIRGINIA SMOKEHOUSE (EDWARDSVAHAM.COM)

A. Sam Wallace Edwards III
B. Salt and black pepper
C. Hickory
D. 13 months
E. The Surryano ham was born from a desire to show the world that domestic traditional country hams can rival the best and most storied European dry-cured hams. A tragic fire in 2016 put a pause in production, but a little over a year later, the fine folks at Edwards were back at it.

8. OLLI SALUMERIA (OLLI.COM)

A. Olli Colmignolihis
B. Sea salt
C. Unsmoked
D. 16 months
E. While not actually a country ham, this is a damn fine ham made in the South. The business started between two friends with three hams from pigs raised by my friend Emile de Felice of Caw Caw Creek Farm. Olli cured the hams in the traditional Italian way and aged them, unsmoked, for over a year. The resulting ham was good enough to start a curing business selling hams, coppas, and salami across the country.

9. KITE'S HAMS (KITESHAMS.COM)

A. James (Jim) P. Kite
B. Salt and brown sugar
C. Unsmoked
D. 6 to 12 months
E. Jim Kite combined his desire to have an "honest job" and a secret family recipe for country ham passed down from his father to build a curing operation that has been selling country hams for almost sixty years. Kite's produces about 20,000 hams per year, curing them on wooden racks.

SUMMER MELON

with Country Ham and Grilled Honey–Black Pepper Vinaigrette

SERVES 6

GRILLED HONEY–BLACK PEPPER VINAIGRETTE

¼ cup honey, preferably local

¼ cup honey vinegar, preferably Lindera Farms (see Resources, page 369)

½ teaspoon kosher salt

½ teaspoon freshly ground black pepper, preferably Bourbon Barrel Smoked Black Pepper (see Resources, page 368)

½ cup peanut oil, preferably Oliver Farm Green Peanut Oil (see Resources, page 369)

TO COMPLETE

Two 2- to 2½-pound melons of your choice, quartered, rind removed, seeded, and cut into 1-by-1½-inch pieces

2 teaspoons grated lime zest

24 very thin slices country ham (about 12 ounces), preferably Bob Wood's (see Resources, page 368)

½ recipe Spicy Peanuts (page 365)

½ cup wood sorrel leaves, washed and dried

Wood sorrel flowers (optional)

Many cuisines are known to pair sweet, juicy melon with the saltiness of a good cured ham. For a Southern version, instead of prosciutto or *jamón serrano*, I use a beautiful country ham. The grilled honey vinaigrette incorporates the flavor of the hearth while the other ingredients remain fresh and uncooked.

NOTE: Make this vinaigrette on a day when you've already fired up the grill so you can easily (and carefully) get the hot coal you need.

FOR THE VINAIGRETTE: If you don't have the grill fired up for another recipe (see Note), light the smallest amount of hardwood charcoal you can (see page 96); you need only one hot coal.

Put the honey in a small nonreactive saucepan with a lid. Using a pair of long-handled tongs, take a red-hot coal from the grill, drop it into the honey, and immediately put the lid on the saucepan. Let the honey cool completely.

Strain the honey through a fine-mesh sieve into a blender. Add the honey vinegar, salt, and pepper and blend to incorporate. With the motor running, slowly drizzle in the peanut oil and blend until emulsified. Transfer to a container, cover, and refrigerate. *(Tightly covered, the vinaigrette will keep for up to 1 week in the refrigerator. Whisk before using to re-emulsify if necessary.)*

TO COMPLETE: Combine the melon pieces, lime zest, and about ¼ cup of the vinaigrette in a large bowl and gently toss to combine. Divide the melon among six plates, top each with 4 slices of country ham, and sprinkle with the peanuts. Garnish with the sorrel leaves and sorrel flowers, if desired.

PEACH AND TOMATO SALAD

with Cottage Cheese, Watercress, and Pawpaw Vinaigrette

SERVES 4

PAWPAW VINAIGRETTE

⅓ cup Lindera Farms Pawpaw Vinegar (see Resources, page 369) or raspberry vinegar

¼ teaspoon kosher salt

¼ teaspoon freshly ground black pepper

⅔ cup grapeseed oil

1 tablespoon very finely diced shallot

1 teaspoon minced garlic

1 tablespoon finely chopped basil

SALAD

2 large ripe peaches (about 1 pound), pitted and cut into 8 wedges each

2 pounds heirloom tomatoes, cored and cut into 1-inch-thick wedges

Coarse finishing salt, preferably J.Q. Dickinson's (see Resources, page 368)

Freshly ground black pepper

½ cup Cottage Cheese (page 360) or other high-quality cottage cheese

½ cup watercress leaves, washed and dried

GOES WELL WITH:

Cured Duck Breasts with Rice Porridge (page 136)
Cornmeal-Dusted Grouper with Herb Puree (page 105)

Peaches and cottage cheese was one of my dad's favorite things to eat, but when I was a little kid, the combination totally grossed me out. Fast-forward a couple of decades, and now I get it. In fact, I crave the thing I used to think was inedible! I also love pairing ripe tomatoes with ripe fruits, especially stone fruits at their summer peak. This salad marries peaches, tomatoes, and cottage cheese with a vinaigrette made from pawpaw vinegar. The vinegar adds a tropical flavor that you might not expect in a simple salad like this. It's like a modern interpretation of the type of dish you'd find in the classic 1960s Time-Life cookbooks. If you can't get pawpaw vinegar, use raspberry vinegar instead.

FOR THE VINAIGRETTE: Combine the vinegar, kosher salt, and pepper in a small bowl. Whisking constantly, slowly drizzle in the grapeseed oil and whisk until emulsified. Stir in the shallot, garlic, and basil. Transfer to a container, cover, and refrigerate. *(Tightly covered, the vinaigrette will keep for up to 1 week in the refrigerator. Whisk before using to re-emulsify if necessary.)*

FOR THE SALAD: Using a sharp knife, cut away the skin from each piece of peach and discard. Lay the peaches and tomatoes on a platter in a single layer. Drizzle with the pawpaw vinaigrette and season lightly with coarse salt and pepper.

Divide the peaches and tomatoes among four plates. Spoon the cottage cheese in between the peaches and tomatoes and top the salads with the watercress.

GRILLED ASPARAGUS AND CRACKLIN' SALAD with "Amazake" Vinaigrette

Asparagus is one of those ephemeral, fleeting vegetables that can be enjoyed for only a couple of weeks during the short season, but that makes it all the more special. My friend Brian Baxter came up with this dish, and the consistency of the vinaigrette is inspired by the traditional Japanese fermented rice beverage *amazake*. Although the recipe gives instructions for cooking the rice for the vinaigrette, it's also a great way to use leftover rice you already have in your fridge.

SERVES 4

RICE

¼ cup Anson Mills Carolina Gold Rice (see Resources, page 368)

½ cup water

¼ teaspoon kosher salt

"AMAZAKE" VINAIGRETTE

¼ cup minced shallots

1 teaspoon grated fresh ginger

1¼ teaspoons minced garlic

2½ tablespoons thinly sliced scallion, white part only

¼ teaspoon crushed red pepper flakes

2 tablespoons canola oil

⅓ cup plus 1 tablespoon soy sauce, preferably Bourbon Barrel Bluegrass Soy Sauce (see Resources, page 368)

⅓ cup plus 2 teaspoons Lindera Farms Hickory Vinegar (see Resources, page 369) or apple cider vinegar

½ teaspoon Surig 25% Vinegar (see Resources, page 368) or apple cider vinegar

2 tablespoons plus 1 teaspoon pickling liquid from Pickled Green Tomatoes (page 249)

PORK CRACKLIN'S

One 12-inch square piece of pork skin, cut into 4 squares

2 cups Pork Stock (page 346) or Chicken Stock (page 344)

Canola oil for deep-frying

½ cup Anson Mills Carolina Gold Rice Flour (see Resources, page 368)

Kosher salt

FOR THE RICE: Combine the rice, water, and salt in a small saucepan and bring to a boil over medium-high heat. Reduce the heat to low, cover, and simmer until the rice is soft and all the water has been absorbed, about 12 minutes. Transfer to a bowl and cool to room temperature. (*The rice can be cooked ahead. Tightly covered, it will keep for up to 3 days in the refrigerator.*)

FOR THE VINAIGRETTE: Combine all the ingredients for the vinaigrette and ¼ cup of the cooked rice in a blender and blend on high until smooth and emulsified, about 1 minute. Strain through a fine-mesh sieve into a container, cover, and set aside at room temperature. (*You will need only ½ cup of the vinaigrette for this dish. Tightly covered, the remaining vinaigrette will keep for up to 5 days in the refrigerator. Whisk before using to re-emulsify if necessary.*)

FOR THE PORK CRACKLIN'S: Combine the pork skin and the pork stock in the pressure cooker. Lock on the lid, bring the cooker up to high pressure, and cook the skin for 90 minutes.

Line a rimmed baking sheet with parchment paper. Carefully release the steam from the pressure cooker. Using a slotted spatula, carefully remove the squares of pork skin and lay them in a single layer on the prepared baking sheet, then refrigerate until cool. Strain the stock left in the cooker and freeze for another use.

When they are cool, cut the squares of skin into ¼-inch-wide strips. (*The pork skins can be prepared to this point ahead. Tightly covered, they will keep for up to 1 day in the refrigerator. Bring to room temperature before frying.*)

TO FRY THE CRACKLIN'S: Fill a deep fryer with canola oil according to the manufacturer's directions and heat the oil

GRILLED PEANUTS

½ cup dried raw peanuts

¼ teaspoon kosher salt

GRILLED ASPARAGUS AND SNAP PEAS

2 pounds asparagus, tough ends cut off

2 tablespoons plus 2 teaspoons canola oil

Kosher salt and freshly ground white pepper

8 ounces sugar snap peas

TO COMPLETE

4 slices Pickled Green Tomatoes (page 249), cut into eighths

½ cup thinly sliced basil leaves

¼ cup cilantro leaves

¼ cup mint leaves

2 tablespoons green peanut oil, preferably Oliver Farm Green Peanut Oil (see Resources, page 369)

EQUIPMENT

Electric pressure cooker (see Note, page 43)

Round 15-inch open-top fine-mesh wire grill basket

GOES WELL WITH:

Grilled Catfish with Barely Cooked Tomatoes (page 94)

to 350°F. Alternatively, fill a deep heavy pot half full with canola oil and heat the oil over medium heat to 350°F. The oil will splatter, so have a splatter guard or a lid at hand.

Cover a wire rack with paper towels. Place the rice flour in a shallow bowl. Working in batches, dredge the pork skin strips in the rice flour, shake off any excess, and fry until golden brown and crisp, about 1 minute. Transfer them to the rack and season lightly with salt. *(The cracklin's can be fried ahead. Tightly covered, they will keep for up to 1 day at room temperature in a container lined with paper towels.)*

FOR THE PEANUTS: Prepare a hot fire in a charcoal grill (see page 96), removing the grill rack and distributing the hot coals in an even layer in the bottom of the grill.

Put the peanuts in the grill basket, place directly on the coals, and grill, stirring constantly with long-handled tongs, until the peanuts are a deep brown and are just starting to char, about 1 minute. Transfer the peanuts to a cutting board, sprinkle with the salt, and roughly chop, then transfer to a container, cool, cover, and set aside. Clean the grill basket to use for the asparagus and snap peas.

FOR THE ASPARAGUS AND SNAP PEAS: Place the asparagus in a bowl, add 2 tablespoons of the canola oil, season liberally with salt and white pepper, and toss to coat. Transfer to the grill basket (set the bowl aside), place it directly on the coals, and grill the asparagus, shaking often, until lightly charred and tender, about 3 minutes. Transfer to a cutting board.

Put the snap peas in the bowl you used for the asparagus, add the remaining 2 teaspoons canola oil, season liberally with salt and white pepper, and toss to coat. Transfer to the grill basket, place it directly on the coals, and grill the snap peas, shaking often, until lightly charred and tender, about 1½ minutes. Transfer them to a large bowl.

Cut the asparagus into pieces about 2½ inches long and add to the bowl with the snap peas. Shake or stir the amazake vinaigrette to make sure it is well emulsified, then add ½ cup to the asparagus and snap peas and toss well to combine.

TO COMPLETE: Add the pickled green tomatoes, peanuts, basil, cilantro, and mint and toss gently. Divide the salad among four plates. Drizzle with the green peanut oil and finish with the pork cracklin's.

FISH and SHELLFISH

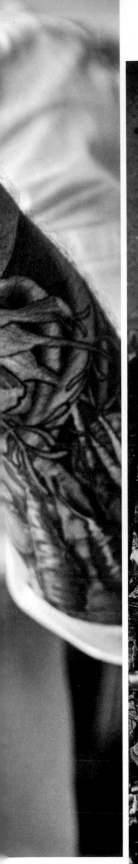

GRILLED CATFISH with Barely Cooked Tomatoes

BARELY COOKED TOMATOES

3 pounds heirloom tomatoes

3 tablespoons fish sauce

1 tablespoon Lindera Farms Turmeric Vinegar (see Resources, page 369)

CATFISH

Four 5- to 7-ounce skinless farm-raised catfish fillets (such as Carolina Classics; see Resources, page 368), about ½ inch thick

1 tablespoon canola oil

Kosher salt and freshly ground white pepper

1 tablespoon benne oil (see Resources, page 369)

2 teaspoons Anson Mills Antebellum Benne Seeds (see Resources, page 368)

2 tablespoons finely chopped flat-leaf parsley

GOES WELL WITH:

No-Peek Rice (page 233)
Pepper Vinegar (page 262)
Pepper Mash (page 263)
Pickled Fennel (page 252)

This dish captures the essence of picking a ripe tomato off the plant and eating it under the blazing-hot sun of the South. That tomato is probably pushing 100°F during the hottest part of the day—almost starting to cook. To translate the experience to the plate, I peel the tomatoes, dice them, and marinate them in a little bit of fish sauce for a couple of hours before warming them in a pan until they hit that internal temperature of 100°F. The result is a tomato that is at the intersection of raw and cooked.

Adding benne seeds to the plate brings it into the fold of classic Gullah Geechee food traditions. You could swap the catfish for some steamed Carolina Gold rice for an incredible vegetarian dinner.

FOR THE TOMATOES: Bring a medium pot of water to a boil over high heat. Make an ice bath with equal parts ice and water in a large bowl. Working in batches, lightly score the skin on the bottom of each tomato with an X and submerge the tomatoes in the boiling water for 10 seconds. Remove and submerge them in the ice bath to cool; do not leave them in there for longer than 5 minutes. Drain, then peel, halve, and seed the tomatoes and cut them into medium dice.

Combine the diced tomatoes, fish sauce, and vinegar in a medium nonreactive saucepan, cover, and set aside at room temperature for at least 1 hour and up to 4 hours.

FOR THE CATFISH: Prepare a hot fire in a charcoal grill (see page 96), removing the grill rack and distributing the hot coals in an even layer in the bottom of the grill. Place the grill rack as close to the coals as possible.

Meanwhile, reheat the tomatoes over low heat until they are just warmed through, about 10 minutes. Remove from the heat and cover to keep warm.

Using a pastry brush, lightly brush the catfish fillets with canola oil on both sides and season liberally with salt and white pepper. Grill the fillets skinned side up until lightly charred and opaque, about 2 minutes. Turn the fillets over and grill them for 2 minutes more.

TO SERVE: Arrange the catfish fillets on four warm plates. Spoon the tomatoes over the fillets, drizzle with the benne oil, and sprinkle with the benne seeds and chopped parsley.

GRILLING

I know the average home grill setup is far simpler than what I'm used to in a professional kitchen, and I developed and tested the recipes in this book keeping that in mind. To that end, all the recipes can be made with a standard Weber-style kettle grill, good-quality hardwood lump charcoal, and a few other essential tools. Once you're comfortable starting and maintaining a charcoal grill, everything that follows is just a variation on a theme. (For a look at how I cook over a hearth, see Fireplace Cookery, page 30.)

LIGHTING THE GRILL

Grilling starts with lighting your charcoal, and the best way to do this is by using a chimney starter. Essentially a perforated metal tube with a handle on the side and a grate at one end, it uses the airflow principle of drafting to draw oxygen over the coals, allowing them to light and burn quickly in an easily handled container.

Crumple a few sheets of newspaper and put them in the bottom of your kettle grill. Set the chimney starter over the paper with the grate end down. Fill the chimney with charcoal (it usually takes 3 to 4 pounds of charcoal). Light the newspaper using a match or lighter and let the chimney do the rest of the work. Generally speaking, it will take 20 to 25 minutes for the coals to light completely and be ready. They should be evenly lit and glowing, without any large flames coming out of the top of the starter.

Carefully pour the glowing-hot coals into the bottom of the grill. The handle on the side of the chimney will be hot, so don't grab it without using a thick kitchen towel or oven mitt. Set the hot chimney out of the way where it won't set anything on fire or burn anyone.

From here, each recipe will differ a little bit. Where (or if) you position the grill rack, and whether you spread the coals evenly or off to one side, depends on what you're cooking.

ESSENTIAL TOOLS

Having these tools on hand will make your grilling life much easier.

- **Metal Tongs.** A pair of sturdy long-handled tongs and another smaller pair are crucial for moving food around on the grill surface, whether on the rack or in a basket. The long-handled version is also a great tool for moving hot coals around in the bottom of your grill.

- **Grill Baskets.** There are tons of different types of grilling baskets available. For me, the most versatile one is a round open-top fine-mesh wire basket. A good grill basket will let you cook things over the coals you otherwise couldn't, from delicious English peas to squid or even peanuts. It also lets you get more conventional grilling ingredients far closer to the coals than you can using the grill rack.

- **Kitchen Towels.** A stash of dry, heavy-duty kitchen towels is a must when you're grilling.

- **Grill Brush.** Cleaning the grill rack before and after grilling is crucial to ensuring that the food you cook doesn't stick to the grate or pick up any unwanted flavors. Select a good brush with stiff metal bristles and a sturdy handle.

GRILLED CATFISH with Hoppin' John

SERVES 4

RED PEAS

2 cups Vegetable Stock (page 348)

½ cup Anson Mills Sea Island Red
Peas (see Resources, page 368),
soaked in water to cover in the
refrigerator overnight

¼ cup roughly chopped drained
Preserved Tomatoes (page 278)
or canned whole tomatoes

1 ounce bacon, preferably Benton's
(see Resources, page 368), cut
into ¼-inch pieces

1 small garlic clove, peeled

1 fresh bay leaf

5 thyme sprigs

Kosher salt

RICE

2 cups water

½ teaspoon kosher salt

⅛ teaspoon cayenne pepper

½ cup Anson Mills Carolina Gold
Rice (see Resources, page 368)

2 tablespoons unsalted butter,
diced

CATFISH

Four 5- to 7-ounce skinless farm-
raised catfish fillets (such as
Carolina Classics; see Resources,
page 368), about ½ inch thick

1 tablespoon canola oil

Kosher salt and freshly ground
white pepper

1 teaspoon fresh lemon juice

¼ teaspoon Espelette pepper

1 tablespoon thinly sliced scallion
greens

32 pea or bean flowers (optional)

Hoppin' John made with red peas and rice is certainly a
meal in itself. But it can share the plate with simply grilled
catfish or even shrimp. Here the flavor of the catfish com-
plements the Hoppin' John without overwhelming it.

NOTE: You'll need to start this recipe a day ahead of time
to soak the red peas.

FOR THE RED PEAS: Combine the vegetable stock, drained
peas, tomatoes, bacon, garlic, bay leaf, and thyme in the
pressure cooker, lock on the lid, bring the cooker up to high
pressure, and cook for 15 minutes. Carefully release the
steam from the pressure cooker. Drain the peas, reserving
¼ cup of the cooking liquid. Remove and discard the garlic,
bay leaf, and thyme sprigs.

Transfer the peas to a small saucepan and season lightly
with salt. Let cool, then cover and refrigerate until ready to
use. (Tightly covered, the peas will keep for up to 3 days in
the refrigerator.)

Preheat the oven to 300°F. Prepare a hot fire in a charcoal
grill (see page 96), removing the grill rack and distributing
the hot coals in an even layer in the bottom of the grill. Place
the grill rack as close to the coals as possible.

FOR THE RICE: While the grill is heating, combine the water,
salt, and cayenne in a small saucepan, bring to a boil over
medium-high heat, and stir to completely dissolve the salt.
Reduce the heat to medium, add the rice, stir once, and
bring to a simmer. Simmer gently, uncovered, stirring occasionally, until the rice is al dente, about 10 minutes.

Drain the rice and spread it out on a rimmed baking sheet.
Place the rice in the oven to dry for 10 minutes, stirring it
occasionally. Scatter the butter evenly over the rice and
return it to the oven for about 5 minutes, stirring it twice
during that time, until the rice is dry. All the excess moisture
should have evaporated and the grains should be separate.

FOR THE CATFISH: While the rice is in the oven, using a pastry
brush, lightly brush the catfish fillets with canola oil on both
sides and season liberally with salt and white pepper. Grill
the fillets skinned side up until lightly charred and opaque,
about 2 minutes. Turn the fillets over and grill them for
2 minutes more. Transfer them to a platter, sprinkle with

Electric pressure cooker (see Note,
page 43)

GOES WELL WITH:

*Rice-and-Shrimp Croquettes
with Tomato Chili Sauce
(page 24)*

the lemon juice and Espelette pepper, and lightly cover with
foil to keep warm.

Meanwhile, remove the peas from the refrigerator and warm
them over low heat.

TO SERVE: Lay a catfish fillet slightly off center on each
of four warm plates. Using a slotted spoon, spoon a line of
peas right next to each fillet. Spoon some of the rice, slightly
overlapping the peas, in a line down each fillet. Sprinkle the
sliced scallions and pea flowers, if using, over the rice.

GRILLED SWORDFISH with Green Gumbo

SERVES 6

SMOKED VEGETABLES

1 cup small dice sweet onion

⅔ cup small dice peeled carrots

GREEN GUMBO

2 pounds greens (see headnote)

4 tablespoons unsalted butter

¼ cup all-purpose flour

4 cups Vegetable Stock (page 348)

3 tablespoons soy sauce, preferably Bourbon Barrel Bluegrass Soy Sauce (see Resources, page 368)

Kosher salt and freshly ground black pepper

SWORDFISH

Six 6 ounce skinless swordfish steaks, about 1½ inches thick

2 tablespoons extra-virgin olive oil

Kosher salt and freshly ground white pepper

1 tablespoon fresh lemon juice

TO COMPLETE

2 tablespoons fresh lemon juice

2 tablespoons thinly sliced scallion

EQUIPMENT

Smoker

Meat grinder

GOES WELL WITH:

Charleston Ice Cream (page 234)
No-Peek Rice (page 233)
Limpin' Susan (page 184)

Green gumbo, or gumbo z'herbes, doesn't bear much resemblance to the more well known versions you're probably familiar with. More often than not completely meatless, green gumbo sometimes doesn't even feature the iconic roux that defines the typical gumbos of the Gulf Coast. When there is a roux in green gumbo, it is usually far lighter than the deep-brown one found in the traditional version. This dish is especially popular in and around New Orleans during the Lenten season, when a lot of folks abstain from meat.

Green gumbo will be different each time you make it, because the idea is to use all the fresh greens you can find. So one day it might be kale, turnip greens, Swiss chard, and parsley, and the next it could be collard greens, arugula, radish tops, and sorrel. Use the widest variety of the freshest leafy greens and herbs you can get your hands on—the more, the better. Tradition has it, the more types of greens you use, the more friends you'll make in the coming year. You also don't have to stop at farmed produce; green gumbo is a great way to use any wild greens that you can forage.

FOR THE VEGETABLES: Prepare the smoker with hardwood charcoal and hickory (see page 57); maintain the temperature at between 125°F and 150°F.

Combine the onion and carrot in a shallow baking dish that will fit in your smoker and spread them out in a thin single layer. Smoke the diced vegetables until they have developed a rich smoky flavor but still retain their fresh texture, 20 to 25 minutes. Remove from the smoker and set aside to cool to room temperature.

FOR THE GUMBO: Wash the greens in the sink or a large bowl of cold water, changing the water several times if they are sandy. Drain and dry.

Grind the cleaned greens through the large die of a meat grinder; set aside.

Heat the butter in a large pot over medium heat until foamy. Add the smoked onion and carrot and cook, stirring occasionally, until the onion is translucent, about 7 minutes. Stir in the flour and cook, stirring constantly, until the flour just begins to turn light brown, about 4 minutes. Gradually whisk in the vegetable stock and bring to a simmer, whisking. Add

the greens, reduce the heat to medium-low, and cook, stirring occasionally, until the greens are just tender but still vibrant in flavor, about 30 minutes. Stir in the soy sauce and season with salt, if necessary, and black pepper. Remove from the stove, cover, and set aside. *(The gumbo can be made ahead. Tightly covered once cooled, it will keep for up to 4 days in the refrigerator.)*

FOR THE SWORDFISH: Prepare a hot fire in a charcoal grill (see page 96), removing the grill rack and distributing the hot coals in an even layer in the bottom of the grill. Place the grill rack as close to the coals as possible.

Using a pastry brush, lightly brush the swordfish steaks with the olive oil on both sides. Season liberally with salt and white pepper. Grill the swordfish steaks on the hottest part of the grill for about 5 minutes, without moving them. When the steaks can easily be moved without any resistance, turn them over and grill, moving the fish around the grill if necessary to avoid flare-ups, until the flesh just begins to flake when gently prodded with a fork, about 5 minutes. Transfer to a platter, sprinkle with the lemon juice, and lightly cover with foil to keep warm.

TO COMPLETE: Reheat the gumbo gently over medium-low heat, then stir in the fresh lemon juice. Divide the gumbo among six warm bowls, place a swordfish steak in each bowl, and sprinkle with the scallion.

GRILLED TROUT with Cornbread Puree

SERVES 4

CORNBREAD PUREE

¼ recipe Basic Cornbread (page 216), made a day ahead, broken into small pieces

1 cup whole milk

½ cup full-fat buttermilk (see Note, page 27)

2 teaspoons kosher salt

½ teaspoon freshly ground white pepper

TROUT

Four 7-ounce skin-on trout fillets, about ½ inch thick

2 teaspoons canola oil

Kosher salt and freshly ground white pepper

1 teaspoon fresh lemon juice

Coarse finishing salt, preferably J.Q. Dickinson's (see Resources, page 368)

GOES WELL WITH:

Potatoes and Ramps Cooked in Ham Fat (page 172)
Ramp Leaf Oil (page 365)

Grilling is the first thing that pops into my head when I think about cooking trout. I'm not even sure if there is any other way. The aroma of the trout grilling elicits so many memories of fishing and camping trips from my youth, and I love to relive those at home. Using the lid allows the grill to cook like an oven, resulting in trout with a delicate texture.

The cornbread puree is very much the result of a late-night "What if?" Sometimes those ideas don't work out, but this one did. It's fun to see the reaction from my dinner guests when I serve it. Try it with grilled pork too.

FOR THE CORNBREAD PUREE: Combine the cornbread, milk, and buttermilk in a medium saucepan and warm through over low heat. Transfer to a blender and blend on high until completely smooth, about 3 minutes. Blend in the salt and white pepper. Transfer the puree to a small saucepan, cover, and set aside.

FOR THE TROUT: Prepare a hot fire in a charcoal grill (see page 96), removing the grill rack and distributing the hot coals in an even layer in the bottom of the grill. Place the grill rack at its normal height.

Using a pastry brush, lightly brush the skin of the trout with the canola oil to keep it from sticking to the grill rack. Lightly season the fillets on both sides with salt and white pepper. Place the fillets skin side down on the grill, cover the grill, and grill until the flesh is just cooked but still slightly trans-lucent, 3 to 4 minutes. Sprinkle the fillets with lemon juice.

TO SERVE: Reheat the cornbread puree over low heat. Lay a trout fillet on each of four warm plates and sprinkle with a few grains of finishing salt. Put a spoonful of the cornbread puree beside each fillet.

CORNMEAL-DUSTED GROUPER

with Herb Puree

SERVES 4

HERB PUREE

Kosher salt

1 cup tightly packed mixed herb
    leaves, such as basil and parsley

¼ teaspoon grated garlic

2 tablespoons extra-virgin olive oil

GROUPER

1 cup fine white cornmeal,
    preferably Anson Mills
    (see Resources, page 368)

2 tablespoons kosher salt, plus
    more for seasoning

2 teaspoons freshly ground white
    pepper, plus more for seasoning

Four 6-ounce skinless grouper
    fillets, about ¾ inch thick

2 tablespoons canola oil

Herbs and edible flowers, such as
    basil, fennel, and elderflower
    (optional)

GOES WELL WITH:

*Crowder Pea and Hominy
    Succotash (page 178)*

Dredging a pristine fillet of your favorite fish in seasoned high-quality cornmeal is a great way to give it a crispy texture without dealing with messy breading that can mask the flavor of the fish. As the cornmeal toasts and browns in the hot skillet, it gives off an aroma reminiscent of cornbread, which is never a bad thing. This herb puree is amazing with fish, but you can add it to almost any dish for a burst of bright, fresh flavor.

FOR THE HERB PUREE: Bring a large saucepan of salted water to a boil over high heat. Make an ice bath with equal parts ice and water in a large bowl. Put the herb leaves in a large mesh strainer and submerge them in the boiling water until tender and bright green, about 30 seconds. Leaving them in the strainer, transfer the herbs to the ice bath and submerge until completely cold. Remove from the ice bath, shake off the excess water, and drain the leaves on paper towels. Reserve ¼ cup of the ice water.

Combine the herbs, garlic, and reserved ¼ cup water in a blender and blend on high until completely smooth, about 1 minute. With the blender running on low, slowly drizzle in the olive oil. Blend in ½ teaspoon salt. Transfer to a container, cover, and set aside. *(The herb puree can be made ahead. Tightly covered, it will keep for up to 1 day in the refrigerator. Remove from the refrigerator 30 minutes before using.)*

FOR THE GROUPER: Combine the cornmeal, salt, and white pepper in a large shallow bowl and mix well. Season the grouper fillets liberally with salt and white pepper. Dredge the fillets in the cornmeal, gently shaking off any excess, and put them on a large plate.

Line a rimmed baking sheet with paper towels. Heat the canola oil in a large cast-iron skillet over medium-high heat until it shimmers. Place the fillets in the skillet skinned side up and sear them for 2 minutes, without moving them. Reduce the heat to medium and cook until the fillets are golden brown on the first side, about 3 minutes. (Peek under a fillet to check.) Turn them over and continue to cook just until the flesh flakes when gently prodded with a fork, 3 to 4 minutes. Transfer the fillets to the prepared baking sheet to drain briefly.

TO SERVE: Place a grouper fillet on each of four warm plates. Spoon the herb puree next to the fillets. Garnish with the herbs and flowers, if using.

FRIED CATFISH with Green Tomato Tartar Sauce

SERVES 6

Canola oil for deep-frying

1 cup all-purpose flour

1 cup full-fat buttermilk (see Note, page 27)

1 cup fine yellow cornmeal

Six 5- to 7-ounce skinless farm-raised catfish fillets (such as Carolina Classics; see Resources, page 368), about ½ inch thick, each cut lengthwise into 3 strips

Kosher salt

¼ cup Blackening Seasoning (page 363)

About 1½ cups Green Tomato Tartar Sauce (recipe follows)

2 tablespoons finely sliced chives

GOES WELL WITH:

Green Beans (page 173)
Ladies' Cabbage (page 167)

The inspiration for this dish comes from Arnold's Country Kitchen, a Nashville meat-and-three. It's a cafeteria-style restaurant, and as you make your way down the line, you'll see people from every walk of life. I love Arnold's fried catfish, and here is my interpretation, served with a green tomato version of tartar sauce.

Preheat the oven to 200°F. Fill a deep fryer with canola oil according to the manufacturer's directions and heat the oil to 350°F. Alternatively, fill a deep heavy pot half full with canola oil and heat the oil over medium heat to 350°F. Line a baking sheet with paper towels.

Put the flour, buttermilk, and cornmeal in three separate shallow bowls. Liberally season the catfish strips with salt and about 3 tablespoons of the blackening seasoning. Working in batches, dredge the strips in the flour, then the buttermilk, and finally in the cornmeal and add them to the hot oil. Fry the strips until cooked through, crispy, and golden brown, 4 to 5 minutes. Transfer the fish to the prepared baking sheet and keep warm in the oven while you fry the remaining strips.

Divide the catfish among six plates and sprinkle with the remaining tablespoon of blackening seasoning and the chives. Serve each portion with a spoonful of the tartar sauce.

GREEN TOMATO TARTAR SAUCE

MAKES 2½ CUPS

1¾ cups mayonnaise, preferably Duke's (see Resources, page 369)

3 tablespoons ⅛-inch dice Pickled Green Tomatoes (page 249), plus 2 tablespoons of their pickling liquid

2 tablespoons plus 1 teaspoon chopped capers

2 tablespoons ⅛-inch dice shallot

1 heaping tablespoon chopped dill

1 tablespoon fresh lemon juice

1 cup very thinly sliced sweet onion

Put all the ingredients except the onion in a small bowl and stir to combine. Cover and refrigerate until cold. *(Tightly covered, the tartar sauce base will keep for up to 4 days in the refrigerator.)*

Just before serving, fold the onion into the sauce base.

BEELINER SNAPPER with Fried Peppers

SERVES 4

1 tablespoon Rendered Fresh Lard (page 343) or vegetable oil

Eight 3-ounce skin-on beeliner snapper fillets, about ½ inch thick, lightly scored on the skin side

Kosher salt and freshly ground white pepper

½ cup very thinly sliced red bell pepper

½ cup very thinly sliced green bell pepper

2 tablespoons Pepper Sauce (page 353)

GOES WELL WITH:

Corn Puree (page 152)
Field peas (see page 191)
Sour Corn (page 272)

Beeliner snapper, also called vermilion snapper, is at its peak in the summer season, so I gravitate toward serving it with sweet peppers and other sun-ripened seasonal produce. The snapper fillets are seared in lard, which adds a subtle layer of flavor to the dish. It also makes the fried peppers cooked in the same skillet that much more delicious. But if you don't want to use pork fat, vegetable oil will get the job done.

Preheat the oven to 200°F. Line a rimmed baking sheet with paper towels.

Cook the snapper in two batches: Heat half the lard in a large cast-iron skillet over medium heat until it shimmers. Season the fillets liberally with salt and white pepper. Place a fillet in the skillet skin side down, applying light pressure on it with a spatula for about 30 seconds before adding another and pressing it down. This will help set the skin, keep the skin from curling, and cook the fish evenly. Repeat with 2 more fillets. Cook the fillets until the skin is crisp and golden, 2 to 3 minutes. Turn them over and cook just until the flesh flakes when gently prodded with a fork, 2 to 3 minutes more. Transfer the fillets to the prepared baking sheet and keep warm in the oven while you cook the second batch. Transfer the second batch to the baking sheet and return the skillet to the heat.

Add the bell peppers to the skillet, season them lightly with salt and white pepper, and fry until they start to soften and lightly brown, about 2 minutes. Add the pepper sauce to the pan and stir to coat the bell peppers. Remove from the heat.

Arrange the snapper fillets on a platter and top with the fried peppers.

SHEEPSHEAD "ON THE HALF SHELL" with Tomato Gravy

SERVES 4

TOMATO GRAVY

1 tablespoon Rendered Bacon Fat (page 342)

1 tablespoon fine white cornmeal, preferably Anson Mills (see Resources, page 368)

1½ cups Preserved Tomatoes (page 278) or canned whole tomatoes, with their juices

1½ teaspoons kosher salt

1½ teaspoons freshly cracked black pepper

1 teaspoon Hot Sauce (page 260) or Red Clay Original Hot Sauce (see Resources, page 369)

SHEEPSHEAD

Four 6- to 7-ounce skin-on sheepshead fillets, about ½ inch thick, scales left on (see Note)

2 teaspoons extra-virgin olive oil

Kosher salt and freshly ground white pepper

¼ cup Parsley Sauce (page 367)

GOES WELL WITH:

Petit Vert Peas (page 173)

The sheepshead is an Atlantic saltwater fish found from Nova Scotia all the way south to Brazil. Its mouth, with its eerily human-looking teeth, allows it to eat barnacles off rocks and pilings, which is where you'll find the fish. There's a bit of a ritual to catching sheepshead, from digging the fiddler crabs for bait in the morning to rigging your pole for the particular challenge of hooking one (they're so good at stealing bait, they're called "saltwater bandits"), which makes fishing for them damn enjoyable.

My favorite way to cook a sheepshead is "on the half shell," a technique used with redfish all along the Gulf Coast. I leave the scales on the fillets and gently cook them skin side down on the grill; the scales protect the skin, which holds in the moisture as the fish cooks, rendering it succulent and tender. As a result of its diet, sheepshead has a mild shellfish flavor, which is accentuated when you cook it this way. When it's time to serve, simply lift the fillets away from the skin.

NOTE: You'll need to request scale-on fillets from your fishmonger. If you can't get sheepshead, you could substitute triggerfish or tilefish.

FOR THE TOMATO GRAVY: Heat the bacon fat in a small saucepan over medium-high heat until it shimmers. Stir in the cornmeal with a wooden spoon, reduce the heat to low, and cook, stirring constantly, until the cornmeal turns a light brown color, about 3 minutes.

Put the tomatoes in a bowl and crush them into bite-sized pieces with your hands. Add the tomatoes and their juices to the saucepan and stir to combine. Increase the heat to medium, bring the gravy to a simmer, and cook, stirring occasionally, until it has thickened slightly and the cornmeal is soft, about 10 minutes; be careful that it doesn't stick or scorch. Add the salt, black pepper, and hot sauce and stir to combine. Remove from the stove, cover, and set aside.

FOR THE SHEEPSHEAD: Prepare a hot fire in a charcoal grill (see page 96), removing the grill rack and distributing the hot coals over one side of the bottom of the grill. Place the grill rack at its normal height.

Place the sheepshead skin side up on a rimmed baking sheet and use a pastry brush to lightly brush the skin with olive oil

to keep it from sticking to the grill rack. Liberally season the fillets with salt and white pepper.

Place the fillets skin side down on the cooler side of the grill, cover the grill, and grill for about 3 minutes. Rotate the fillets 180 degrees and grill until the flesh is just starting to flake when gently prodded with a fork but still moist, 2 to 4 minutes more. Transfer the grilled fillets to a clean rimmed baking sheet and brush the tops with the parsley sauce.

TO SERVE: Spoon a circle of the tomato gravy in the center of each of four warm plates. Carefully lift the sheepshead fillets away from the skin and lay a fillet on top of the tomato gravy on each plate.

POTLIKKER-STEAMED SEA BASS with Corn Dodgers

TURNIP GREEN POTLIKKER

1 pound turnip greens

¾ cup diced fat from a country ham (or from really fatty bacon)

¼ cup plus 1 tablespoon dried shrimp (see Resources, page 369)

5 Dried Oysters (page 298)

12 cups water

½ cup turnip vinegar (see page 259) or apple cider vinegar

1½ teaspoons crushed red pepper flakes

CORN DODGERS

½ cup fine yellow cornmeal, preferably Anson Mills (see Resources, page 368)

½ cup all-purpose flour

1½ teaspoons kosher salt

¾ cup water

6 tablespoons unsalted butter

3 large eggs

½ cup grated Gruyère-type cheese (about 2 ounces), preferably Kenny's Farmhouse Norwood Cheese (see Resources, page 369)

¼ cup finely chopped flat-leaf parsley

SEA BASS

Canola oil for the steamer insert

Six 6- to 7-ounce skin-on black sea bass fillets, about ½ inch thick

Steaming is, no question, my favorite way to cook a fresh piece of black sea bass. There is something so delicate about this fish; the skin, the flesh, and the flavor all demand simplicity to allow them to shine. I use an aromatic liquid to steam the bass—in this case, one that has a Southern context: potlikker. This recipe treats the potlikker less like the result of cooking a pot of greens and more like the star of its own show.

Traditionally, corn dodgers are simply cornmeal mixed with a liquid, and perhaps some fat and onions, shaped into balls, and poached or simmered in potlikker or water. The texture of those traditional versions can often leave a lot to be desired, though. These corn dodgers are more delicate but still deliver that cornmeal flavor. They are poached in the same potlikker used to steam the fish, another example of my drive to echo flavors throughout a dish in different ways.

FOR THE POTLIKKER: Remove the stems from the turnip greens and discard. Make stacks of the leaves, roll them up into cylinders, and slice the cylinders into ribbons about ½ inch wide. Wash them in the sink or a large bowl of cold water, changing the water several times if they are sandy. Drain and dry.

Combine the ham fat, dried shrimp, and dried oysters in a large pot and cook over medium heat, stirring often, until the fat renders, 5 to 7 minutes. Add the water, vinegar, and red pepper flakes, increase the heat to high, and bring to a boil. Add the turnip greens, reduce the heat to medium, cover, and cook for 30 minutes to allow the flavor to develop.

Strain the potlikker through a fine-mesh sieve set over a large container and set aside. You will need 7 cups of potlikker for the dish. If you like, you can reheat the greens in some of the extra potlikker and serve them alongside the dish, or just discard them. (*Tightly covered, the extra potlikker will keep for up to 3 days in the refrigerator or up to 3 months in the freezer. Use it for cooking the Braised Turnips on page 193 or a pot of greens or field peas.*)

Kosher salt and freshly ground
white pepper

EQUIPMENT

Pastry bag fitted with a ½-inch
round tip

Large saucepan with a steamer
insert

GOES WELL WITH:

Braised Turnips (page 193)
Grilled Ramps (page 204)

FOR THE CORN DODGERS: Heat a large skillet over medium heat. Add the cornmeal and cook, stirring constantly, for 2 to 3 minutes, until it is toasted and starts to smell a little nutty. Spread the cornmeal out on a plate and cool to room temperature.

Combine the cornmeal, flour, and salt in a small bowl.

Combine the water and butter in a large saucepan and bring to a boil over high heat. Reduce the heat to medium, stir in the cornmeal mixture with a wooden spoon, and cook, stirring constantly, until the mixture has thickened, about 2 minutes. Remove from the stove and cool until just warm, about 10 minutes.

Transfer the cornmeal mixture to the bowl of a stand mixer fitted with the paddle attachment (or use a hand mixer and a large bowl). With the mixer on low speed, mix in the eggs one at a time, being sure each one is completely incorporated before adding the next. Add the cheese and parsley and mix until just combined. Transfer the mixture to the pastry bag.

Put 3 cups of the potlikker in a medium saucepan and bring to a simmer over medium heat. Form the corn dodgers by piping the batter directly into the potlikker, cutting off ¾-inch lengths of batter with a knife as you pipe it; work in batches of about 15 so that you don't overcrowd the saucepan. Cook the corn dodgers until they are set and cooked through: They will initially sink into the potlikker and then will float to the surface; once they rise to the surface, cook for about 1 minute more. Transfer the cooked corn dodgers to a large skillet, along with about ¼ cup of the potlikker, and cover to keep warm while you cook the remaining batches. You want 42 corn dodgers.

FOR THE SEA BASS: Preheat the oven to 200°F. Line a rimmed baking sheet with parchment paper. Lightly oil the steamer insert to prevent the fish from sticking.

Cut each fillet crosswise in half and lightly season with salt and white pepper. Put 4 cups of the potlikker in the saucepan with the steamer insert and bring to a simmer over medium heat. Place 6 fillets skin side up in the steamer insert in one layer, without touching. Cover the saucepan and steam the fillets for 3 to 4 minutes, until they just begin to flake when lifted from the insert. Transfer the first batch to the prepared baking sheet and keep warm in the oven while you cook the second batch.

TO SERVE: Warm the corn dodgers over medium heat. Carefully place 2 pieces of fish in each of six warm shallow bowls and pour in some of the hot potlikker from the steamer. Divide the corn dodgers among the bowls.

LOWCOUNTRY FISH-HEAD STEW

SERVES 4

FISH-HEAD STOCK

3 pounds fish heads (see Note), scaled and rinsed under cold water to remove any traces of blood

10 cups water

1 large sweet onion (about 8 ounces), thinly sliced

2 ribs celery, thinly sliced

1 large carrot, thinly sliced

2 fresh bay leaves

5 thyme sprigs

1 tablespoon white peppercorns

1 tablespoon kosher salt

STEW

1 cup medium dice sweet onion

2 garlic cloves, chopped

2 teaspoons chopped seeded jalapeño pepper

½ teaspoon Bourbon Barrel Bourbon Smoked Salt (see Resources, page 368)

½ teaspoon Bourbon Barrel Bourbon Smoked Black Pepper (see Resources, page 368)

1 tablespoon canola oil

3 tablespoons small dice celery

2 tablespoons all-purpose flour

1⅓ cups Preserved Tomatoes (page 278) or canned whole tomatoes, passed through a food mill, with their juices

1 fresh bay leaf

¼ teaspoon Aleppo pepper (see Resources, page 369)

CONTINUED

Fish-head stew is one of the many great contributions to the food of the Lowcountry from the Gullah Geechee community. It's not something you're likely to find on a restaurant menu these days, so I hope you'll cook it at home. The rich stew, served over rice, epitomizes the practice of using every part of an ingredient and not wasting a thing. But using the heads is not just frugality for frugality's sake; some of the most flavorful meat is found in the head. A little extra time and effort spent picking through the cracks and crevices of the heads will yield all the delicious fat and collagen with its sticky, wonderful goodness. I've eaten versions of this dish on my visits to Senegal, and I combined what I saw there with the flavors of Charleston to create this take on it.

NOTE: Ask your fishmonger for fresh fish heads with the collars still attached, preferably from 2- to 3-pound whole fish.

FOR THE STOCK: Combine the fish heads and water in a large pot and bring to a simmer over medium-high heat, skimming off any scum that rises to the surface. Add the onion, celery, carrot, bay leaves, thyme, white peppercorns, and salt and return to a simmer. Reduce the heat to medium-low and cook until the flesh on the fish heads pulls away easily when picked with a fork, about 30 minutes.

Carefully transfer the fish heads to a rimmed baking sheet and cool. Strain the fish-head stock. (*The stock can be made ahead. Once cooled, it can be tightly covered and refrigerated for up to 3 days or frozen for up to 3 months.*) Pour 3½ cups of the stock into a heatproof container and set aside. (*The remaining stock can be refrigerated for up to 3 days—or up to 1 day if you made it ahead—or frozen for up to 3 months.*)

When the fish heads have cooled enough to handle, carefully pick the flesh, discarding the skin, eyes, bones, cartilage, and any remaining scales. Put the flesh in a container, cool to room temperature, cover, and refrigerate. (*Tightly covered, the fish will keep for up to 2 days in the refrigerator.*)

FOR THE STEW: Combine the onion, garlic, jalapeño, smoked salt, and smoked pepper in a mortar and crush with the pestle until the mixture becomes a wet paste.

CONTINUED

RICE

4 cups water

2 teaspoons kosher salt

¼ teaspoon freshly ground white pepper

1 fresh bay leaf

1 cup Anson Mills Carolina Gold Rice (see Resources, page 368)

4 tablespoons unsalted butter, diced

1 tablespoon Anson Mills Antebellum Benne Seeds (see Resources, page 368)

2 tablespoons flat-leaf parsley leaves for garnish

1 tablespoon thinly sliced scallion greens for garnish

2 teaspoons onion flowers for garnish (optional)

Heat the canola oil in a large saucepan over medium heat until it shimmers. Add the celery and cook until translucent, about 5 minutes. Add half the onion mixture and cook, stirring frequently, until some of the moisture evaporates, 3 to 5 minutes. Add the flour and cook, stirring constantly, for 2 minutes to make a light roux. Slowly add 1½ cups of the reserved fish-head stock to the roux, stirring constantly to prevent lumps. Stir in the tomatoes, bay leaf, and Aleppo pepper and simmer for 15 minutes to develop the flavors.

Stir in the remaining onion mixture and simmer for 3 minutes more. Remove from the stove and cover to keep warm. (The stew can be made ahead. Tightly covered once cooled, it will keep for up to 3 days in the refrigerator.)

FOR THE RICE: While the stew is simmering, preheat the oven to 300°F. Combine the water, salt, white pepper, and bay leaf in a medium saucepan, bring to a boil over medium-high heat, and stir to be sure the salt has dissolved completely. Reduce the heat to medium, add the rice, stir once, and bring to a simmer. Simmer gently, uncovered, stirring occasionally, until the rice is al dente, about 10 minutes. Drain.

Spread the rice out on a rimmed baking sheet; remove and discard the bay leaf. Place the rice in the oven to dry for 10 minutes, stirring it occasionally. Scatter the butter evenly over the rice and return it to the oven for 5 minutes, stirring it twice during that time, until the rice is dry. All the excess moisture should have evaporated and the grains should be separate.

While the rice is in the oven, heat a large skillet over medium heat. Add the benne seeds and cook, stirring constantly, for 2 to 3 minutes, until they are toasted and start to smell a little nutty. Transfer to a plate to cool.

Combine the reserved fish and the remaining 2 cups fish-head stock in a small saucepan and gently reheat over low heat. Reheat the stew over medium heat; remove and discard the bay leaf.

TO SERVE: Divide the rice among four warm bowls. Leaving any stock in the saucepan, divide the fish among the bowls, placing it beside the rice. Ladle the stew over everything, sprinkle with the benne seeds, parsley, scallion, and onion flowers, if using, and serve.

SHRIMP AND OYSTER PURLOO

SERVES 6

2 tablespoons canola oil

6 ounces andouille sausage, cut into ¼-inch-thick slices

2 ounces fatty country ham scraps, preferably Bob Wood's Country Ham Trimmings (see Resources, page 368), diced

1 cup small dice sweet onion

⅓ cup small dice red bell pepper

⅓ cup small dice green bell pepper

2 teaspoons minced garlic

1 cup Anson Mills Carolina Gold Rice (see Resources, page 368)

1 cup Chicken Stock (page 344)

24 oysters, shucked, liquor reserved

⅔ cup Preserved Tomatoes (page 278) or canned whole tomatoes, drained and roughly chopped

⅛ teaspoon cayenne pepper

¼ teaspoon crushed red pepper flakes

1 teaspoon kosher salt

¼ teaspoon freshly ground white pepper

Thirty 26–30-count shrimp, preferably local, peeled and deveined

1½ tablespoons fresh lemon juice

1 tablespoon Hot Sauce (page 260) or Red Clay Original Hot Sauce (see Resources, page 369)

3 tablespoons chopped flat-leaf parsley

¼ cup thinly sliced scallion greens

GOES WELL WITH:

She-Crab Soup (page 73)
Peach and Tomato Salad with Cottage Cheese, Watercress, and Pawpaw Vinaigrette (page 86)

Shrimp and oyster purloo is 100 percent my kind of dish. First, it's a timeless recipe that doesn't get the culinary credit it deserves. I like to think of it as the South's version of paella, and when it's cooked well, it evokes the same emotions but reflects the culture and tradition of the microregion where it's made. Second, it's truly a one-pot dish, from start to finish to serving, making it a perfect meal to cook at home.

Heat the canola oil in a large cast-iron Dutch oven or other heavy pot with a lid over medium heat until it shimmers. Add the sausage and ham scraps and cook, stirring frequently, until the ham fat has rendered and the sausage is lightly browned, about 2 minutes. Add the onion and bell peppers and cook, stirring frequently, until the onion is translucent, about 5 minutes. Add the garlic and cook, stirring frequently, until translucent and very fragrant, about 2 minutes.

Stir in the rice and cook, stirring, to toast the rice, about 1 minute. Add the chicken stock, oyster liquor, tomatoes, cayenne, red pepper flakes, salt, and white pepper and stir to combine. Once the mixture comes to a simmer, reduce the heat to low, cover, and cook until the rice is tender and just starting to make a caramelized crust on the bottom of the pot, about 18 minutes. Watch carefully, because you want to add the shrimp in a single layer about 3 minutes before the rice is done, then cover the pot to let the rice finish cooking.

Remove the pot from the heat and add the oysters. Gently stir in the lemon juice, hot sauce, and parsley. Sprinkle with the scallion greens and serve family-style, directly from the Dutch oven.

POULTRY
and MEAT

CHICKEN BREASTS

with Black Pepper and Peanut Butter Gravy

SERVES 4

CHICKEN BREASTS

Four 10-ounce skin-on, bone-in chicken breasts

Kosher salt

1 tablespoon canola oil, or as needed

Freshly ground black pepper

5 thyme sprigs

GRAVY

¼ cup very finely diced sweet onion

1½ tablespoons all-purpose flour

½ cup whole milk

½ cup Chicken Stock (page 344)

¼ cup plus 2 tablespoons creamy peanut butter

1 tablespoon plus 2 teaspoons Oliver Farm Green Peanut Oil (see Resources, page 369)

1 teaspoon fresh lime juice

¾ teaspoon freshly ground black pepper

Kosher salt

TO COMPLETE

¾ cup flat-leaf parsley leaves

½ cup mint leaves

¼ cup shelled green peanuts (about 4 ounces in the shell; see page 22, and Resources, page 369), roughly chopped

4 teaspoons Oliver Farm Green Peanut Oil (see Resources, page 369)

1 teaspoon fresh lime juice

Kosher salt and freshly ground black pepper

Coarse finishing salt, preferably J.Q. Dickinson's (see Resources, page 368)

The taste of crispy-skinned pan-roasted chicken with pan gravy will never, ever get old for me. The big lesson from this recipe is to salt the chicken ahead of time. Letting the breasts air-dry in the refrigerator wicks away the excess moisture that can keep the skin from crisping up in the pan. The pan gravy is a riff on the classic Groundnut Soup (page 69) I learned while working in Richmond, Virginia.

NOTE: The seasoned chicken must be refrigerated overnight before cooking.

***

FOR THE CHICKEN: Liberally season the chicken breasts with salt, place on a rack set over a nonreactive baking dish, and refrigerate, uncovered, for 24 hours.

The next day, remove the chicken from the refrigerator and leave at room temperature for 30 minutes before cooking. Preheat the oven to 350°F.

Heat the canola oil in a large cast-iron skillet over medium-high heat until it shimmers. Pat the chicken breasts dry with paper towels and season them liberally with pepper. Place the chicken breasts in the skillet skin side down and sear until the skin is golden and crispy, about 4 minutes.

Add the thyme sprigs to the skillet, turn the breasts over, transfer the skillet to the oven, and roast for about 10 minutes, until an instant-read thermometer inserted in the thickest part of a breast reads 140°F. Transfer the chicken to a cutting board, lightly cover with aluminum foil, and rest for 5 minutes. Remove the thyme from the skillet and set the skillet aside.

FOR THE GRAVY: There should be about 1½ tablespoons of fat left in the skillet from cooking the chicken; add a little more oil if you need to. Place the skillet over medium heat, add the onion, and cook, stirring occasionally, until it starts to soften. Stir in the flour and cook, stirring constantly, until the flour just begins to turn a light golden color, about 2 minutes. Slowly stir in the milk and chicken stock and bring to a simmer, stirring constantly. Reduce the heat to low, stir in the peanut butter, green peanut oil, lime juice, and pepper, and return the gravy to a simmer. Season lightly with salt, remove from the stove, and set aside.

CONTINUED

Buttermilk Rolls (page 230)

TO COMPLETE: Combine the parsley, mint, peanuts, 2 teaspoons of the green peanut oil, and the lime juice in a small bowl. Season lightly with salt and pepper and toss to combine. Keeping the skin on, carefully carve the chicken away from the bones; discard the bones. Slice each breast crosswise into ¾-inch-thick slices. Using a pastry brush, lightly brush the slices with the remaining 2 teaspoons green peanut oil and sprinkle with a few grains of finishing salt.

Spoon some of the gravy into the center of each of four warm plates and place a sliced chicken breast on each. Divide the herb salad among the plates and serve.

CHICKEN BREASTS with Herb Dumplings

SERVES 4

HERB DUMPLINGS

¾ cup water

8 tablespoons (1 stick) unsalted butter

1 cup all-purpose flour

1½ teaspoons kosher salt

4 large eggs

½ cup grated Tomme-style cheese (about 2 ounces), preferably Sequatchie Cove Cumberland (see Resources, page 369)

¼ cup finely chopped herbs, such as flat-leaf parsley and lovage

CHICKEN

Four 8-ounce skin-on boneless chicken breasts

2 teaspoons canola oil

Kosher salt and freshly ground white pepper

1 recipe Chicken Sauce (page 351)

Coarse finishing salt, preferably J.Q. Dickinson's (see Resources, page 368)

Lemon balm leaves for garnish (optional)

GOES WELL WITH:

Butter beans (see page 191)
Grilled Ramps (page 204)
Confit Tomatoes (page 199)

I tried for a long time to "refine" my mother's chicken and dumplings so I could bring it into one of my restaurants. It never worked, because the recipe is perfect as is. So I ditched that idea and used my mom's recipe as the inspiration for this dish. My dumplings are much lighter than the hearty traditional version and can be made with whatever herbs you love. Serving them with grilled skin-on chicken breasts and a simply seasoned chicken jus, you end up with something fancy but familiar.

FOR THE DUMPLINGS: Combine the water and 6 tablespoons of the butter in a large saucepan and bring to a boil over high heat. Reduce the heat to medium and stir in the flour and salt with a wooden spoon, then cook, stirring constantly, until the mixture has thickened, about 2 minutes. Remove from the stove and cool until just warm, about 10 minutes.

Transfer the mixture to the bowl of a stand mixer fitted with the paddle attachment (or use a hand mixer and a large bowl). With the mixer on low speed, add the eggs one at a time, being sure each one is completely incorporated before adding the next. Add the cheese and chopped herbs and mix until just combined. Transfer the mixture to a container and cover to keep warm.

Prepare a hot fire in a charcoal grill (see page 96), removing the grill rack and distributing the hot coals in an even layer in the bottom of the grill. Place the grill rack at its normal height.

Bring a medium saucepan of water to a boil over medium heat. To form the dough into quenelles, dip two soupspoons into cold water. Scoop up about 1 tablespoon of the dough with one spoon and form it into a roughly oval shape using the second spoon, then carefully transfer the dumpling to the simmering water, maintaining the shape. Work in batches of about 6 at a time so the dumplings cook evenly and you don't overcrowd the saucepan. Cook the dumplings until they are set and cooked through, 2 to 3 minutes. Transfer them to a large skillet, add the remaining 2 tablespoons butter, and cover to keep warm. Repeat to make a total of 24 dumplings.

CONTINUED

FOR THE CHICKEN: Using a pastry brush, lightly brush the chicken skin with the canola oil. Liberally season the breasts with salt and white pepper. Grill the breasts skin side down for 2 minutes, without moving them. Use a metal spatula to carefully lift up the breasts and turn them over. Grill them on the other side, moving them around the grill if necessary to avoid flare-ups, until an instant-read thermometer inserted in the thickest part of the breast registers 140°F, about 10 minutes. Transfer the breasts to a cutting board, cover lightly with foil, and let rest for 5 minutes.

TO SERVE: Warm the chicken sauce in a small saucepan over low heat. Divide the dumplings among four warm bowls. Slice each chicken breast into 4 slices and place them on top of the dumplings. Drizzle the chicken with the sauce, sprinkle with some finishing salt, and garnish with the lemon balm leaves, if using.

FRIED CHICKEN

MAKES 8 PIECES

CHICKEN

8 cups water

¾ cup kosher salt

3 tablespoons sorghum syrup, preferably Muddy Pond (see Resources, page 369)

One 3- to 3½-pound chicken

BREADING

1½ dried bay leaves

1 teaspoon rubbed sage

½ teaspoon ground ginger

½ teaspoon ground coriander

½ teaspoon dried summer savory

½ teaspoon Bourbon Barrel Bourbon Smoked Paprika (see Resources, page 368)

½ teaspoon ground nutmeg

¼ teaspoon cayenne pepper

¼ teaspoon ground cardamom

¼ teaspoon ground cloves

2 cups all-purpose flour

1 tablespoon kosher salt

2 teaspoons freshly ground black pepper

2 teaspoons freshly ground white pepper

Canola oil for deep-frying

1½ tablespoons Rendered Fresh Lard (page 343)

1½ tablespoons Rendered Bacon Fat (page 342)

½ ounce fatty country ham scraps, preferably Bob Wood's Country Ham Trimmings (see Resources, page 368), diced

1½ tablespoons unsalted butter

Fried chicken is something I'll never stop trying to perfect. This version is the latest in my quest for the ideal. Fried chicken is difficult to make well, and especially tough to make for a crowd. Trying to achieve a perfectly cooked, moist interior while getting that crunchy skin with a breading that stays put is one of the things that can keep any good Southern cook up at night. This recipe is one I couldn't be happier with. That said, since writing it down, I've already thought of a few new ideas!

For this recipe, I skip the common step of dipping the chicken in buttermilk. Buttermilk is delicious, but cooking buttermilk-dipped chicken creates steam. The steam blows off the breading, and you're left with a naked piece of chicken. Nobody wants that! The most important step in the recipe is giving your chicken pieces time to sit in the breading overnight. That allows the breading to form a tight bond with the skin so that it won't disappear as you fry it. The next day, do the second breading before your guests arrive so when you are ready to cook, you can simply grab the chicken from the breading with your tongs and put it straight into the fryer.

As an ode to the fried chicken recipe in my first book, *Heritage*, and to the Nashville hot chicken I love, I finish the fried pieces with a quick toss in some super-flavorful rendered fats. That adds a wonderful depth of flavor and takes the chicken from being really, really good to being really, really, *really* good with a little extra something your guests won't quite be able to place.

NOTE: You'll need to start this recipe up to 2 days ahead of time to brine the chicken and then refrigerate it overnight after the first breading.

TO BRINE THE CHICKEN: Put the water in a pot and bring to a boil over high heat. Remove from the stove, add the salt and sorghum syrup, and stir until completely dissolved. Pour the brine into a nonreactive heatproof container large enough to hold the chicken, cool to room temperature, and then refrigerate until completely cold.

CONTINUED

Cut the chicken into 8 pieces: 2 drumsticks, 2 thighs, 2 wings, and 2 breasts. Cut the skin away from the backbone, transfer the skin to a container, cover, and refrigerate. (Save the backbone for Chicken Stock, page 344, if desired.) Rinse the chicken pieces with cold water, then place in the chilled brine, cover, and refrigerate for at least 12 hours or overnight.

WHILE THE CHICKEN IS IN THE BRINE, MAKE THE BREADING: Place the bay leaves, sage, ginger, coriander, summer savory, paprika, nutmeg, cayenne, cardamom, and cloves in a blender and blend to a fine powder. Combine the blended spice powder, flour, salt, black pepper, and white pepper in a bowl and stir to combine well. Cover and set aside at room temperature.

After the chicken has brined, make an ice bath with equal parts ice and water in a large bowl. Place the chicken in the ice bath for 5 minutes. (The ice will help pull out impurities.) Remove the chicken, lightly rinse it under cold water, and pat it dry. Pour half the breading into a large container, add the chicken, and toss to coat. Cover and refrigerate for at least 8 hours or up to overnight. Cover the remaining breading and set aside.

THE NEXT DAY, FRY THE CHICKEN: Preheat the oven to 200°F. Line a rimmed baking sheet with paper towels. Fill a deep fryer with canola oil according to the manufacturer's directions and heat the oil to 325°F. Alternatively, fill a deep heavy pot half full with canola oil and heat the oil over medium heat to 325°F.

Combine the reserved chicken skins, the lard, bacon fat, and country ham scraps in a small saucepan and let the fats infuse over low heat while you fry the chicken. Put the remaining breading in a large bowl.

Remove the chicken from the chilled breading and toss it lightly in the fresh breading. Working in batches to avoid crowding, fry the breasts for 6 minutes, then turn them over and fry until deep brown and crispy, about 6 minutes more. Transfer the breasts to the prepared baking sheet and keep warm in the oven. Return the oil to 325°F and fry the thighs for 2 minutes. Add the drumsticks and wings and fry for another minute, turning the pieces over halfway through.

Strain the infused fats through a fine-mesh sieve into a small bowl and stir in the butter until melted.

TO SERVE: Put the fried chicken in a large bowl, drizzle with the infused fats, and toss to coat.

PIT-COOKED-CHICKEN SANDWICHES

MAKES 8 SANDWICHES

CHICKEN

One 3-pound chicken

½ cup BBQ Rub (page 363)

1 tablespoon kosher salt

SOUR CABBAGE COLESLAW

3 tablespoons mayonnaise, preferably Duke's (see Resources, page 369)

2 teaspoons apple cider vinegar

1 teaspoon Hot Sauce (page 260) or Red Clay Original Hot Sauce (see Resources, page 369)

1 teaspoon celery seeds

1½ cups Sour Cabbage (page 270), drained

⅓ cup thinly sliced sweet onion

8 potato rolls

4 tablespoons unsalted butter, at room temperature

½ cup Alabama White Sauce (page 353)

EQUIPMENT

Smoker

GOES WELL WITH:

Pressure-Cooker Sea Island Red Peas (page 192)
Butter beans (see page 191)
Fried Apples (page 190)
Charred Corn with Grilled Peppers (page 162)
Cooked greens (see page 177)
Green Beans (page 173)

Pit-cooked whole chicken slathered with Alabama white sauce has a rich history in the barbecue world, going all the way back to Big Bob Gibson, the pitmaster behind his eponymous restaurant in Decatur, Alabama. I was introduced to the mysteries of Alabama white sauce by my dear friend Pat Martin, a barbecue badass. When you first dip the perfectly cooked chicken in the creamy white sauce, you'll ask, "How have I never had this before?" The tang of the vinegar and the mayonnaise is just amazing.

I turned the idea into a barbecue sandwich, cooking the chicken low and slow in the smoker and pushing the deliciousness even further by adding a coleslaw made with sour cabbage. But by all means, feel free to serve it like you would any whole roasted chicken: Carve it up and pair it with all your favorite sides.

FOR THE CHICKEN: Remove the chicken from the refrigerator 30 minutes before smoking to allow it to come to room temperature.

Prepare the smoker with hardwood charcoal and hickory (see page 57); maintain a temperature of between 200°F and 215°F.

Combine the BBQ rub and salt and liberally season the chicken inside and out with the mixture. Transfer the chicken to the smoker and smoke until an instant-read thermometer inserted in the center of one of the thighs reads 165°F, about 4½ hours. Transfer the chicken to a cutting board, cover lightly with aluminum foil, and let rest for 10 minutes.

FOR THE COLESLAW: Combine the mayonnaise, vinegar, hot sauce, and celery seeds in a bowl and mix well. Add the cabbage and onions and stir to combine. Transfer to a nonreactive container, cover, and refrigerate. *(The coleslaw can be made ahead. Tightly covered, it will keep for up to 1 day in the refrigerator.)*

TO CHOP THE CHICKEN: Leave the skin on the chicken and use a knife or your hands to separate the meat from the bones and cartilage. Roughly chop the meat and skin into approximately ½-inch pieces. Transfer to a bowl and cover lightly with foil. *(The chicken can be prepared ahead to this point; let cool completely before covering. Tightly covered, it will keep for up to 3 days in the refrigerator. Reheat the chicken in a large skillet with a little chicken stock before using.)*

TO SERVE: Split the rolls in half and spread the butter on the cut sides. Heat a large cast-iron or other skillet over medium heat. Add the rolls cut side down and toast until golden brown, about 2 minutes.

Divide the sauce among the bottom halves of the rolls and pile on the warm chicken. Spoon the coleslaw on top of the chicken, top with the other halves of the rolls, and serve.

GRILLED QUAIL with Red-Eye Gravy

SERVES 4

RED-EYE GRAVY

1 teaspoon canola oil

1 ounce fatty country ham scraps, preferably Bob Wood's Country Ham Trimmings (see Resources, page 368), cut into ⅛-inch pieces

2 tablespoons very finely diced sweet onion

1 teaspoon minced garlic

1 tablespoon all-purpose flour

½ cup Pork Stock (page 346)

½ cup day-old brewed coffee

1 teaspoon finely chopped sage

½ teaspoon thyme leaves

½ teaspoon kosher salt

½ teaspoon freshly cracked Bourbon Barrel Bourbon Smoked Black Peppercorns (see Resources, page 368)

QUAIL

Four 4-ounce semi-boneless quail, rinsed under cold water and patted dry

2 teaspoons canola oil

Kosher salt and freshly ground black pepper

GOES WELL WITH:

Dirty Farro (page 236)
Sweet Potato Puree (page 153)

Grilled quail and red-eye gravy, that quintessential Southern sauce made with leftover coffee and ham drippings, are a natural pair.

Prepare a hot fire in a charcoal grill (see page 96), removing the grill rack and distributing the hot coals in an even layer in the bottom of the grill. Place the grill rack as close to the coals as possible.

FOR THE RED-EYE GRAVY: While the grill heats, combine the canola oil and ham in a small saucepan and cook over medium heat, stirring frequently, until the fat has rendered and the ham is crisp, about 4 minutes. Add the onion and garlic and cook, stirring occasionally, until translucent, about 3 minutes. Add the flour and cook, stirring constantly, for 2 minutes to make a light roux. Slowly stir in the pork stock and coffee and bring to a simmer, stirring frequently. Reduce the heat to low, stir in the sage, thyme, salt, and cracked pepper, and cover to keep warm.

FOR THE QUAIL: Rub the quail with the canola oil and season liberally with salt and pepper. Grill the quail breast side down, moving them occasionally to avoid flare-ups, until they develop a light char, about 2 minutes. Turn the quail and grill until just cooked through, about 2 minutes longer. Transfer the grilled quail to a cutting board, cover lightly with foil, and let rest for 3 minutes.

TO SERVE: Divide the grilled quail among four warm plates and spoon some of the red-eye gravy over each.

TAKING CARE OF CAST IRON

You'd be hard-pressed to find a Southern kitchen without at least one cast-iron skillet. Cast iron was ubiquitous in the kitchens of the American South from the European settlement onward, but perhaps most so in the hills, hollers, and valleys of the Appalachian Mountains, where settlers and homesteaders relied almost exclusively on a wood fire and the hearth for cooking until the end of the nineteenth century (or, in more isolated communities, even later).

Cast-iron cookware has been used around the world for thousands of years. Molded from molten iron alloyed with about 3 percent carbon, the pots and pans are all one piece, handle and all, with no rivets to come loose or fail. The thickness and durability of cast iron are what make it so versatile. A cast-iron skillet can go from the stove to the oven or straight into a hot fire without skipping a beat. Cast iron's ability to withstand high temperatures makes it the natural choice for cooking a recipe like cornbread, but you can also use it for searing a beautiful piece of fish or getting the perfect crust on a big pork chop.

A good cast-iron skillet or pot will transcend its function as a cooking vessel, becoming a family heirloom—something to cherish and protect—and, to the cook who takes care of it, something to be proud of. Over time, after many uses, a properly cared for cast-iron pan will develop a patina made from the heated fats used to cook in it. The result is a natural nonstick cooking surface that can last for generations.

Following a few simple maintenance and cleaning rules will extend the life of your cast-iron pots and pans and ensure decades of cooking satisfaction. Most new pots and pans come seasoned and ready to use right from the factory, but if you've picked up an older piece from a thrift store or from your grandma's attic, it'll probably need to be seasoned before you use it for the first time. Give it a good cleaning, and skip to the final step below. Here's how I was taught by my mom to clean and reseason a cast-iron skillet (or Dutch oven, or griddle, etc.) and how I do it at home.

· After you've cooked your cornbread or morning bacon, let your skillet cool a little bit and then thoroughly wipe the inside and outside with a clean kitchen towel or paper towels. For a lot of applications, this is all the cleaning you need to do.

· If you're left with some tricky, sticky bits of food in your skillet, you can add a little bit of warm water to the pan and scrape up the pieces with a wooden spoon, but never let the water stand in your skillet. Cast iron is prone to rusting when exposed to water for any extended amount of time. Pour out the water and wipe the skillet completely dry. Warm the skillet over low heat for 5 minutes to ensure that any remaining water evaporates, then add enough flaxseed oil to coat the inside of the skillet, carefully spreading the oil with a clean towel. Turn the heat off and leave the skillet to cool. Then wipe any excess oil from the skillet and store it, ready for its next job.

· If you need to reseason your pan (or if you've picked up one from a thrift shop and it needs some loving care), place the cleaned and dried skillet (or other cast-iron piece) in the oven and heat it to 200°F. When the oven reaches 200°F, remove the skillet and crank the oven up to 500°F. Add a tablespoon or so of flaxseed oil to your pan and wipe it over all the surface. Take a clean towel and wipe away all the oil, leaving behind only a very thin film. This is the fat that will undergo polymerization and give your prized possession its protective coating. Place the skillet in the 500°F oven for 1 hour to complete the reseasoning. Turn the oven off and leave the skillet inside to cool. Repeating this process every so often will keep your cast-iron pieces in working order for generations.

CURED DUCK BREASTS with Rice Porridge

SERVES 4

DUCK BREASTS

Four 8-ounce skin-on, bone-in
   Muscovy duck breasts (see Note
   and box)

Kosher salt

1 tablespoon canola oil

Freshly ground black pepper

RICE PORRIDGE

1 cup Anson Mills Carolina Gold
   Rice Grits (see Resources, page
   368)

3 cups water

1 fresh bay leaf

2 teaspoons kosher salt

¼ ounce firm sheep's-milk cheese,
   grated

1 tablespoon fresh lemon juice

1 recipe Duck Jus (page 351)

GOES WELL WITH:

Grilled Carrots (page 165)
Citrus Condiment (page 366)
*Peach and Tomato Salad with
   Cottage Cheese, Watercress,
   and Pawpaw Vinaigrette
   (page 86)*

You can cure duck at home in a short amount of time—just 3 days—by using breasts only, lightly salting them, and letting them rest in the fridge. Aging duck this way results in moisture loss, which increases the intensity of the duck's meatiness and dries the skin, giving it a succulence and crispiness you can't achieve any other way.

Rice porridge is a perfect example of glorifying an ingredient that once would have been considered waste. On the rice plantations of the eighteenth and nineteenth centuries, the broken pieces of rice would have been thrown out or given away. But the damaged grains (in this case, the rice grits) release more starch than their whole counterparts and give the finished dish a creamy texture, not unlike that of good risotto.

NOTES: You'll need to start several days ahead to salt and age the duck breasts. If your butcher can't provide you with skin-on, bone-in duck breasts, you will need to buy 2 whole ducks and break them down yourself—which will leave you with the bones you need to make Duck Stock (page 345).

FOR THE DUCK BREASTS: Liberally season the duck breasts with salt. Place on a rack set over a nonreactive baking dish and refrigerate, uncovered, for 72 hours.

When you are ready to cook the duck breasts, remove them from the refrigerator and leave at room temperature for 30 minutes. Preheat the oven to 350°F.

MEANWHILE, FOR THE RICE PORRIDGE: Put the rice and water in a medium saucepan, add the bay leaf and salt, and bring to a simmer, stirring, over medium heat. Reduce the heat to low and cook the rice, stirring frequently to prevent sticking, until tender, about 20 minutes. Remove the rice from the stove, remove and discard the bay leaf, and cover to keep warm.

Heat the canola oil in a large cast-iron skillet over medium heat until it shimmers. Pat the duck breasts dry with paper towels and season them with pepper. Place them in the skillet skin side down and sear until the skin is golden and crispy and most of the subcutaneous fat has rendered, 10 to 12 minutes. Turn the breasts, transfer the skillet to the oven, and roast the breasts for about 10 minutes, until an instant-read thermometer inserted in the thickest part of a breast reads 130°F. Transfer the duck breasts to a cutting board, cover lightly with foil, and let rest for 5 minutes.

TO SERVE: Heat the duck jus in a small saucepan over medium heat. Warm the rice porridge over low heat and stir in the cheese and lemon juice.

Carve the duck breasts into slices about ½ inch thick and divide them among four warm plates. Spoon the rice porridge next to the duck and drizzle the breasts with the jus.

HOW TO BREAK DOWN A DUCK

To get duck breasts with the rib cages attached for use in this recipe, you will probably need to buy 2 whole ducks, preferably Muscovy, and butcher them at home, because most stores sell boneless breasts, but it's a great way to acquire the bones needed to make this rich duck stock. Here's how to do it:

Lay each duck breast side down on a cutting board with the legs facing away from you. Using poultry shears, cut down both sides of the backbone and remove it; set aside. Turn the duck over, find the joint that connects one of the thighs to the body, and, using a sharp knife, cut through the joint to release the leg. Repeat with the other thigh and set the legs aside. With the duck breast facing up, use your finger to find the piece of cartilage that separates the two breast halves. Carefully cut along either side of the cartilage through the breast and down to the breastplate, but do not cut all the way through it. Using poultry shears, cut down both sides of the exposed cartilage, separating the two halves. Set the piece of cartilage aside with the backbone. Using a sharp knife, cut the wings away from the breasts and add to the other bones.

At this point, you can either add the whole legs to the reserved bones to make an even richer stock, or you can debone them and use the meat for another purpose, like duck confit or sausage. To debone the legs, lay them skin side down on the cutting board. Using a sharp paring knife, carefully cut the thigh and leg meat from the bones, leaving the skin attached. Add the leg bones to the other reserved bones to use for stock.

CHEESEBURGERS

MAKES 5 CHEESEBURGERS

SPECIAL SAUCE

¾ cup plus 2 tablespoons mayonnaise, preferably Duke's (see Resources, page 369)

½ cup plus 2 tablespoons yellow mustard

2½ tablespoons ketchup

¼ cup Bread-and-Butter Pickles (page 243), drained and cut into ⅛-inch dice

2 tablespoons pickled jalapeño peppers, drained and cut into ⅛-inch dice

1½ teaspoons grated lemon zest

1 tablespoon fresh lemon juice

1 tablespoon Pepper Vinegar (page 262) or Texas Pete Pepper Vinegar

1½ teaspoons Hot Sauce (page 260) or Red Clay Original Hot Sauce (see Resources, page 369)

Kosher salt and freshly ground black pepper

CHEESEBURGERS

One 1½-pound boneless chuck roast

8 ounces flank steak

3 tablespoons unsalted butter, at room temperature

5 hamburger buns, split

½ cup shaved white onion

10 slices American cheese

25 Bread-and-Butter Pickles (page 243)

EQUIPMENT

Meat grinder (see headnote)

Something as ordinary as a cheeseburger can present a surprising number of variables to consider. Seared or grilled? Stuffed? How big should the bun be? Sesame seeds or not? Toasted? With butter or with beef fat? And when you start thinking about the cheese and other accoutrements, the list of possibilities only grows.

I prefer a burger cooked on the flattop to one cooked over charcoal. I love how the juices and fat that escape during the cooking process hang around, caramelizing and working their way back into the patty. I've done a lot of research into cheeseburgers, and my favorite method is the one used for the smash burger. The idea is pretty simple: You portion your meat into a ball, season the outside heavily with salt and pepper, and smash it hard with your spatula onto the hot griddle. The most important part of this technique, after the initial smash, is to leave the burger alone. Right at the beginning, the proteins in the meat make it stick to the flattop, and any attempt to move it would result in a sad mess. But as the patty cooks, the delicious beef fat within renders out, crisping up the bottom and sides of the patty until it releases from the griddle. Most of the time, I don't add any additional fat to the griddle, but sometimes, depending on the fat content of the meat, I may add a touch of beef fat or butter to help the burger cook. After 1½ to 2 minutes, you'll just start to see the edges getting crispy and brown, and the aroma will be off the charts. The deep, almost crunchy crust you achieve by cooking a burger this way gives it an incredible flavor. Then flip the burger very carefully and cook it just long enough to soften the onions and melt the cheese that you've added on top, another minute or so.

I always grind the meat for my burgers myself, using a mix of chuck and flank steak. The freshness really comes through. But if you don't have a meat grinder, you can have the butcher do this—buy the meat the day you plan to make the burgers.

FOR THE SAUCE: Combine all the ingredients for the sauce in a large container and stir to blend well. Cover and refrigerate. *(Tightly covered, the sauce will keep for up to 5 days in the refrigerator.)*

FOR THE CHEESEBURGERS: Grind the chuck and flank steak through the large die of the meat grinder into a bowl. Mix gently to combine. Grind half the mixture through the small die. Mix the two halves together.

GOES WELL WITH:

Ripe, in-season tomatoes
Crispy fried potato wedges

Portion the meat into ten 3-ounce balls; each burger will get 2 patties. *(The balls can be shaped ahead, tightly covered, and refrigerated for up to 1 day. Remove from the refrigerator about 30 minutes before you're ready to cook; it's important that the balls are not ice-cold when they hit the hot pan.)*

Generously butter the cut sides of the buns. Toast on a griddle until golden brown. Transfer to a rimmed baking sheet, toasted side up, and set aside.

Heat two 12-inch cast-iron skillets over high heat until very hot and just barely beginning to smoke, 2 to 3 minutes. Divide the balls between the two hot skillets, smashing each one down with a spatula. When the patties are charred on the bottom, with a dark brown crust, about 2 minutes, turn them over. Place the onion slices on top of 5 of the patties and place a slice of cheese on each patty. Cook for another 1 to 2 minutes, until the onions have softened and the cheese has melted; the burgers will be cooked to medium. Stack the patties without onions on top of the patties with onions. Remove from the heat.

Smear both cut sides of the buns with the sauce. Place 5 pickles on the bottom of each bun. Add the burgers and cover with the tops of the buns.

PORK SHOULDER STEAK

with Grilled Mushrooms

SERVES 4

PORK

Four 6- to 7-ounce pork shoulder
steaks

Kosher salt and freshly ground
black pepper

MUSHROOMS

8 ounces wild mushrooms,
preferably chanterelles, stems
scraped clean, caps swirled in
warm water to clean, and dried

1 tablespoon extra-virgin olive oil

2 teaspoons kosher salt

1 teaspoon freshly ground black
pepper

1½ teaspoons fresh lemon juice

¼ cup chervil leaves

EQUIPMENT

Round 15-inch open-top fine-mesh
wire grill basket

GOES WELL WITH:

Eggplant Purloo (page 189)
Sweet Potato Puree (page 153)
Butterball Potatoes with Crispy
*   Potato Topping (page 170)*
Braised Fennel (page 194)

Pork shoulder steak is totally worth searching out. It reminds me of a country ham steak you might find in a diner, but with that fresh pork flavor I love so much. Grilled quickly, it's unbelievably moist, thanks to all the glorious little pockets of fat that you get in a shoulder from a good pig. As for the mushrooms, during the summer in the South, it's all about chanterelles, but you can use whatever fresh mushroom is in season.

NOTE: Pork shoulder steaks, sometimes called blade steaks, come from a part of the pig more commonly associated with the low-and-slow cooking of barbecue, but cut thin, they are right at home on the grill.

FOR THE PORK: Prepare a hot fire in a charcoal grill (see page 96), removing the grill rack and distributing the hot coals in an even layer in the bottom of the grill. Place the grill rack as close to the coals as possible.

Season the pork shoulder steaks liberally with salt and pepper on both sides. Grill until deep brown on the first side, about 4 minutes. Turn the steaks over and grill until an instant-read thermometer inserted in the middle of a steak reads 130°F, another 1 to 2 minutes. Transfer the steaks to a cutting board, cover lightly with foil, and let rest for 5 minutes.

FOR THE MUSHROOMS: While the steaks rest, combine the mushrooms, olive oil, salt, and pepper in a bowl and toss. Transfer to the grill basket (set the bowl aside), remove the grill rack (set the hot rack aside in a safe place), and place the basket directly on the coals. Grill the mushrooms, shaking the basket frequently to ensure that they cook evenly, until they are tender and have developed a light char around the edges, about 3 minutes. Return them to the bowl, add the lemon juice, and toss to combine.

TO SERVE: Divide the shoulder steaks among four warm plates and top each with some of the grilled mushrooms and the chervil leaves.

STRIP STEAK with Worcestershire

SERVES 4

SAUCE

1 tablespoon Worcestershire sauce, preferably Bourbon Barrel (see Resources, page 368)

1 tablespoon Rendered Fresh Beef Fat (page 342), melted

1 teaspoon fish sauce

1 tablespoon finely sliced chives

1 tablespoon small dice red onion

1 teaspoon minced garlic

1 tablespoon fresh lemon juice

STEAK

Four 10- to 12-ounce strip steaks, about 1 inch thick

Kosher salt and freshly ground black pepper

4 tablespoons unsalted butter, at room temperature

GOES WELL WITH:

Butterball Potatoes with Crispy Potato Toppings (page 170)

Potato and Ramp Puree (page 156)

Grilled Mushrooms (page 206)

Grilled Ramps (see page 204)

This steak marinates in a Bourbon Barrel Worcestershire–based concoction that I like to call "Love Sauce." I don't cook a steak at home that doesn't spend some time resting in this complex and flavorful mixture. You'll want to save some to spoon over your cooked steaks as well.

Prepare a hot fire in a charcoal grill (see page 96), removing the grill rack and distributing the hot coals in an even layer in the bottom of the grill. Place the grill rack as close to the coals as possible.

FOR THE SAUCE: Combine the Worcestershire, beef fat, fish sauce, chives, onion, garlic, and lemon juice in a small bowl. Set aside.

FOR THE STEAK: Season both sides of the steaks liberally with salt and pepper and spread 2 tablespoons of the soft butter over one side of the steaks. Place them butter side down on the grill and cook, moving them as necessary to avoid flare-ups, until they develop a deep brown crust on the first side, about 4 minutes. Turn the steaks, spread the remaining 2 tablespoons butter on the tops, and grill until an instant-read thermometer inserted in the middle of a steak reads 120°F, 5 to 6 minutes. (If you prefer your steaks cooked to medium, grill them for 2 minutes longer.)

Transfer the steaks to a shallow baking dish and pour the sauce over them. Cover lightly with aluminum foil and let rest for 5 minutes. The residual heat in the steaks will cook them to medium-rare while they rest.

TO SERVE: Divide the steaks among four warm plates and top each steak with a spoonful of the sauce.

PORK PRIME RIB with Mustard Onions

SERVES 8

PORK RACK

1 gallon water

1⅓ cups kosher salt

One 8-bone rack of pork (about
   6 pounds), chine bone removed
   (have the butcher do this)

15 thyme sprigs

3 tablespoons freshly ground black
   pepper

MUSTARD ONIONS

1 cup distilled white vinegar

1 cup Dijon mustard

1 tablespoon agave nectar

2 teaspoons kosher salt

½ teaspoon freshly ground white
   pepper

1 large yellow onion (about
   1 pound), cut lengthwise in half
   and then into ¼-inch-wide strips

Coarse finishing salt, preferably
   J.Q. Dickinson's (see Resources,
   page 368)

2 tablespoons thyme leaves

GOES WELL WITH:

---

*Braised and Seared Cabbage
   (page 166)*
Green Garlic Puree (page 160)

"Prime rib" usually makes people think of beef and old-school carveries, but the same low-and-slow technique yields an even doneness throughout a pork rack and a flavorful crust on the outside. I cook my pork prime rib in my wood-burning fireplace; you can use your oven and grill for results every bit as good. The fat melts just right and picks up that addictive smoke flavor, and the meat has that really wonderful soft prime rib texture.

The mustard onions came into my kitchen by way of Dakar. In the street stalls of the Senegalese capital, almost everything grilled over charcoal is served with a healthy portion of them, and they've become a mainstay in my repertoire.

NOTE: You'll need to plan ahead to brine the pork.

FOR THE PORK: Put the water in a pot and bring to a boil over high heat. Remove from the stove, add the salt, and stir until completely dissolved. Pour the brine into a nonreactive heatproof container large enough to hold the pork and cool to room temperature, then refrigerate until completely cold.

Place the pork in the cold brine, cover, and refrigerate for at least 8 hours or up to overnight.

WHILE THE PORK IS IN THE BRINE, MAKE THE MUSTARD ONIONS: Combine the vinegar, mustard, agave nectar, salt, and white pepper in a medium glass or ceramic bowl. Add the onion and toss to mix well. Cover tightly with plastic wrap and refrigerate for at least 4 hours. *(Tightly covered, the mustard onions will keep for up to 2 days in the refrigerator. Bring to room temperature before serving.)*

When you're ready to cook the pork, remove it from the brine (discard the brine), blot it dry with paper towels, and put it in a baking dish. Leave it at room temperature for 1 hour.

TO COOK THE PORK: Preheat the oven to 250°F. Place a rack in a roasting pan and line the rack with the thyme sprigs.

Rub the rack of pork all over with the pepper and place it fat side up on the rack. Roast the pork for about 2 hours, until the internal temperature reads 125°F on an instant-read thermometer. Remove the pan from the oven and cover lightly with aluminum foil; let stand while you prepare the grill.

CONTINUED

Prepare a hot fire in a charcoal grill (see page 96), removing the grill rack and distributing the hot coals in an even layer in the bottom of the grill. Place the grill rack as close to the coals as possible.

Grill the pork fat side down until the fat begins to render and the pork develops a nice crust, about 5 minutes. Move it as necessary to avoid flare-ups. Turn it over and grill on the other side until the entire rack of pork has a nice crust, 4 to 5 minutes more. Transfer the pork to a cutting board, cover lightly with foil, and let rest for 10 to 15 minutes.

TO SERVE: Carefully remove the bones from the pork rack in one piece by running your knife between the meat and the bones, pressing lightly against the bones so you get all the meat, and transfer the bones to a platter. Cut the pork into slices about ½ inch thick. Transfer the slices to the platter, laying them over the bones, and sprinkle with finishing salt. Top with the mustard onions and their juices and sprinkle with the thyme leaves.

SPRING LAMB with Rhubarb Butter

SERVES 4

GLAZE

4 tablespoons extra-virgin olive oil

2 tablespoons white soy sauce

1 tablespoon fish sauce

2 tablespoons sorghum syrup, preferably Muddy Pond (see Resources, page 369)

1½ tablespoons Hominy Miso (page 264)

2 garlic cloves

½ teaspoon grated lemon zest

½ teaspoon grated lime zest

2 teaspoons fresh lemon juice

2 teaspoons fresh lime juice

1 tablespoon finely chopped flat-leaf parsley

¼ teaspoon Espelette pepper

⅛ teaspoon freshly ground black pepper

LAMB

Two 12- to 14-ounce boneless lamb loin roasts

Kosher salt and freshly ground black pepper

½ cup Rhubarb Butter (page 288)

Coarse finishing salt, preferably J.Q. Dickinson's (see Resources, page 368)

GOES WELL WITH:

Rye and Morel Porridge (page 237)
Grilled Mushrooms (page 206)

If you eat lamb at different times throughout the year, you may notice the change in taste based on the season, the animal's age, and the varied forage that the animal grazed on. In the spring, most of the lambs slaughtered are primarily milk-fed, and this yields more tender and delicately flavored meat, with lower levels of the lanolin that some people find off-putting. That subtlety makes spring lamb the perfect choice for an understated dish like this.

Rhubarb is at its best in the spring too, and it cooks down into a delicious fruit butter that serves as a sauce for the lamb.

FOR THE GLAZE: Combine 2 tablespoons of the olive oil, the white soy sauce, fish sauce, sorghum syrup, miso, and garlic in a small saucepan. Blend with an immersion blender until smooth and emulsified, about 1 minute. Set aside.

FOR THE LAMB: Prepare a hot fire in a charcoal grill (see page 96), removing the grill rack and distributing the hot coals in an even layer in the bottom of the grill. Place the grill rack as close to the coals as possible.

Transfer ¼ cup of the glaze to a small bowl and set aside. Season the lamb loins liberally with salt and black pepper and lightly brush with some of the remaining glaze. Grill the lamb fat side down until the fat begins to render and the lamb is golden brown on the first side, about 3 minutes. Turn the lamb (you want to keep turning the meat to prevent the glaze from charring too much), brush with more glaze, and cook for about 5 minutes more for medium-rare; an instant-read thermometer inserted in the thickest part of the lamb should read 125°F. Transfer the lamb to a cutting board, cover lightly with aluminum foil, and let rest for 5 minutes.

While the lamb is resting, add the remaining 2 tablespoons olive oil, the lemon zest, lime zest, lemon juice, lime juice, parsley, Espelette pepper, and black pepper to the reserved glaze and stir to combine.

Warm the rhubarb butter in a small saucepan over low heat.

TO SERVE: Slice the lamb into ½-inch-thick pieces. Divide the lamb among four warm plates and spoon the glaze mixture over it. Sprinkle with finishing salt and spoon some rhubarb butter beside each portion.

VEGETABLES AND SIDES

CORN PUREE

SERVES 4 AS A SIDE

1½ cups fresh sweet corn kernels
(from about 3 ears)

1 cup Vegetable Stock (page 348)

¼ cup Sour Corn (page 272),
drained

¼ teaspoon kosher salt

¼ teaspoon freshly ground white
pepper

1 tablespoon unsalted butter

GOES WELL WITH:

*Grilled Catfish with Hoppin' John
(page 98)*

*Beeliner Snapper with Fried
Peppers (page 108)*

Normally when I cook fresh sweet corn, I do it quickly. It takes only a matter of seconds to be perfectly cooked. But this puree is different. Simmering the kernels slowly and gently in some stock brings out a deep, rich, almost soul-food flavor that will keep you coming back. The puree is brightened by the addition of Sour Corn, one of my favorite funky fermented flavors. You could also try this thinned out with more vegetable stock to turn it into a soup; eat it with a nice, hot wedge of cornbread alongside.

Pictured on page 154

Combine the corn and vegetable stock in a small saucepan and bring to a simmer over high heat. Reduce the heat to low and cook until the corn is very soft and the stock has reduced by about half, about 45 minutes. Drain the corn, reserving the cooking liquid.

Combine the cooked corn, sour corn, salt, and white pepper in a blender and blend on high until completely smooth, about 2 minutes. If the puree needs more liquid to blend properly, add some of the reserved cooking liquid 1 teaspoon at a time. Transfer to a small saucepan, stir in the butter, and serve. Or transfer to a container, cool to room temperature, cover, and refrigerate for up to 2 days; reheat before serving.

SWEET POTATO PUREE

SERVES 4 AS A SIDE

2 large sweet potatoes (about 1½ pounds total), scrubbed and patted dry

½ cup Vegetable Stock (page 348)

½ cup whole milk

1 teaspoon kosher salt

¼ teaspoon freshly ground white pepper

2 tablespoons fresh orange juice

GOES WELL WITH:

Pork Shoulder Steak with Grilled Mushrooms (page 141)
Chicken Breasts with Black Pepper and Peanut Butter Gravy (page 120)

A simple sweet potato baked slowly in the oven gives off the most enticing aroma. The natural sugars transform into a sort of magical sticky glaze that keeps the flesh nice and moist, and when it's scooped out and simmered with a touch of vegetable stock and milk, it becomes almost decadent. Seasoning the puree with freshly squeezed orange juice makes it pop, elevating that familiar and comforting sweet potato flavor.

Pictured on page 155

Preheat the oven to 375°F.

Place the sweet potatoes in a baking dish and bake for about 1 hour and 15 minutes, until completely tender. Let cool completely.

Cut the sweet potatoes lengthwise in half, scoop out the flesh, and roughly chop it (discard the skins). Combine the flesh, vegetable stock, and milk in a medium saucepan and bring to a simmer over medium heat, stirring occasionally to prevent scorching. Simmer, stirring occasionally, until the liquid has reduced by about half, about 15 minutes.

Transfer the mixture to a blender, add the salt and white pepper, and blend on high until completely smooth, about 2 minutes. Blend in the orange juice and serve. Or transfer to a container, cool to room temperature, cover, and refrigerate for up to 2 days; reheat before serving.

POTATO AND RAMP PUREE

SERVES 6 AS A SIDE

Kosher salt

2 pounds Yukon Gold potatoes, scrubbed

⅓ cup whole milk

½ pound (2 sticks) unsalted butter, diced

¾ teaspoon freshly ground white pepper

8 ounces ramps, cleaned, dried, hairy root ends removed, and thinly sliced

---

GOES WELL WITH:

Strip Steak with Worcestershire (page 142)

Spring Lamb with Rhubarb Butter (page 148)

The perfect potato puree is an ethereal thing. It should melt in your mouth, leaving behind that wonderful, buttery potato flavor. There are a couple of things that will help you achieve that perfection time and again. First, don't let your potatoes come to a rolling boil. You want them to cook at just a little bit above a simmer, no more. And don't let them cool before you puree them and add the milk and butter. If they cool too much, they won't blend well and will turn waxy and starchy. This potato puree is great on its own, but it reaches new heights of deliciousness when you add an intense fresh ramp puree. I do that every spring when ramps first make their way into my kitchen.

Pictured on page 143

Put the potatoes in a large pot of salted water and bring just to a boil over high heat. Reduce the heat to medium-high and boil gently until a fork inserted in a potato meets no resistance, about 35 minutes.

While the potatoes are cooking, heat the milk and butter in a small saucepan over low heat until the butter melts; set aside.

Drain the potatoes, return them to the pot, and cover with a kitchen towel. Then, using another towel to hold the potatoes and avoid being burned, peel them one at a time. Roughly chop the peeled potatoes and, working in batches if necessary, process them in a food processor, slowly adding the melted butter and milk, just until completely smooth, about 2 minutes. Be careful not to overprocess, or the potatoes will get gummy.

Transfer the potato puree to a medium saucepan, stir in 1 tablespoon salt and ½ teaspoon of the white pepper, cover, and set aside.

Bring a large pot of salted water to a boil over high heat. Make an ice bath with equal parts ice and water in a large bowl. Place the ramps in a large fine-mesh sieve and submerge them in the boiling water just until the whites are tender and the green parts are a vibrant green color, about 1 minute. Leaving them in the sieve, transfer the ramps to the ice bath and submerge until completely cool.

Drain the ramps, reserving about ¼ cup of the ice water. Transfer the ramps to a blender and blend on high until very smooth, about 1 minute. If the puree needs more liquid to blend properly, add some of the reserved ice water 1 teaspoon at a time. Blend in ½ teaspoon salt and the remaining ¼ teaspoon white pepper. Strain the puree through a fine-mesh sieve. *(The puree can be made ahead. Tightly covered, it will keep for up to 2 days in the refrigerator.)*

Add the ramp puree to the potato puree and reheat over medium heat, stirring occasionally. Transfer to a serving bowl and serve.

CREAMED RAMPS

SERVES 4 AS A SIDE

2 tablespoons unsalted butter

6 ounces ramps, cleaned, dried, hairy root ends removed, and thinly sliced

1 recipe Ramp Sauerkraut (page 269)

½ cup heavy cream

2 ounces Asiago cheese, preferably Kenny's Farmhouse Dry Fork Reserve (see Resources, page 369), grated

Pinch of ground nutmeg

Kosher salt and freshly ground white pepper

GOES WELL WITH:

Hot-Water Cornbread (page 219)
Grilled Quail with Red-Eye Gravy (page 133)

I've made creamed ramps for years, but it wasn't until recently that I had the idea to add some funky ramp sauerkraut. It adds a whole other layer of flavor to an already complex and delicious recipe.

Heat the butter in a medium skillet over medium heat until foamy. Add the ramps and cook, stirring constantly, until softened, about 3 minutes. Drain the ramp sauerkraut, add it to the skillet, and stir until warmed through. Add the cream and cook until it has reduced by half, about 3 minutes.

Remove from the stove and add the cheese, stirring until it has completely melted. Season lightly with the nutmeg, salt, and white pepper and serve.

GREEN GARLIC PUREE

SERVES 8 AS A SIDE

10 whole green garlic stalks (about 12 ounces)

3 tablespoons unsalted butter

⅓ cup Anson Mills Carolina Gold Rice (see Resources, page 368)

Kosher salt

½ teaspoon freshly ground white pepper

GOES WELL WITH:

Strip Steak with Worcestershire (page 142)

Grilled Catfish with Barely Cooked Tomatoes (page 94)

Green garlic season is pretty brief in the South. I always like to treat fleeting ingredients in the simplest ways so I can enjoy their flavor. This puree tastes like a slightly tame cross between garlic and ramps. Catching fresh green garlic at the right time in its growth is essential: It should not have formed a bulb but should resemble a small leek.

When I was first toying around with green garlic puree, it always turned into a lumpy, cottage cheese–like mess. The cellulose in the green garlic does strange things when it's cooked. I was able to counter it with a classic technique: using rice as an emulsifier.

Separate the white and green parts of the garlic. Wash and dry. Thinly slice the whites and chop the greens, keeping them separate.

Heat the butter in a large saucepan over medium-high heat until foamy. Add the white parts of the garlic and cook, stirring frequently, until soft, about 7 minutes, adding a splash of water if the whites start to stick. Add the rice, stir to coat, and stir until the rice is toasted and starts to smell slightly nutty, about 1 minute. Add ½ cup water and bring to a simmer, then reduce the heat to low, cover, and cook, stirring often, until the garlic and rice are very soft, about 15 minutes. Remove from the stove and cool slightly.

Transfer the garlic mixture to a blender and blend on high until very smooth, about 2 minutes. Blend in 1 teaspoon salt and the white pepper. Strain through a fine-mesh sieve into a small saucepan and set aside.

Bring a large pot of salted water to a boil over high heat. Make an ice bath with equal parts ice and water in a large bowl. Put the green parts of the garlic in a fine-mesh sieve and submerge in the boiling water until tender and a vibrant green color, 1 to 2 minutes. Leaving them in the sieve, transfer to the ice bath and submerge until completely cold.

Remove the greens from the ice bath and transfer to a blender; reserve about ¼ cup of the ice water. Blend the greens on high until very smooth, about 1 minute; if the puree needs more liquid to blend properly, add some of the reserved ice water about 1 teaspoon at a time. Strain through a fine-mesh sieve into the saucepan with the pureed garlic whites and stir together until uniform in color.

Reheat the puree gently over low heat and serve. Or cover and refrigerate for up to 2 days; reheat before serving.

SLOW-COOKED ONIONS

SERVES 4 AS A SIDE

1 pound sweet onions, sliced ⅛ inch thick

6 tablespoons unsalted butter

1 teaspoon kosher salt

¼ teaspoon freshly ground white pepper

GOES WELL WITH:

Cured Duck Breasts with Rice Porridge (page 136)

HOW TO MAKE A CARTOUCHE

A cartouche is a parchment paper lid used to control evaporation during the cooking process. To make one, cut a square of parchment paper slightly larger than the pan you will be using and fold it in half from right to left to make a rectangle, then in half again from bottom to top to make a square. Keeping the folded seam on the bottom, fold the top right corner over to the bottom left corner to form a triangle. Fold the triangle over itself, then fold in the same manner one more time. Hold the point at the center of your pan and cut off the wider end of the paper at a point just inside the pan. Cut a ½-inch piece from the pointed end. Unfold the paper and place it directly over the ingredients you are cooking.

This recipe takes a little bit of patience, but the result is completely worth it. When sweet onions are cooked with butter over low heat for a long time, they essentially dissolve into their own onion bisque. You don't want any browning at all to sneak onto the onions, so stir them well and often. These slow-cooked onions are an excellent accompaniment to a nice piece of roasted meat, but I also love to add a little stock or milk to them for a simple but delicious onion soup.

Combine the onions, butter, salt, and white pepper in a medium skillet, spreading the onions in an even layer. Cover the mixture with a cartouche (see box) and cook over low heat, stirring occasionally, until the onions are extremely tender, about 45 minutes.

Serve the onions immediately. Or transfer to a container, cool to room temperature, cover, and refrigerate for up to 3 days; reheat before serving.

CHARRED CORN with Grilled Peppers

SERVES 4 AS A SIDE

GRILLED JALAPEÑO VINAIGRETTE

2 red jalapeño peppers

2 teaspoons grated lime zest

2½ tablespoons fresh lime juice

½ teaspoon kosher salt

2 tablespoons extra-virgin olive oil

SHISHITO PEPPERS

4 ounces shishito peppers (about 8 peppers), cut into ¼-inch-thick rings

Kosher salt and freshly ground black pepper

CHARRED CORN

2 cups fresh sweet corn kernels (from about 4 ears)

1 tablespoon extra-virgin olive oil

2 teaspoons kosher salt

1 teaspoon freshly ground black pepper

2 teaspoons grated lime zest

2 tablespoons fresh lime juice

2 tablespoons small dice Manchego cheese (about 1 ounce)

2 tablespoons ⅛-inch-thick slices scallion, white part only

8 basil leaves, torn into smaller pieces

EQUIPMENT

Round 15-inch open-top fine-mesh wire grill basket

GOES WELL WITH:

Arugula or other greens

When summer is at its peak, I like to grill fresh sweet corn over the fire, dress it with a chili-lime vinaigrette, and scatter some diced Manchego cheese and charred shishito peppers over it all.

FOR THE VINAIGRETTE: Prepare a hot fire in a charcoal grill (see page 96), removing the grill rack and distributing the hot coals in an even layer in the bottom of the grill.

Put the jalapeños in the grill basket and place the basket directly on the coals. Grill the peppers, rotating them with long-handled tongs as they cook to char them evenly on all sides, for about 3 minutes. Transfer to a cutting board and cool to room temperature.

Remove the stems and seeds from the jalapeños, roughly chop them, and transfer to a blender. Add the lime zest, lime juice, and salt and pulse just enough to break up the charred peppers but not puree them. Transfer to a small bowl and stir in the olive oil to make a broken vinaigrette (it will not emulsify). Set aside at room temperature.

FOR THE SHISHITO PEPPERS: Arrange the peppers in the grill basket in an even layer and place the basket directly on the coals. Grill the peppers until they have developed a nice char on the first side, about 30 seconds, then transfer to a bowl, season lightly with salt and black pepper, and cover to keep warm. Clean the grill basket to use for the corn.

FOR THE CORN: Put the kernels in a large bowl, add the olive oil, salt, and black pepper, and toss. Transfer the corn to the grill basket and place the basket directly on the coals. Grill the kernels, stirring them with long-handled tongs so they cook evenly, until they have lightly charred and softened, about 1 minute. Transfer the kernels to a medium bowl, add the lime zest and juice, and stir to combine.

TO SERVE: Spoon the vinaigrette into the middle of a serving bowl. Add the charred corn, sprinkle the shishito peppers, cheese, and scallions on top, and garnish with the torn basil leaves.

GRILLED CARROTS

SERVES 4 AS A SIDE

20 baby carrots with tops
(about 1½ pounds)

¾ cup water, plus more as needed

2 teaspoons sugar

1 teaspoon kosher salt

1 tablespoon citrus vinegar,
preferably Jean-Marc
Montegottero Calamansi Vinegar
(see Resources, page 369)

1 tablespoon sunflower oil
(see Resources, page 369)

3 tablespoons chopped chervil

EQUIPMENT

Round 15-inch open-top fine-mesh
wire grill basket

GOES WELL WITH:

*Cornmeal-Dusted Grouper with
Herb Puree (page 105)*

Grilling dense root vegetables like carrots can be challenging. Achieving the perfect balance of doneness and char is almost impossible from raw. So I came up with this method—sort of a high-heat, low-moisture braise—to make it easier to nail the ideal texture. The carrots are essentially cooked al dente before they hit the grill but in a way that adds much more flavor than a simple blanch would. The braise can be done ahead of time so the carrots just need to be grilled, a matter of minutes, when you're ready to eat.

Remove the tops from the carrots. Pick the 12 nicest-looking tops and reserve in ice water to use as a garnish, if desired. Peel and rinse the carrots.

Arrange half the carrots in a single layer in a large cast-iron skillet. Add ¼ cup plus 2 tablespoons of the water, 1 teaspoon of the sugar, and ½ teaspoon of the salt. Cover the skillet with a cartouche (see box, page 161) and cook the carrots over medium heat until all the water has evaporated, about 10 minutes. Remove the cartouche and continue to cook the carrots, shaking the skillet frequently and deglazing it with water, adding it 1 tablespoon at a time as necessary, until the carrots are just tender and evenly browned, 8 to 10 minutes. Transfer to a rimmed baking sheet and set aside. Repeat with the remaining carrots, using the remaining ¼ cup plus 2 tablespoons water, 1 teaspoon sugar, and ½ teaspoon salt.

Prepare a hot fire in a charcoal grill (see page 96), removing the grill rack and distributing the hot coals in an even layer in the bottom of the grill.

Transfer the carrots to the grill basket and place directly on the coals. Grill the carrots, shaking the basket frequently with long-handled tongs to ensure that they cook evenly, until they are lightly charred and hot throughout, about 4 minutes.

Transfer the carrots to a serving bowl, add the vinegar, sunflower oil, and chervil, and toss to coat. Garnish with the reserved carrot tops, if desired, and serve.

BRAISED AND SEARED CABBAGE

SERVES 8 AS A SIDE

1 medium head green cabbage (about 2 pounds), tough outer leaves discarded, cut into 8 equal wedges

¼ cup cabbage vinegar (see page 259) or apple cider vinegar

1½ teaspoons kosher salt

1 teaspoon freshly ground white pepper

2 tablespoons canola oil

GOES WELL WITH:

Pork Prime Rib with Mustard Onions (page 144)

This recipe combines two techniques I've always been particularly enamored of: cooking a vegetable as you would a nice piece of meat—in this case, braising the cabbage—and seasoning it with a vinegar made from the vegetable itself.

Remove all but the lower rack from the oven and preheat the oven to 400°F.

Place the cabbage wedges on a rimmed baking sheet and season them with the vinegar, salt, and white pepper. Transfer the wedges to a large Dutch oven or other heavy pot with a lid and arrange them in a single layer on the bottom, or in as close to a single layer as possible. Drizzle with any remaining liquid from the baking sheet and cover the pot.

Place the Dutch oven in the oven and cook the cabbage, basting it with the juices and rotating the pot every 10 minutes or so, for about 30 minutes, until it is just tender and beginning to turn translucent, about 3 minutes.

Remove the Dutch oven from the oven and set aside, covered, to keep the cabbage warm. (*The cabbage can be made up to this point ahead. Tightly covered once cooled, it will keep for up to 2 days in the refrigerator.*)

Heat the canola oil in a large skillet over medium-high heat. Working in batches if necessary, add the cabbage wedges cut side down and sear until dark brown on the first side, about 3 minutes. Turn onto the other cut side and sear until dark brown on that side, about 2 minutes (if working in batches, retrieve and reserve the juices in the Dutch oven before searing the second batch).

Transfer the cabbage to a serving dish, spoon some of the juices from the Dutch oven over it, and serve.

LADIES' CABBAGE

SERVES 6 AS A SIDE

Butter for the pan

Kosher salt

1 medium green cabbage (about 2 pounds), tough outer leaves removed, halved lengthwise

¼ cup thinly sliced leek, white part only, washed and dried

¼ cup small dice cooked egg whites (from about 2 boiled eggs)

2 large eggs

1 cup heavy cream

2 teaspoons Asian mushroom seasoning (see Note)

½ teaspoon ground mace

¼ teaspoon freshly ground white pepper

GOES WELL WITH:

Fried Catfish with Green Tomato Tartar Sauce (page 106)

I first read about Ladies' Cabbage in *The Unrivaled Cookbook and Housekeeper's Guide.* As you might surmise, the dish was invented to be a more "delicate" vegetable option for ladies. The cabbage is boiled in two changes of water until it is quite tender and the flavor is pretty subtle, then it's baked in a light custard. It reminds me of Japanese *chawanmushi*, the steamed savory custard, made with braised vegetables.

NOTE: Asian mushroom seasoning can be found in your local Asian foods store or from online retailers.

Pictured on page 106

Preheat the oven to 375°F. Butter a 9-by-13-inch baking dish.

Bring a large pot of salted water to a boil over high heat. Add the cabbage, reduce the heat to medium, and simmer for 15 minutes. Drain Fill the pot with fresh salted water, add the cabbage, and bring to a simmer over high heat, then reduce the heat to medium and simmer until the cabbage is completely tender, about 5 minutes. Drain the cabbage and cool completely.

While the cabbage is cooling, blanch the leeks: Bring a small saucepan of salted water to a boil over high heat. Put the leeks in a small sieve and submerge them in the water until tender, about 1 minute. Drain the leeks, transfer to a plate, spread them out evenly, and cool to room temperature.

Core the cabbage and roughly chop it into pieces no bigger than 1 inch. Combine the cabbage, leeks, and cooked egg whites in a large bowl. Whisk the eggs in a small bowl. Whisk in the cream, mushroom seasoning, mace, 2 teaspoons salt, and the white pepper and add to the cabbage mixture. Stir to combine and transfer the mixture to the prepared baking dish.

Bake the cabbage, uncovered, until bubbling and starting to brown around the edges, about 35 minutes. Remove from the oven and serve. Or cool to room temperature, cover, and refrigerate for up to 1 day; reheat in a 325°F oven for 15 minutes before serving.

FRIED CABBAGE

SERVES 4 AS A SIDE

2 tablespoons Rendered Fresh Lard
(page 343)

1 tablespoon Rendered Bacon Fat
(page 342)

½ medium head green cabbage
(about 1 pound), tough outer
leaves discarded, cored and cut
into 1-inch chunks

1½ teaspoons kosher salt

2 teaspoons honey vinegar,
preferably Lindera Farms
(see Resources, page 369)

¼ teaspoon Hot Sauce (page 260)
or Red Clay Original Hot Sauce
(see Resources, page 369)

1 teaspoon fresh lemon juice

GOES WELL WITH:

Salt-Roasted Beets (page 196)
Braised Turnips (page 193)
*Pressure-Cooker Sea Island Red
  Peas (page 192)*
*Potatoes and Ramps Cooked in
  Ham Fat (page 172)*
Sweet Potato Puree (page 153)
Basic Cornbread (page 216)

Where I'm from, "fried" doesn't always mean deep-fried, like French fries. Most of the time, in fact, it means skillet-fried. The trick with this recipe is to start with high heat so you caramelize the bottom layer of cabbage while the rest of the cabbage, stacked on top, releases its juices. Don't cook the cabbage to death; it should still have a little bite. Try this technique with potatoes or turnips too. You won't be disappointed.

Heat the lard and bacon fat in a large cast-iron skillet over high heat until just starting to smoke. Add one-third of the cabbage, season with ½ teaspoon of the salt, and cook, undisturbed, for about 1 minute to begin to caramelize the cabbage. Stir, add another one-third of the cabbage, season with another ½ teaspoon of the salt, and cook, stirring occasionally, for a minute or so, until the cabbage has decreased slightly in volume. Add the remaining cabbage and ½ teaspoon salt and cook, stirring, for 1 minute. Reduce the heat to medium, cover, and cook until the cabbage is just tender and starting to break down, 4 to 5 minutes.

Remove the cabbage from the stove and stir in the vinegar, hot sauce, and lemon juice. Serve straight from the skillet.

BUTTERBALL POTATOES

with Crispy Potato Topping

SERVES 4 AS A SIDE

CRISPY POTATOES

2 medium russet potatoes (about 12 ounces total)

Canola oil for deep-frying

Kosher salt and freshly ground white pepper

1 ounce Gruyère-type cheese, preferably Kenny's Farmhouse Norwood Cheese (see Resources, page 369), finely chopped

2 tablespoons finely sliced chives

BUTTERBALL POTATOES

1½ cups whole milk

6 tablespoons unsalted butter

2 teaspoons kosher salt, plus more for seasoning

½ teaspoon freshly ground white pepper

1 pound small Butterball potatoes (about ½ inch wide and 2 inches long) or new potatoes (about 1½ inches in diameter), washed and dried

GOES WELL WITH:

Strip Steak with Worcestershire (page 142)

Pork Shoulder Steak with Grilled Mushrooms (page 141)

The technique for cooking these potatoes is the result of a happy accident. I lost track of some potatoes that were on the stove, gently simmering away in milk. The heat was too high, so the milk split into curds and whey, but it didn't scorch. The potatoes were just sitting there, covered in clumpy curds, when it struck me how delicious all that milk protein would be if it were caramelized. I threw my accidental tubers into a hot skillet to get the outsides beautifully brown, then poured in a little bit of the whey and simmered it until it reduced and caramelized. The results ended up far exceeding the original idea! The flavors kicked into overdrive, and the crispy, fried potato coating I added stuck to the outside of the Butterball potatoes even better.

This recipe is a great example of how messing up doesn't necessarily mean starting over. Always taste your food, even if it didn't end up the way you had imagined. Things can almost always be saved or altered, and sometimes you'll even get a pleasant surprise.

To make a faster, simpler dish, you can omit the crispy potatoes. They're amazing and worth the effort, but if you don't have the time, that shouldn't keep you from trying the Butterball potatoes.

Pictured on page 143

FOR THE CRISPY POTATOES: Fill a large bowl with water and line a baking sheet with paper towels. Peel the russet potatoes and grate on the large holes of a box grater, adding them to the bowl of water as you go. Swirl them around in the water, then change the water several times, until it remains clear. Working in two batches, transfer the potatoes to a kitchen towel and wring out as much of the water as you possibly can. Transfer the potatoes to the prepared baking sheet and fluff them out in one layer.

Fill a deep fryer with canola oil according to the manufacturer's directions and heat the oil to 300°F. Alternatively, fill a deep heavy pot half full with canola oil and heat the oil over medium heat to 300°F. Line a rimmed baking sheet with paper towels.

Working in two batches, fry the potatoes until golden brown and completely crispy, about 4 minutes. Transfer the potatoes to the prepared baking sheet and season lightly with salt and white pepper. Once they cool to room temperature, transfer the potatoes to an airtight container lined with paper towels. *(The crispy potatoes will keep well for up to 2 hours.)*

FOR THE BUTTERBALL POTATOES: Combine the milk, 4 tablespoons of the butter, the salt, and the white pepper in a skillet large enough to hold the potatoes in a single layer and heat over medium-low heat, stirring occasionally, until the butter has melted and the salt has dissolved. Add the Butterball potatoes, cover them with a cartouche (see box, page 161), and gently cook over medium-low heat until a knife inserted in a potato meets no resistance and the milk has curdled, about 15 minutes. Drain the potatoes, reserving ½ cup of the cooking liquid.

Heat the remaining 2 tablespoons butter in a large skillet over medium-high heat until foamy. Add the potatoes and cook, stirring occasionally, until they start to brown, about 2 minutes. Add the reserved cooking liquid and cook until the liquid has almost evaporated, about 3 minutes. Season liberally with salt. Remove from the stove and cover to keep warm.

TO SERVE: Lightly crush the crispy potatoes until they are just a little larger than bread crumbs and mix with the cheese and chives. Transfer the Butterball potatoes to a warm serving dish and top with the crispy potatoes.

POTATOES AND RAMPS COOKED IN HAM FAT

SERVES 4 AS A SIDE

1 cup Rendered Ham Fat (page 343)

1 pound small Butterball potatoes (about ½ inch wide and 2 inches long) or new potatoes (about 1½ inches in diameter), cut into ½-inch-thick slices

8 ounces ramps, cleaned, dried, and hairy root ends removed

1 tablespoon fresh lemon juice

Kosher salt and freshly ground black pepper

¼ cup sliced Pickled Ramps (page 251)

GOES WELL WITH:

Grilled Trout with Cornbread Puree (page 103)
Grilled Swordfish with Green Gumbo (page 101)

After a spring day of ramp hunting with chef David Chang and me, legendary curemaster Allan Benton pulled his car off the road on the creek side and set up a camp kitchen. He pulled out a cast-iron skillet, some of his famous ham and bacon, a sack of potatoes, black walnut brownies, and a plate of cornbread that his wife, Sharon, had sent us out with. Dave and I washed the ramps in the creek while Allan tended the fire. He fried up the ham and bacon, added the potatoes and ramps, covered the skillet, and cooked up some of the best food I've ever eaten. Sitting around that creekside campfire, eating the ham and potatoes and ramps with two great friends after a day in the mountains, is an experience I won't forget. This plate of food is my homage to that meal. Serve this dish in spring, when ramps are in season, and thank Mr. Benton.

Melt the ham fat over medium heat in a deep saucepan just large enough to hold the potatoes in a loose single layer. Add the potatoes (they should be submerged in the fat) and cook until a knife inserted in a potato meets no resistance, about 15 minutes. Remove from the stove and let the potatoes cool in the fat.

Heat a large cast-iron skillet over medium-high heat. Spoon 2 tablespoons of the ham fat from the potatoes into the skillet, add the potatoes in a single layer, and cook until golden brown on the bottom and starting to crisp, about 2 minutes. Turn the potatoes over and cook until the other side is golden brown and starting to crisp, about 2 minutes. Add the fresh ramps to the skillet, cover, and cook until just wilted, 2 to 3 minutes. Uncover, add the lemon juice, and season liberally with salt and pepper.

Transfer to a serving bowl, sprinkle with the pickled ramps, and serve.

GREEN BEANS

SERVES 6 AS A SIDE

4 cups Vegetable Stock (page 348)

One 8-ounce smoked ham hock

2 pounds fresh heirloom pole
beans, such as greasy, cut-short,
half-runner, or Turkey Craw, any
strings removed and beans cut
into 1-inch pieces

1 tablespoon Rendered Fresh Lard
(page 343)

1 tablespoon kosher salt

1 teaspoon freshly ground black
pepper

GOES WELL WITH:

Hot-Water Cornbread (page 219)
Pickled Pig's Feet (page 294)

These beans are braised low and slow with some salty
pork until they're practically falling apart, and by the time
they're ready, the umami flavor is off the charts.

Combine the vegetable stock and ham hock in a large pot
and bring to a boil over high heat. Reduce the heat to low
and simmer, covered, for 1 hour to develop the flavors.

Add the beans, lard, salt, and pepper to the pot and bring
to a simmer. Reduce the heat to low, cover, and cook until
the beans are very tender, about 1 hour, adding water if
needed to keep the beans covered. Remove from the stove
and serve. Or transfer to a container, cool to room temperature, cover, and refrigerate for up to 3 days; reheat before
serving.

PETIT VERT PEAS

SERVES 4 AS A SIDE

½ cup Anson Mills Petit Vert Peas
(see Resources, page 368),
soaked in 1 cup of water in the
refrigerator overnight

1½ cups water

¾ teaspoon kosher salt

¼ teaspoon freshly ground black
pepper

GOES WELL WITH:

Sheepshead "on the Half Shell"
with Tomato Gravy (page 110)

Petit vert peas are barely the size of a lentil and were orig-
inally cultivated in the Lowcountry as an important part
of the crop rotation for Carolina Gold rice. Cooking them
yields a naturally thickened potlikker and deep, vegetal
flavor that make them the ideal accompaniment to grilled
seafood.

Drain the peas and rinse thoroughly under cool running
water. Combine the peas and the water in a small saucepan and bring to a boil over high heat, stirring frequently to
prevent sticking. Reduce the heat to low and simmer until
the peas are tender and the cooking liquid has thickened,
about 30 minutes. Stir in the salt and pepper, remove from
the stove, and cover to keep warm.

PURPLE CAPE BEANS AND GRILLED GREENS

SERVES 4 AS A SIDE

2 teaspoons canola oil

½ sweet onion (about 3 ounces), trimmed and cut in half through the root end (leave the root intact so that the halves hold together)

2½ cups Vegetable Stock (page 348)

1 tablespoon apple cider vinegar

1 fresh bay leaf

3 thyme sprigs

1 cup Anson Mills Sea Island Purple Cape Beans (see Resources, page 368), soaked in water to cover in the refrigerator overnight

Kosher salt

Freshly ground white pepper

4 tablespoons unsalted butter, diced

1 teaspoon fresh lemon juice

1 teaspoon Hot Sauce (page 260) or Red Clay Original Hot Sauce (see Resources, page 369)

6 ounces mixed sturdy greens, such as kale, Swiss chard, and mustard greens

Freshly ground black pepper

EQUIPMENT

Round 15-inch open-top fine-mesh wire grill basket

GOES WELL WITH:

Sheepshead "on the Half Shell" with Tomato Gravy (page 110)
Chicken Breasts with Black Pepper and Peanut Butter Gravy (page 120)

Glenn Roberts, the heirloom crusader behind Anson Mills, first encountered dried Purple Cape beans in the galley of a shrimp boat he was working on years ago. The Cape bean had traditionally been a staple on the fleet of fishing boats working the waters around Cape Romain, South Carolina, but it had all but disappeared in the first half of the twentieth century. Thanks to Glenn's efforts and commitment, we get to taste something that could have been gone forever.

NOTE: You'll need to start this recipe a day ahead of time to soak the beans.

Heat 1 teaspoon of the canola oil in a medium saucepan over medium-high heat until it shimmers. Add the onion halves cut side down and cook, undisturbed, until the bottoms are caramelized to a very dark brown, about 3 minutes. Add the vegetable stock, vinegar, bay leaf, thyme, and beans and bring to a boil. Reduce the heat to low and simmer until the beans are tender, about 1 hour and 15 minutes.

Drain the beans and discard the bay leaf, thyme, and onion. Transfer the beans to a medium saucepan and season lightly with salt and white pepper. Add the butter, lemon juice, and hot sauce and stir to combine. Cover and set aside.

Prepare a hot fire in a charcoal grill (see page 96), removing the grill rack and distributing the hot coals in an even layer in the bottom of the grill.

Remove the stems and ribs from the greens. Make stacks of the leaves, roll them into cylinders, and cut them into very thin ribbons. Wash the greens in the sink or a large bowl of cold water, changing the water several times, to remove any sand. Drain and dry with paper towels.

Combine the greens and the remaining teaspoon of canola oil in a bowl, season with salt and black pepper, and toss. Transfer the greens to the grill basket and place the basket directly on the coals. Grill the greens, stirring them frequently with long-handled tongs so they cook evenly, until they are wilted and lightly charred, about 2 minutes. Add the grilled greens to the beans, stir to combine, and serve.

HOW TO COOK A POT OF GREENS

I cook greens a different way almost every time, depending on what I've found at the market, the time of year, and even whom I'm cooking them for. But at the core of my method is a simple idea: adding as little liquid as possible. It's all about extracting the natural "pot-likker" from whatever greens you're cooking, whether collards, turnip or mustard greens, or some combination. Success starts with your pot selection: Go for one that is wider than it is tall, like a French-style *rondeau*, with a tight-fitting lid.

At the base of a good pot of greens is a smoky, meaty, umami-rich ingredient. This could be any number of things, from belly and jowl bacon or a ham hock to something less traditional, like dried shrimp or dried oysters. I set the pot over high heat and add a tablespoon or two of fresh rendered lard, depending on how much (if any) fat is going to render out of whatever umami ingredient I'm using. Then I cook the umami ingredient until its fat has rendered and it is evenly browned and fragrant, stirring frequently to keep it from burning and turning bitter.

At this point, I throw in a julienned large sweet onion and cook, stirring, until the onion just starts to give way and turn translucent. Then it's time to start adding the greens. I add three or four good handfuls of greens that have been thoroughly washed, stemmed (if the stems are tough), and cut into ribbons about an inch wide. After a quick sprinkling of salt (more for releasing liquid than seasoning), I get in there with my hands (double up on latex gloves to do this, because the pot is hot, and the gloves also make it easier to manipulate the greens; or just use a pair of tongs) and start pushing the greens into the bottom of the pot, kind of smearing them around in the onions and lard, squeezing them to encourage them to give up their flavorful juices. As they wilt slightly, I add another three or four handfuls—mixing, squeezing, pushing—along with another sprinkling of salt, and I repeat the process until I've added all the greens.

By now, the greens should have released quite a bit of liquid, and the cooking process becomes more like a braise. If it seems that the greens are being stubborn and there isn't quite enough liquid to cook them, I add moisture to the pan in the form of beer. You need to be careful here, though. You want to add it only a splash at a time, just enough liquid to encourage a little more steam in the pot, or you run the risk of adding too much liquid and diluting that flavor you've worked so hard for.

When all the greens are wilted, I reduce the heat to low, cover the pot, and braise the greens. A tight-fitting lid is really important here. It keeps all that hard-earned natural pot-likker in the pot, and the greens cook faster than they would just boiling away uncovered. From this point on, I check the greens every few minutes, making sure I don't overcook them. How far to take them depends on the greens, the time of year (late-season collards, for example, can be pretty tough), and how they're going to be served. I prefer greens at the moment when they are just tender, before they lose that vegetal flavor, that vibrancy. When cooked this way, they have a lot more to offer from a nutritional standpoint too.

The last thing to do is a final seasoning, if necessary. Simplicity reigns supreme here. The greens ought to be just salty enough, as I've added a little salt with each addition of greens to the pot, but I taste to make sure. Then I finish them off with a little cider vinegar for acidity and hot sauce for bite. With patience, effort, and time, you can cook a pot of greens that captures those natural flavors that too often get diluted or hidden, giving you a dish that warms the body and the soul.

CROWDER PEA AND HOMINY SUCCOTASH

SERVES 4 AS A SIDE

PEAS

1 teaspoon canola oil

½ sweet onion (about 3 ounces), trimmed and cut in half through the root end (leave the root intact so that the halves hold together)

2 cups Vegetable Stock (page 348)

1 tablespoon apple cider vinegar

1 fresh bay leaf

3 thyme sprigs

2 cups fresh or frozen crowder peas (about 1 pound beans in the pod)

Kosher salt and freshly ground white pepper

SUCCOTASH

3 tablespoons unsalted butter

½ cup thinly sliced sweet onion

1 teaspoon minced garlic

¼ cup fine dice red bell pepper

¼ cup fine dice yellow bell pepper

2 tablespoons fine dice green bell pepper

½ recipe Hominy (page 213)

½ cup Vegetable Stock (page 348)

½ cup heavy cream

Kosher salt and freshly ground white pepper

1 tablespoon fresh lemon juice

½ ounce Asiago cheese, preferably Kenny's Farmhouse Dry Fork Reserve (see Resources, page 369), grated

3 tablespoons Fines Herbes (page 356)

In the middle of a cold January when you're craving the flavors of the summer garden, instead of going for the ears of corn grown Lord knows where, make hominy. The best dried corn captures that corn flavor from the field and stores it, ready to be enjoyed in the colder months. Because crowder peas are a summer crop, in the winter you're more likely to see them frozen than fresh. But when they're shelled fresh and frozen right out of the field, they keep their intensity of flavor with very little change in texture. You can stockpile crowder peas in the summer months and freeze them to enjoy in the winter.

FOR THE PEAS: Heat the canola oil in a medium saucepan over medium-high heat until it shimmers. Add the onion halves to the pan cut side down and cook, undisturbed, until the bottoms are caramelized to a very dark brown, about 3 minutes. Add the vegetable stock, vinegar, bay leaf, thyme, and peas and bring to a boil. Reduce the heat to low and simmer until the peas are tender, about 25 minutes.

Drain the peas, reserving ¼ cup of the cooking liquid, and discard the bay leaf, thyme, and onion. Transfer the peas to a medium saucepan and season lightly with salt and white pepper. Add the reserved cooking liquid, cover, and set aside.

FOR THE SUCCOTASH: Heat the butter in a large skillet over medium-high heat until foamy. Add the onion and garlic and cook, stirring frequently, until the onion is translucent, about 4 minutes. Add the bell peppers and cook, stirring frequently, until they soften, about 5 minutes.

Add the hominy, the crowder peas and their liquid, and the vegetable stock to the skillet and bring to a simmer. Cook, stirring occasionally, until the stock has reduced by half, about 3 minutes. Add the cream and cook, stirring occasionally, until the liquid has reduced by half and slightly thickened, 1 to 2 minutes.

Season the succotash liberally with salt and white pepper and stir in the lemon juice. Fold in the cheese and fines herbes and serve.

GRILLED OKRA

SERVES 4 AS A SIDE

20 small okra pods

1 tablespoon canola oil

Kosher salt and freshly ground
  black pepper

2 teaspoons fresh lemon juice

2 tablespoons Benne Tahini (page
  357)

EQUIPMENT

Round 15-inch open-top fine-mesh
  wire grill basket

GOES WELL WITH:

*Traditional Shrimp and Grits
  (page 61)*
*Beeliner Snapper with Fried
  Peppers (page 108)*

The okra served on my family's table in Virginia (see recipe opposite) was almost always dredged in cornmeal and fried. I was in my twenties before I tried okra grilled. Okra cooked on a grill doesn't have that (in)famous slimy texture that is often associated with it, because the high heat and the quick cooking technique don't draw out as much of that mucilaginous cellulose from the vegetable. Grilled okra needs only a touch of fresh lemon juice and a drizzle of benne tahini to make an easy side dish you can eat all summer long.

Prepare a hot fire in a charcoal grill (see page 96), removing the grill rack and distributing the hot coals in an even layer in the bottom of the grill.

Combine the okra and canola oil in a small bowl and toss, then season with salt and pepper and toss again. Transfer the okra to the grill basket, place directly on the coals, and grill, stirring occasionally with long-handled tongs, until the okra develops a light char and is just tender, about 2 minutes. Transfer to a large bowl, drizzle with the lemon juice and benne tahini, toss, and serve.

FRIED OKRA

SERVES 4 AS A SIDE

Canola oil for deep-frying

2 large eggs

1½ pounds small okra pods, caps removed and pods cut into ½-inch-thick pieces

1 cup fine yellow cornmeal, preferably Anson Mills (see Resources, page 368)

2 teaspoons kosher salt, plus more for seasoning

½ teaspoon freshly ground black pepper, plus more for seasoning

---

GOES WELL WITH:

Tomato Jam (page 281)
Hot Sauce (page 260)

I learned this technique from chef Joseph Lenn while I was filming *The Mind of a Chef*. He showed me how his mom makes fried okra. I'd never seen anybody do it this way before—all the ingredients, including the okra, go into one bowl, and you end up with something closer to a cornmeal batter than a breading. The result is a satisfying, crispy cornmeal coating on the outside and fresh, vibrant green okra underneath. The only problem? It's so good that when the okra comes out of the hot oil, it's going to be tough to share.

Fill a deep fryer with canola oil according to the manufacturer's directions and heat the oil to 350°F. Alternatively, fill a large deep cast-iron skillet half full with canola oil and heat the oil over medium heat to 350°F. Preheat the oven to 200°F. Line a rimmed baking sheet with paper towels.

Put the okra in a large bowl, add the eggs, and stir thoroughly to lightly beat the eggs and completely coat the okra. Add the cornmeal, salt, and pepper to the okra mixture and stir to evenly coat the okra.

Working in three batches, fry the okra until the cornmeal coating is crisp and golden brown and the okra is a vibrant green, about 2 minutes. Transfer to the prepared baking sheet and season liberally with salt and pepper. Keep the first batches warm in the oven while you fry the remaining okra.

Transfer the fried okra to a bowl or plate and serve.

LIMPIN' SUSAN

SERVES 6 AS A SIDE, 4 AS A MAIN COURSE

VEGETABLE BASE

2 tablespoons canola oil

1¼ cups very finely diced sweet onion

1 cup very finely diced celery

1 cup very finely diced green bell pepper

2 teaspoons minced garlic

1 tablespoon kosher salt

RICE

4 cups water

1 tablespoon kosher salt

¼ teaspoon freshly ground white pepper

1 fresh bay leaf

1¼ cups Anson Mills Carolina Gold Rice (see Resources, page 368)

4 tablespoons unsalted butter, diced

OKRA

3 tablespoons unsalted butter

1 pound small okra pods, caps removed, pods cut into ½-inch-thick slices

Kosher salt and freshly ground black pepper

1 tablespoon Pepper Vinegar (page 262)

1½ teaspoons okra seed oil (see Resources, page 369)

2 tablespoons Fines Herbes (page 356)

1 tablespoon Anson Mills Antebellum Benne Seeds (see Resources, page 368)

Rumor has it that Limpin' Susan was Hoppin' John's secret girlfriend. Whereas Hoppin' John is a rich and filling blend of rice and field peas, Limpin' Susan, rice and okra, is a little more delicate and fresh. I like to make this when the market is full of small, green, tender okra pods. It's a simple dish that becomes memorable when cooked with care and drizzled with a touch of okra seed oil.

FOR THE VEGETABLE BASE: Heat the canola oil in a large skillet over medium heat until it shimmers. Add the onion, celery, bell pepper, garlic, and salt and cook, stirring occasionally, until the vegetables are softened, about 6 minutes. Remove from the stove and set aside.

FOR THE RICE: Combine the water, salt, white pepper, and bay leaf in a medium saucepan, bring to a boil over medium-high heat, and stir to be sure the salt has dissolved completely. Reduce the heat to medium, add the rice, stir once, and bring to a simmer. Simmer gently, uncovered, stirring occasionally, until the rice is al dente, about 10 minutes. Drain.

Transfer the rice to another medium saucepan, discarding the bay leaf, stir in the butter, and cover to keep warm.

FOR THE OKRA: Heat the butter in a large skillet over high heat until foamy. Add the vegetable base and okra and cook, gently stirring often, until the butter begins to brown and the okra is just tender, about 6 minutes. Season lightly with salt and black pepper and stir in the pepper vinegar.

TO SERVE: Put the rice in a serving bowl and spoon the okra mixture on top. Drizzle with the okra seed oil and sprinkle with the fines herbes and benne seeds.

TOMATO-OKRA STEW

SERVES 6 AS A SIDE, 4 AS A MAIN COURSE

STEW

4 ounces slab bacon, preferably Benton's (see Resources, page 368)

¼ cup small dice green bell pepper

2 tablespoons small dice celery

10 ounces small okra pods, caps removed, cut into ½-inch-thick slices

1 tablespoon all-purpose flour

2 cups Preserved Tomatoes (page 278) or canned whole tomatoes, with their juices

2 tablespoons Pepper Sauce (page 353)

2¼ teaspoons kosher salt

½ teaspoon freshly ground black pepper

1 teaspoon Bourbon Barrel Bourbon Smoked Paprika (see Resources, page 368)

2 tablespoons small dice sweet onion

1 teaspoon minced garlic

RICE

4 cups water

2 teaspoons kosher salt

¼ teaspoon freshly ground white pepper

1 fresh bay leaf

1 cup Anson Mills Carolina Gold Rice (see Resources, page 368)

4 tablespoons unsalted butter, diced

1 tablespoon organic palm oil

¼ cup thinly sliced scallions

When the okra starts to come in every summer, this is the first dish I make at home. It's delicious, and it comes together quickly, which means you won't have to keep the stove on for very long. This recipe calls for smoky bacon, but you could use country ham if that's what you have.

This dish, along with okra itself, made its way into Lowcountry cuisine via the food culture of enslaved West Africans brought to South Carolina's shores during the seventeenth, eighteenth, and nineteenth centuries. Along the coastal plains and barrier islands of South Carolina and Georgia, the stew takes this form, but in the Gulf communities of Louisiana, Cajun and Creole influences turned it into variations of gumbo. Dishes like this give us a chance to reflect on the history of Southern cooking.

FOR THE STEW: Make lardons by cutting the bacon into ¼-inch-thick strips and then cutting the strips into ¼-inch-thick matchsticks. Put the bacon in a medium saucepan and cook over medium heat, stirring frequently, until the fat has rendered and the bacon is crisp. Using a slotted spoon, remove the bacon and drain it on paper towels, leaving the rendered fat in the saucepan.

Add the bell pepper and celery to the pan and cook, stirring occasionally, until translucent, about 5 minutes. Add the okra and cook, stirring occasionally, until it begins to soften, about 3 minutes. Add the flour and cook, stirring constantly, for about 2 minutes to make a light roux. Stir in the tomatoes, pepper sauce, 2 teaspoons of the salt, the black pepper, and the paprika and bring to a simmer. Reduce the heat to low and cook, uncovered, stirring occasionally, until the okra is soft and the tomatoes have fallen apart, about 30 minutes.

Meanwhile, combine the onion, garlic, and the remaining ¼ teaspoon salt in a mortar and crush with the pestle until the mixture becomes a wet paste. Set aside.

FOR THE RICE: While the stew is simmering, preheat the oven to 300°F.

Combine the water, salt, white pepper, and bay leaf in a medium saucepan and bring to a boil over medium-high heat. Stir to be sure the salt has dissolved, then reduce the heat to medium. Add the rice, stir once, and bring to a simmer. Simmer gently, uncovered, stirring occasionally, until the rice is al dente, about 10 minutes. Drain.

CONTINUED

GOES WELL WITH:

Baby Collards with Benne Caesar Dressing and Cornbread Croutons (page 80)

Spread the rice out on a rimmed baking sheet; discard the bay leaf. Dry the rice in the oven, stirring occasionally, for 10 minutes. Scatter the butter evenly over the rice, return to the oven, and dry, stirring every few minutes for about 5 minutes more; the excess moisture should have evaporated and the grains should be separate.

TO SERVE: Stir the onion paste and palm oil into the stew. Divide the rice among four warm bowls and spoon the stew over the top. Sprinkle with the bacon and scallions.

EGGPLANT PURLOO

1½ cups medium dice peeled eggplant

3 tablespoons canola oil

Kosher salt and freshly ground white pepper

1 cup small dice yellow onion

⅓ cup small dice peeled celery

2 garlic cloves, shaved paper-thin on a mandoline or very thinly sliced with a knife

⅓ cup small dice red bell pepper

½ cup Anson Mills Carolina Gold Rice (see Resources, page 368)

⅓ cup Preserved Tomatoes (page 278) or canned whole tomatoes, drained and roughly chopped

1 cup Vegetable Stock (page 348)

1 fresh bay leaf

⅛ teaspoon Aleppo pepper (see Resources, page 369)

¼ teaspoon Bourbon Barrel Bourbon Smoked Paprika (see Resources, page 368)

1 tablespoon fresh lemon juice

EQUIPMENT

Round 15-inch open-top fine-mesh wire grill basket

GOES WELL WITH:

Pork Shoulder Steak with Grilled Mushrooms (page 141)

My version of eggplant purloo was inspired by an afternoon cooking alongside chef BJ Dennis, one of the champions of traditional Gullah Geechee cookery and history. It was his idea to replace the seafood or other protein in a traditional purloo with some meaty grilled eggplant. The eggplant goes beyond standing in for the meat; it makes you not even miss it at all.

Prepare a hot fire in a charcoal grill (see page 96), removing the grill rack and distributing the hot coals in an even layer in the bottom of the grill.

Put the eggplant in a bowl, toss with 2 tablespoons of the canola oil, and season lightly with salt and white pepper. Transfer to the grill basket and place directly on the coals. Grill, stirring frequently with long-handled tongs, until the eggplant pieces have a light char and start to soften, about 5 minutes. Transfer the eggplant to a bowl and set aside. Cover the grill to maintain the temperature for cooking the pork; add a few more pieces of charcoal if necessary.

Heat the remaining tablespoon of canola oil in a medium pot over medium heat until it shimmers. Add the onion and cook, stirring frequently, until translucent, about 5 minutes. Add the celery and garlic and cook, stirring frequently, until tender, 3 to 5 minutes. Add the eggplant and bell pepper and cook for another minute.

Stir in the rice and cook, stirring, to toast the rice, about 1 minute. Add the tomatoes, vegetable stock, bay leaf, Aleppo pepper, and paprika and stir to combine. Once the mixture comes to a simmer, reduce the heat to low, cover, and cook until the rice is tender and just starts to make a caramelized crust on the bottom of the pot, about 15 minutes.

Remove the purloo from the heat, stir in the lemon juice, and season lightly with salt. Transfer to a serving dish, discarding the bay leaf, and serve.

FRIED APPLES

SERVES 6 AS A SIDE

2 tablespoons Rendered Fresh Lard
(page 343)

2 pounds Granny Smith apples,
peeled, cored, and cut into
¾-inch-thick wedges

½ cup packed light brown sugar

4 tablespoons unsalted butter

½ teaspoon kosher salt

GOES WELL WITH:

*Cured Duck Breasts with Rice
Porridge (page 136)*
*Pork Prime Rib with Mustard
Onions (page 144)*
*Grilled Quail with Red-Eye Gravy
(page 133)*

In Appalachia, "fried" means cooked in a skillet, not a deep fryer. I can hardly remember a breakfast at my grandmother's table without fried apples. They're equally at home on the dinner table. Try these with roasted or grilled pork and you'll see why I can never pass up this dish.

Heat the lard in a large cast-iron skillet over medium-high heat until it shimmers. Add the apples and cook, stirring frequently, until they start to brown and soften, about 6 minutes. Add the brown sugar and butter and stir to combine and melt the butter. Reduce the heat to low and cook until the apples are completely tender but not falling apart, about 3 minutes.

Remove the apples from the stove, stir in the salt, and serve directly from the skillet. Or transfer to a heatproof container, cool to room temperature, cover, and refrigerate for up to 2 days; reheat over medium heat before serving.

HOW TO COOK FRESH FIELD PEAS OR BUTTER BEANS

A well-cooked pot of shelled fresh field peas or butter beans is one of the staples in the Southern cook's arsenal of vegetable dishes. There are a lot of ways to cook them, but this way is my favorite. It retains the freshness of the ingredient but also delivers on that low-and-slow soulful flavor that makes so much of Southern cooking irresistible. I start by making a base of onion and garlic and then fold that into the cooked peas or beans and braise them until they just give way and glaze up.

To serve 4 as a side, here's what you'll need:

BASE

1½ teaspoons canola oil

1 tablespoon unsalted butter

½ small sweet onion (about 2½ ounces), very finely diced

1 small clove garlic, minced

1 to 2 tablespoons Vegetable Stock (page 348)

Kosher salt

BEANS

4 cups shelled fresh field peas or butter beans

About 2 cups Vegetable Stock (page 348)

1 tablespoon unsalted butter

Kosher salt

1 to 2 tablespoons finely chopped herbs (I like flat-leaf parsley and lovage)

1 to 2 teaspoons vinegar (apple cider vinegar is the classic choice, but this is a great place to use something homemade; see How to Make Vinegar, page 258)

Freshly ground black pepper

Hot Sauce (page 260) or Red Clay Original Southern Hot Sauce (see Resources, page 369), or other hot sauce of your choice

FOR THE BASE: The process starts with making a rich onion base, which will give the relatively quick-cooking peas or beans a depth of flavor that belies how fast they cook. Heat the oil and butter in a medium skillet over low heat. When the butter is melted but not quite foaming, stir in the onion and cook, stirring frequently, until translucent and starting to soften; you're not looking to get any color on the onion. Add the garlic and cook, stirring, for another minute or so. At this point, the onion and garlic will have given up some of their moisture, so I add vegetable stock 1 tablespoon at a time to make sure they're never frying but instead gently braising and breaking down. When the mixture is completely soft and the liquid you've added has just cooked away, season with a pinch of salt and remove from the stove.

FOR THE BEANS: Put your field peas or butter beans in a medium saucepan, add enough vegetable stock so they're almost but not quite covered, and bring to a boil over high heat. Add the base, lower the heat to medium-high, and cook, adding more stock as necessary to keep the peas or beans almost covered, until just tender and cooked through. The timing will vary depending on the size of the peas or beans, so taste them often as they cook.

When the peas or beans are right in that sweet spot, drain off all but about 3 tablespoons of the cooking liquid, add the butter, season liberally with salt, and cook a little further, just to glaze the peas or beans. Then the cooking is done and it's up to you to season them just how you like, with chopped fresh herbs, vinegar, black pepper, and hot sauce.

I love to serve peas and beans cooked this way with a skillet of fresh cornbread (see page 216) or simply steamed Carolina Gold rice (see No-Peek Rice, page 233), but they're good with just about anything from fried fish to grilled pork chops.

PRESSURE-COOKER SEA ISLAND RED PEAS

SERVES 4 AS A SIDE

4 cups Vegetable Stock (page 348)

1 cup Anson Mills Sea Island Red Peas (see Resources, page 368), soaked in water to cover in the refrigerator overnight

½ cup roughly chopped drained Preserved Tomatoes (page 378) or canned whole tomatoes

2 ounces bacon, preferably Benton's (see Resources, page 368), cut into ¼-inch strips

1 small garlic clove

2 fresh bay leaves

5 thyme sprigs

Kosher salt

EQUIPMENT

Electric pressure cooker (see Note, page 43)

GOES WELL WITH:

Grilled Quail with Red-Eye Gravy (page 133)
Beeliner Snapper with Fried Peppers (page 108)
Cured Duck Breasts with Rice Porridge (page 136)

This technique for cooking dried peas and beans is pure magic. Using an electric pressure cooker opens up a whole range of flavors and textures that would take hours to achieve otherwise. With this recipe, everything goes into the cooker, you bring it up to pressure, and, in a matter of minutes, you have perfectly cooked peas. I love how the tomatoes become part of the potlikker under the high pressure.

NOTE: You'll need to start this recipe a day ahead of time to soak the red peas.

Combine all the ingredients except the salt in the pressure cooker, lock on the lid, bring the cooker up to high pressure, and cook for 15 minutes.

Carefully release the steam from the pressure cooker. Drain the peas, reserving ½ cup of the cooking liquid, and discard the garlic, bay leaves, and thyme sprigs. Season the peas lightly with salt and serve. Or transfer the peas to a container, cool to room temperature, cover, and refrigerate for up to 3 days; reheat before serving.

BRAISED TURNIPS

SERVES 6 AS A SIDE

2 tablespoons unsalted butter

3 pounds baby turnips, tops removed and reserved for another use if desired, washed, and quartered

About ¾ cup Turnip Green Potlikker (see page 112) or Vegetable Stock (page 348)

2 teaspoons turnip vinegar (see page 259) or apple cider vinegar

Kosher salt and freshly ground black pepper

GOES WELL WITH:

Potlikker-Steamed Sea Bass with Corn Dodgers (page 112)

Braising is my preferred way to cook nearly every vegetable under the sun. Coating the vegetables in the soft but not quite melted butter creates a glaze as the liquid starts to come out of the turnips and naturally emulsifies. Try this with carrots or diced butternut squash in the winter and tender young onions in the spring.

Melt the butter in a large skillet over medium heat. Add the turnips and stir to coat, then add ½ cup of the potlikker and bring to a simmer, gently stirring. Cover the skillet and braise the turnips until tender when tested with a knife, 5 to 7 minutes. Check the turnips halfway through the cooking time and add more liquid if necessary to maintain the same level.

Remove the turnips from the stove, stir in the vinegar, and season liberally with salt and pepper. Transfer to a warm serving bowl and serve.

BRAISED FENNEL

SERVES 4 AS A SIDE

1 large fennel bulb (about 1 pound), stalks removed, some fronds reserved for garnish

1 cup Vegetable Stock (page 348)

2 tablespoons unsalted butter

1 teaspoon kosher salt

¼ teaspoon freshly ground white pepper

GOES WELL WITH:

Shrimp and Grits with Roasted Tomatoes, Fennel, and Sausage (page 62)

Grilled Catfish with Hoppin' John (page 98)

Grilled Swordfish with Green Gumbo (page 101)

Pork Shoulder Steak with Grilled Mushrooms (page 141)

This is one of my absolute favorite ways to cook seasonal vegetables, especially a vibrant one like licorice-y fennel. Combining a little stock with good butter, adding the fennel, bringing it up to a simmer, and slowly cooking until the fennel just gives way traps all its flavor. As the stock reduces, the butter and pan juices emulsify, leaving you with beautifully glazed fennel ready to be served on its own or added to another dish, such as Shrimp and Grits with Roasted Tomatoes, Fennel, and Sausage (page 62).

Cut the fennel bulb into wedges about ½ inch thick; trim away some of the core from each wedge, leaving enough of it so the wedges stay intact. Combine the fennel, vegetable stock, butter, salt, and white pepper in a medium saucepan and bring to a simmer over high heat. Reduce the heat to low and cook until the fennel wedges are tender and easily pierced with a fork and the stock has reduced by about half, 10 to 12 minutes.

Transfer the glazed fennel pieces to a serving dish if serving as a side. If using the fennel in another recipe, such as shrimp and grits, transfer it to a plate to cool to room temperature; reserve the cooking liquid.

BROWN-BUTTER CAULIFLOWER

SERVES 4 AS A SIDE

1 small head cauliflower with a
 1-inch stem (about 1 pound)

Kosher salt

3 tablespoons unsalted butter

½ cup canola oil

Freshly ground white pepper

1 teaspoon fresh lemon juice

GOES WELL WITH:

*Strip Steak with Worcestershire
 (page 142)*
*Potlikker-Steamed Sea Bass with
 Corn Dodgers (page 112)*

Cooking a whole head of cauliflower in a skillet with butter results in a beautifully golden brown, moist, tender, and nutty cauliflower. As delicious as it is, it may be even more fun to make. I love showing people this technique for the first time. Spooning the hot butter over the whole cauliflower as it cooks is most satisfying.

Remove the green leaves from the cauliflower but leave the stem intact. Press a small ring mold or round metal cookie cutter into the bottom of the stem so that the head of cauliflower will stand upright. Liberally season the cauliflower with salt.

Heat the butter and canola oil in a large deep skillet over medium heat until the butter melts. Stand the cauliflower up in the skillet and cook, occasionally spooning the hot butter-oil mixture over the cauliflower, until the outside of the cauliflower is golden brown, about 10 minutes. Transfer the cauliflower to a cutting board and cool to room temperature.

Cut the cauliflower away from the stem into 8 equal wedges and discard the stem. Transfer the wedges to a container, cover, and refrigerate. *(Tightly covered, the cauliflower will keep for up to 1 day in the refrigerator. Remove from the refrigerator 30 minutes before you plan to grill.)*

Prepare a hot fire in a charcoal grill (see page 96), removing the grill rack and distributing the hot coals in an even layer in the bottom of the grill. Place the grill rack as close to the coals as possible.

Season the cauliflower lightly with white pepper. Grill the cauliflower wedges, turning frequently to develop an even, light char and warm them through, for about 3 minutes. Transfer to a serving dish, sprinkle with the lemon juice, and serve.

SALT-ROASTED BEETS

SERVES 4 AS A SIDE OR 6 AS PART OF A SALAD

1 large egg white

3 cups kosher salt

20 baby beets (about 1 ounce each), preferably of various varieties, scrubbed and tops trimmed to 1 inch

---

GOES WELL WITH:

Cured Duck Breasts with Rice Porridge (page 136)
Spring Lamb with Rhubarb Butter (page 148)

Salt-roasting in the oven, or in my fireplace, has become one of my go-to ways to cook root vegetables, and the technique is especially good with earthy beets. The egg-white-and-salt crust lets the beets steam in their own juices without losing any of that amazing pure beet flavor. And the kid in me loves cracking through the salt crust like it's some sort of dinosaur egg, revealing the steaming red or golden orbs.

Preheat the oven to 400°F.

Lightly beat the egg white in a medium bowl. Add the salt and mix until completely incorporated; the mixture should feel slightly tacky to the touch. Spread a thin layer of the salt mixture in the bottom of a 9-by-13-inch baking dish. Put the beets on the salt mixture and cover them with the remaining salt mixture, lightly packing it down and making sure the beets are evenly covered.

Roast the beets for about 1 hour, until fork-tender. Remove from the oven and let cool slightly.

When the beets are cool enough to handle, crack the salt crust and pull it off. Remove the skin and tops of the beets by rubbing them with a kitchen towel. Wipe off any salt that remains on the beets, cut them lengthwise in half, and transfer to a bowl.

The beets are ready to be used in any of several ways. Try them glazed in a little vegetable stock and butter, grill them to perfection, or cool, slice, and dress in an acidic vinaigrette. If not using them immediately, transfer them to a container, cool to room temperature, cover, and refrigerate for up to 2 days.

OVEN-ROASTED TOMATOES

1 pound heirloom plum tomatoes, cut lengthwise in half

4 garlic cloves, quartered lengthwise

2 tablespoons extra-virgin olive oil

Kosher salt and freshly ground black pepper

GOES WELL WITH:

Grilled Catfish with Hoppin' John (page 98)

Grilled Swordfish with Green Gumbo (page 101)

Beeliner Snapper with Fried Peppers (page 108)

I love oven-roasting ripe tomatoes; it takes me back to the sun-dried-tomato craze of the late 1980s and early '90s. My favorite thing about the technique is the intensity of flavor that results from the dehydration during cooking. You end up with something rich and concentrated, with a flavor almost like that of tomato paste. Roasted tomatoes are great as a summer side on their own, incorporated into succotash or pasta dishes, or spooned on top of some good grilled bread for bruschetta.

Preheat the oven to 450°F.

Stud the cut sides of the tomatoes with the garlic and lay the tomatoes cut side up on a rimmed baking sheet. Drizzle with the olive oil and lightly season with salt and pepper. Roast for about 25 minutes, until the tomatoes start to lose their shape and are lightly browned. Remove from the oven.

When the tomatoes are cool enough to handle, remove their skins and discard. Try to keep the tomatoes as intact as possible. If serving as a side, transfer to a warm serving dish. Otherwise, cool on the baking sheet to room temperature, then leave the tomatoes whole or roughly chop for use in another recipe. Transfer to a container, cover, and refrigerate for up to 3 days.

CONFIT TOMATOES

MAKES 16 CONFIT PETALS

4 heirloom tomatoes (about
   8 ounces each)

4 thyme sprigs

5 small garlic cloves, peeled

Kosher salt and freshly ground
   black pepper

1 cup extra-virgin olive oil

GOES WELL WITH:

Cream of Morel Soup (page 70)

I've been infatuated with the confit technique since I first pored over Thomas Keller's *French Laundry Cookbook*. This is a recipe of transformation. Carefully peeling the tomatoes and cutting them into petals, laying them out in the foil-lined baking dish, and covering them with the best olive oil is like a ritual to me. Then, as the tomato petals slowly cook, their texture changes, developing a pleasant chew and resilience. As a bonus, you're left with the tomato-infused olive oil, which can be drizzled on everything from roasted meats or fish to a big piece of burrata. Or add some to a vinaigrette or marinade, or use it to confit more tomatoes.

Preheat the oven to 200°F. Line a 9-by-13-inch baking dish with a rectangle of aluminum foil large enough to come about 1 inch up the sides.

Bring a large pot of water to a boil over high heat. Make an ice bath with equal parts ice and water in a large bowl. Lightly score the skin on the bottom of each tomato with an X. Submerge the tomatoes in the boiling water for 20 seconds, remove, and submerge them in the ice bath to cool; do not leave them in the ice bath for longer than 5 minutes. Drain.

Peel and quarter the tomatoes. Cut away the seeds and pulp, resulting in flat tomato petals.

Lay the tomatoes in the prepared baking dish in an even layer with no overlap, then add the thyme sprigs and garlic cloves. Sprinkle with salt and pepper and pour in the olive oil.

Transfer to the oven and cook for about 1½ hours, until the tomatoes are softened but not falling apart. Remove from the oven and cool to room temperature.

Using a slotted spoon, carefully transfer the tomatoes to a container. If not using immediately, add a couple of tablespoons of the oil from the baking dish, tightly cover, and refrigerate for up to 2 days.

Strain the oil through a fine-mesh sieve into a container, discarding the solids. Tightly cover and refrigerate the oil for another use; it will keep for up to 7 days.

GRILLED ASPARAGUS

SERVES 4 AS A SIDE

VINAIGRETTE

8 ounces asparagus spears, tough ends cut off

1 tablespoon apple cider vinegar

1 tablespoon Rendered Fresh Chicken Fat (page 342), melted

ASPARAGUS

20 medium asparagus spears, tough ends cut off

2 tablespoons extra-virgin olive oil

1½ teaspoons kosher salt

½ teaspoon freshly ground black pepper

EQUIPMENT

Juice extractor

GOES WELL WITH:

Grilled Trout with Cornbread Puree (page 103)
Chicken Breasts with Herb Dumplings (page 125)

Few things are better than simply grilled fresh asparagus dressed with a vinaigrette made from asparagus juice and chicken fat. It completely amplifies the spears, adding a fresh asparagus flavor to the charred tastes of the grill.

Prepare a hot fire in a charcoal grill (see page 96), removing the grill rack and distributing the hot coals in an even layer on the bottom of the grill. Place the grill rack as close to the coals as possible.

FOR THE VINAIGRETTE: Roughly chop the asparagus and run it through the juice extractor. Remove the pulp and run it through the juice extractor again to extract all the juice. Strain the juice through a fine-mesh sieve into a small bowl. Add the vinegar and chicken fat and stir to combine. Set aside.

FOR THE ASPARAGUS: Put the asparagus spears in a baking dish and toss with the olive oil, salt, and pepper. Transfer them to the grill (set aside the baking dish) and cook, turning frequently, until lightly charred and just tender, about 5 minutes.

TO SERVE: Return the asparagus to the baking dish, add the vinaigrette, and toss to coat. Transfer to a serving dish.

GRILLED SPRING ONIONS

SERVES 4 AS A SIDE

8 spring onions with bulbs about
 1 inch in diameter, trimmed and
 cut in half through the root end
 (leave the root intact so that the
 halves hold together)

4 tablespoons unsalted butter,
 at room temperature

Kosher salt and freshly ground
 white pepper

1 tablespoon fresh lemon juice

GOES WELL WITH:

---

*Strip Steak with Worcestershire
 (page 142)*

*Grilled Catfish with Hoppin' John
 (page 98)*

Grilled spring onions are delicious and extremely versatile. They can be eaten on their own as a side or used as an ingredient in a simple salad. Think arugula, fresh lemon, and salty cheese.

Prepare a hot fire in a charcoal grill (see page 96), removing the grill rack and distributing the hot coals on one side of the bottom of the grill. Place the grill rack at its normal height.

Spread the cut sides of the onion bulbs with a thin layer of the soft butter, using about 2 tablespoons of it, and season them liberally with salt and white pepper.

Place the onions cut side down on the grill rack on the side opposite the coals, cover the grill, and grill the onions until they start to brown and soften, about 10 minutes. Turn the onions over, brush them with the remaining butter, cover, and grill until tender, about 5 minutes.

Transfer the onions to a serving dish. Add the lemon juice, toss, and serve.

GRILLED RAMPS

6 ounces ramps, cleaned, dried, and hairy root ends removed

2 teaspoons Rendered Fresh Beef Fat (page 342), melted

Kosher salt and freshly ground black pepper

½ teaspoon fresh lemon juice

EQUIPMENT

Round 15-inch open-top fine-mesh wire grill basket

GOES WELL WITH:

Potlikker-Steamed Sea Bass with Corn Dodgers (page 112)
Chicken Breasts with Herb Dumplings (page 125)

I've been known to literally hide grilled ramps to have them all to myself. I like to use beef fat to cook them, but you should experiment to find your favorite—whether chicken, bacon, or pork fat, or even good olive oil. You won't go wrong.

Pictured on page 143

Prepare a hot fire in a charcoal grill (see page 96), removing the grill rack and distributing the hot coals in an even layer in the bottom of the grill.

Toss the ramps with the beef fat in a medium bowl, then season liberally with salt and pepper and transfer to the grill basket. Place the basket directly on the coals and grill the ramps, shaking the basket occasionally with long-handled tongs, until they are wilted and lightly charred, about 3 minutes.

Transfer the ramps to a small serving bowl. Add the lemon juice, toss to combine, and serve.

CHARRED TURNIPS with Their Greens

SERVES 4 AS A SIDE

TURNIPS

2 medium turnips (about
  2½ inches in diameter)

Kosher salt and freshly ground
  white pepper

GREENS

10 ounces mixed young, tender
  greens, such as turnip greens,
  mizuna, and tatsoi, washed in
  several changes of water and
  dried

2 teaspoons extra-virgin olive oil

Kosher salt and freshly ground
  black pepper

2 teaspoons fresh lemon juice

EQUIPMENT

Round 15-inch open-top fine-mesh
  wire grill basket

GOES WELL WITH:

---

*Sheepshead "on the Half Shell"
  with Tomato Gravy (page 110)
Cornmeal-Dusted Grouper with
  Herb Puree (page 105)
Pork Prime Rib with Mustard
  Onions (page 144)*

This basic recipe works for nearly anything in the brassica family. If you have Brussels sprouts, use them instead of the turnips. If you have local broccolini, use it. Here I use fresh turnips and young, tender greens. Grilling the vegetable and greens separately and then combining them ensures the best results.

FOR THE TURNIPS: Prepare a hot fire in a charcoal grill (see page 96), removing the grill rack and distributing the hot coals in an even layer in the bottom of the grill. Place the grill rack as close to the coals as possible.

Cut the turnips lengthwise in half. Season lightly with salt and let sit for 2 minutes. Grill the turnip pieces, turning frequently, until the outsides are evenly charred and the insides are just tender, 8 to 10 minutes. Transfer the turnips to a cutting board and cut in half, making 8 equal wedges. Season lightly with white pepper and lightly cover with foil to keep warm.

FOR THE GREENS: Remove the grill rack (set the hot rack aside in a safe place). Combine the greens and olive oil in a large bowl and toss. Season liberally with salt and black pepper and toss again. Divide the greens into two batches. Transfer half the greens to the grill basket and place the basket directly on the coals. Grill the greens, turning them frequently with long-handled tongs so they cook evenly, until wilted and lightly charred around the edges, about 2 minutes. Transfer the greens to a clean bowl and cover to keep warm while you cook the second batch. Add the second batch to the bowl, add the lemon juice, and toss well.

TO SERVE: Add the charred turnips to the greens and toss to combine. Transfer to a serving dish.

GRILLED MUSHROOMS

½ teaspoon kosher salt (plus
    1½ cups more if using morels)

8 ounces fresh mushrooms, such as
    morels, shiitake, and oyster

1 tablespoon Rendered Fresh Beef
    Fat (page 342), melted, or extra-
    virgin olive oil

½ teaspoon soy sauce, preferably
    Bourbon Barrel Bluegrass Soy
    Sauce (see Resources, page 368)

Freshly ground black pepper

½ teaspoon fresh lemon juice

EQUIPMENT

Round 15-inch open-top fine-mesh
    wire grill basket

GOES WELL WITH:

Strip Steak with Worcestershire
    (page 142)
Creamed Rice (page 234)
Cornmeal Porridge (page 221)

Cooking mushrooms over the heat of a fire, whether on the grill or perhaps in your fireplace, intensifies their natural umami flavor. Here the smoke, the char, the depth added by soy sauce, and the brightness of fresh lemon juice all come together to make an addictive side dish. This recipe calls for a mix, so use any fresh mushrooms you like (other than for morels, you can skip the soaking and drying and just do a quick wash and dry for most).

If using morels, fill a large deep container with 2½ gallons warm water, add ½ cup of the salt, and stir until it is dissolved. Add the morels and let them soak for 1 hour. Meanwhile, wash and dry the other mushrooms.

Using a wire rack, push the morels down a little and, with your other hand, skim any leaves and debris off the top with a mesh strainer. Remove the rack and gently lift out the morels, being careful not to disturb the debris that has settled at the bottom. Repeat this procedure twice, using ½ cup salt each time, then lay the morels out on a wire rack and let them air-dry at room temperature for 30 minutes to 1 hour, until completely dry.

Prepare a hot fire in a charcoal grill (see page 96), removing the grill rack and distributing the hot coals in an even layer in the bottom of the grill.

Toss the mushrooms with the beef fat in a small bowl, then add the soy sauce and the ½ teaspoon salt and season lightly with pepper. Toss again and transfer to the grill basket. Place the basket directly on the coals and grill the mushrooms, shaking the basket occasionally with long-handled tongs, until tender and slightly crispy on the edges, about 3 minutes.

Transfer the mushrooms to a small serving bowl, add the lemon juice, and stir to combine. Serve immediately.

GRAINS

HOMINY AND POKEWEED GRIDDLE CAKES

MAKES ABOUT 20 GRIDDLE CAKES; SERVES 6 TO 8

1 recipe Hominy (page 213)

4 cups fresh pokeweed leaves (about 8 ounces)

Kosher salt

2 cups fine yellow cornmeal, preferably Anson Mills (see Resources, page 368)

¼ teaspoon baking soda

½ teaspoon baking powder

¼ teaspoon cayenne pepper

1 large egg

¾ cup plus 1 tablespoon full-fat buttermilk (see Note, page 27)

About ½ pound (2 sticks) unsalted butter for cooking

GOES WELL WITH:

Sour Corn (page 272)
Pimento Cheese (page 361)

Here griddle cake batter is the stage for pokeweed and hominy. The hominy supercharges the flavor of the cornmeal and adds texture thanks to the nixtamalization process (see box, page 213). Eat the griddle cakes hot out of the pan, on their own or smeared with cultured butter. If you can't find pokeweed, you can substitute ramps or fresh corn kernels, or just use the hominy alone.

Working in batches, transfer the hominy to a food processor and pulse until the kernels are broken up into the size of dried lentils. Transfer to a bowl and set aside.

Wash the pokeweed leaves in the sink or a bowl of cold water, changing the water twice, to remove any sand. Drain and dry with kitchen towels. Remove the stems. Stack the leaves, roll them into cylinders, and cut them into fine ribbons.

Bring a large pot of salted water to a boil over high heat. Make an ice bath with equal parts ice and water in a large bowl. Add the pokeweed to the boiling water and cook until the leaves are tender but still a vibrant green, about 1 minute. Drain and submerge in the ice bath until completely cold. Drain the pokeweed again and, working in batches, squeeze in a kitchen towel to remove as much water as possible. Finely chop the pokeweed and set aside.

Combine the cornmeal, baking soda, baking powder, 2 teaspoons salt, and the cayenne in a large bowl. Put the egg and buttermilk in a small bowl, whisk to combine, and stir into the cornmeal mixture. Do not overmix; there should still be some small lumps. Fold in the pokeweed and hominy.

Preheat the oven to 200°F. Line a rimmed baking sheet with paper towels.

Cook the griddle cakes in batches so you don't overcrowd the skillet: Heat 3 tablespoons of the butter in a cast-iron skillet over medium heat. When the butter is foamy, spoon heaping tablespoons of the batter into the skillet to make 4 cakes about 2½ inches in diameter. Cook until the bottoms are golden and crispy, about 2 minutes. Turn them and cook for another 2 minutes, until golden and crispy. Transfer the cakes to the prepared baking sheet and keep warm in the oven. Wipe out the skillet with paper towels and add 3 tablespoons butter after each batch.

Serve the griddle cakes immediately.

HOMINY

MAKES ABOUT 3 CUPS

1⅓ cups (8 ounces) Anson Mills Yellow Hominy Corn (see Resources, page 368)

11 cups water

1 teaspoon culinary lime (see box and Resources, page 368)

2½ tablespoons kosher salt

3 cups Chicken Stock (page 344)

GOES WELL WITH:

Grilled Swordfish with Green Gumbo (page 101)
Sheepshead "on the Half Shell" with Tomato Gravy (page 110)
Chicken Breasts with Herb Dumplings (page 125)

CULINARY LIME

Culinary lime, also known as edible lime or hydrated lime (or, in Spanish, *cal*), is the compound calcium hydroxide. It is used in food preparation in various ways, including to create an alkaline solution with water to break down the outer hulls of dried corn or other dried grains. This process, referred to as nixtamalization, produces corn kernels that grind more easily, have more nutrition, and taste better. It is used to the same effect with the rye berries in Rye and Morel Porridge (page 237).

One of my most prized possessions is a card with a recipe for hominy written in my grandmother's hand. I don't recall eating hominy very often growing up. It was a special-occasion dish because it's a bit time-consuming to make. Well-cooked hominy is in and of itself delicious, but it is also the basis for some of the tastiest things on the planet. Think tortillas, corn nuts, posole, Doritos—the list goes on.

Adding culinary lime to the cooking liquid creates an alkaline solution that breaks down the outer hulls of the dried corn, changing the corn's texture and flavor. Treating the corn this way also chemically alters it, releasing all the nutritious vitamins and amino acids within the hominy.

Combine the corn, 3 cups of the water, and the culinary lime in a large nonreactive saucepan and bring to a boil over high heat, stirring occasionally. Reduce the heat to low and simmer, stirring occasionally, until the hulls of the kernels begin to soften, about 35 minutes.

Drain the corn in a colander and rinse very well under cold running water. Transfer to a large nonreactive pot, add the remaining 8 cups water and 1½ teaspoons of the salt, and bring to a boil over high heat. Reduce the heat to low and simmer, stirring occasionally, until the kernels are soft but not splitting, about 1 hour. Drain the corn, reserving 4 cups of the cooking liquid.

Combine the corn, reserved cooking liquid, chicken stock, and remaining 2 tablespoons salt in a large nonreactive saucepan and bring to a boil over high heat. Reduce the heat to low, cover, and cook, stirring often, until the kernels are completely soft and splitting, about 45 minutes. Drain the corn, spread it out on a rimmed baking sheet, and cool to room temperature.

Transfer the cooled hominy to a container, cover, and refrigerate for up to 3 days.

CORNBREAD

To me, cornbread is *the* iconic Southern staple. Dried corn was a part of Native American foodways of the region long before European settlement, used in breads, cakes, and fritters, and corn has remained an important crop to this day. The different climates in the microregions throughout the South are, generally speaking, more conducive to corn cultivation than to that of wheat, making it and rice the Southern grains of choice, historically. A summer's crop of corn could be dried, milled, and stored all year, providing a family with hearty bread every day. That has made cornbread one of the few constants in the evolution of Southern cuisine.

Cornbread is very simple and quick to make. But, like so many "simple" things, it takes a lot of practice to master. When you examine what makes a good cornbread, you realize right away that it's a very personal preference from one cook to the next. For me, the best cornbread has to tick a few boxes. First, it has to be cooked in a cast-iron skillet, started on the stove and finished in the oven. The crispy, deep brown, caramelized crust achieved when you cook cornbread this way is unbeatable. Then, when you bite into the soft crumb inside, you want to taste a tangy sourness that only buttermilk can give. The corn and buttermilk are the two ingredients that make or break a skillet of cornbread. Even if you're still searching for your ideal skillet of cornbread, if you start with great full-fat buttermilk and high-quality cornmeal, the result will be memorable. But "high quality" doesn't have to mean "the most expensive." High quality means a flavorful variety of corn, organically grown, dried in the field, harvested, and ground, all with care. That means when it gets to you, all you have to do is cook it with the same care to enjoy something truly special.

I keep my cornbread as simple as possible. I don't add flour or sugar, and I always use lard as the fat. The ratios of baking soda, baking powder, salt, and cornmeal remain the same each time, as do those of egg and lard; the variable is the amount of buttermilk. Every batch of cornmeal you buy is going to be slightly different, depending on factors such as the variety of corn, how it was grown, how dry it was when it was harvested, when it was ground, and how long it has been stored, and all these can affect how the cornmeal will hydrate with the buttermilk. What you want to look for in your finished batter is a smooth and creamy flow, like that of a thick pancake batter. The best way I can describe it is as a relaxing pour.

After getting the batter right, the way you cook the cornbread is important—specifically, how you start it. The minute you think of making cornbread, get your oven preheating with your cast-iron skillet in it. Crank the oven up as high as possible at first. The longer you can wait and the hotter you get your skillet, the better the cornbread crust will be. If the temperature drops too much when the batter is added to the skillet, that crust will steam and soften.

When you're ready to bake, carefully remove the skillet from the oven and set it on the stove over medium-high heat. Add your fat, pour in the batter, and pay attention to how the batter bubbles and sizzles around the edges of the pan. If it stops sizzling too quickly, turn up the heat to high and continue to cook until you see that crust starting to form. Transfer the cornbread to the oven and bake until a toothpick inserted in the center comes out clean. Cornbread is a quick bread; it takes only about 15 minutes in the oven.

The Basic Cornbread recipe on the following page is my gold standard. It's the cornbread I grew up with. I use different cornmeals every now and again, but for the past few years, I've been consistently using Jimmy Red cornmeal. It has the perfect earthiness and sweetness. If you're using the right corn, there's no need to add sugar. I've also included some of my favorite riffs on the traditional recipe. I love them all just as much in their own ways.

BASIC CORNBREAD

MAKES ONE 10-INCH ROUND LOAF

2 cups coarse cornmeal, preferably
Geechie Boy Jimmy Red (see
Resources, page 368)

1½ teaspoons kosher salt

½ teaspoon baking soda

½ teaspoon baking powder

1½ cups full-fat buttermilk
(see Note, page 27)

1 large egg, lightly beaten

¼ cup plus 1 tablespoon Rendered
Fresh Lard (page 343), melted

Preheat the oven to 450°F. Put a 10-inch cast-iron skillet in the oven to preheat for at least 10 minutes.

Combine the cornmeal, salt, baking soda, and baking powder in a medium bowl. Combine the buttermilk, egg, and ¼ cup of the melted lard in a small bowl. Stir the wet ingredients into the dry ingredients just to combine; do not overmix.

Move the skillet from the oven to the stove, placing it over high heat. Add the remaining tablespoon of melted lard and swirl to coat the skillet. Pour in the batter, distributing it evenly. It should sizzle.

Transfer the skillet back to the oven and bake the cornbread for about 15 minutes, until a toothpick inserted in the center comes out clean. Serve warm, directly from the skillet.

VARIATIONS

CRACKLIN' CORNBREAD

I like to use the salty, smoky bacon from my friend Allan Benton in cracklin' cornbread, a traditional Southern bread that became famous during my years at Husk Charleston. It's a treat to find little pieces of bacon in every bite.

Run 4 ounces bacon, preferably Benton's (see Resources, page 368), through a meat grinder, or very finely mince it. Put the bacon in a skillet large enough to hold it in one layer and cook over medium-low heat, stirring frequently, until the fat has rendered and the bits of bacon are crispy, 4 to 5 minutes. Remove the bits of bacon with a slotted spoon and place on a paper towel to drain, reserving the fat. You need 5 tablespoons bacon fat.

Prepare the cornbread mixture as directed in the basic cornbread recipe. Add the crispy bacon bits to the cornmeal mixture (omitting the lard). Add ¼ cup of the rendered bacon fat to the buttermilk mixture. Add the remaining tablespoon of bacon fat to the skillet when you're ready to cook the cornbread (omitting the tablespoon of lard) and continue as directed in the basic recipe.

SOUR CORNBREAD

I love sourness in almost anything. Here a short fermentation is an easy way to add more flavor and complexity to basic cornbread.

Combine the cornmeal, salt, and buttermilk in a clean quart-size canning jar. Wipe the rim and threads clean, place the lid and ring on the jar, and tighten the ring. Let the cornmeal mixture ferment in a dark area no warmer than 75°F for 3 days.

Replace the lard in the basic recipe with bacon fat. Combine the cornmeal mixture, baking soda, and baking powder in a medium bowl and stir to mix thoroughly. Combine the egg and 4 tablespoons melted bacon fat in a small bowl. Stir the egg mixture into the cornmeal mixture just to combine; do not over-mix. Continue as directed in the basic recipe, using bacon fat in the skillet in place of the lard.

NOTE: You'll need to start this recipe 3 days ahead of time to allow the cornmeal mixture to ferment.

RICE CORNBREAD

I'd never heard of cornbread with rice until I started researching Lowcountry cuisine while I was attending culinary school in Charleston. Adding rice to cornbread was a traditional way to use any rice left over from the night before. I love the interplay between aromatic Carolina Gold rice and freshly milled cornmeal. The result is an especially flavorful cornbread.

Combine 4 cups water and 2 teaspoons kosher salt in a medium saucepan, bring to a boil over medium-high heat, and stir to be sure the salt has dissolved completely. Reduce the heat to medium, add ⅓ cup Anson Mills Carolina Gold Rice (see Resources, page 368), stir once, and bring to a simmer. Simmer gently, uncovered, stirring occasionally, until the rice is al dente, about 10 minutes. Drain the rice, spread it out on a rimmed baking sheet, and cool to room temperature. Transfer the cooked rice to a large bowl.

Add the dry ingredients to the cooked rice and continue as directed in the basic recipe, adding a couple of minutes to the baking time.

HOT-WATER CORNBREAD

**MAKES FIFTEEN 2-INCH PIECES;
SERVES 4 TO 6**

3 ounces country ham, preferably
Bob Wood's (see Resources,
page 368)

3 to 4 tablespoons Rendered Fresh
Lard (page 343)

2 cups water

2 cups fine yellow cornmeal,
preferably Anson Mills
(see Resources, page 368)

1 teaspoon kosher salt

¼ teaspoon freshly ground black
pepper

1 large egg, lightly beaten

Hot-water cornbread is like a cornbread fritter. It's not a recipe seen as often as its skillet-baked cousin, but it's every bit as delicious. It's the cornbread that was eaten and served before chemical leaveners came to the South. The cornmeal is cooked into a thick porridge on the stove, then combined with rendered ham bits and egg and fried up in a skillet. The steam causes any bit of leavening. The contrast between the crispy, crunchy outside and the soft, almost melting inside of the fritters is so satisfying.

Run the ham through the large die of a meat grinder, or very finely mince it. Combine the ham and 1 tablespoon of the lard in a small skillet over medium heat and cook, stirring frequently, until the ham is crispy, about 5 minutes. Remove the bits of ham with a slotted spoon and transfer to a paper towel to drain. Strain the fat through a fine-mesh sieve into a heatproof container. Cool to room temperature, cover, and refrigerate. *(Tightly covered, the ham fat will keep for up to 3 weeks in the refrigerator.)*

Bring the water to a boil in a medium saucepan over high heat. Stirring constantly with a wooden spoon, slowly add the cornmeal and cook, stirring, until the cornmeal is very thick, all the water has been absorbed, and no grittiness remains, about 2 minutes. Stir in the salt, pepper, and ham. Remove from the heat and cool for 5 minutes, then stir in the egg until completely combined.

Preheat the oven to 200°F. Line a rimmed baking sheet with paper towels.

When the dough is cool enough to handle, divide it into 15 pieces and shape them into disks about 2 inches in diameter and ½ inch thick. Heat 2 tablespoons of the lard in a large cast-iron skillet over medium-high heat. Add half the fritters and fry until golden and crispy on the first side, about 2 minutes. Turn them over and fry until golden and crispy on the second side, 1 to 2 minutes more. Transfer the fritters to the prepared baking sheet and keep warm in the oven. Wipe out the skillet with paper towels if the lard has scorched and add another tablespoon of lard, then cook the remaining fritters. Place the second batch on the baking sheet to drain for just a minute. Serve the cornbread fritters immediately.

STOVETOP GRITS

SERVES 4 AS A SIDE

One 1-liter bottle (4¼ cups) spring water

1 cup Anson Mills Rosebank Gold Grits (see Resources, page 368)

1 fresh bay leaf

1 tablespoon kosher salt

½ teaspoon freshly ground white pepper

2 tablespoons unsalted butter

1 tablespoon fresh lemon juice

1½ teaspoons Hot Sauce (page 260) or Red Clay Original Hot Sauce (see Resources, page 369)

GOES WELL WITH:

Everything

This stovetop method is the traditional way of cooking grits, and it requires a lot of your attention and time. It's the most romantic way as well. You'll have a close connection with the finished product after having carefully and stressfully watched over the pot as the grits cook.

The two most important steps are soaking the grits for at least 8 hours beforehand and skimming off the chaff before you start cooking. Soaking the grits will jump-start the hydration process, and that—along with removing the chaff—results in creamier, more delicate cooked grits.

NOTE: You'll need to plan ahead to soak the grits.

Combine the water and grits in a container, cover, and refrigerate for at least 8 hours or up to overnight.

Use a fine-mesh sieve to skim off any hulls or chaff from the surface of the water, being careful not to disturb the water too much so that none of the bits sink back into the grits. Transfer the grits and their soaking water to a large saucepan and bring to a boil over high heat, stirring constantly with a silicone spatula. Then continue to boil, stirring, until the starch in the corn is hydrated and the grits thicken, 1 to 2 minutes. Remove from the stove, cover, and let stand for 10 minutes to let the grits relax.

Uncover the grits, add the bay leaf, and cook over low heat, stirring often, until very soft and tender, about 1 hour. Taste the grits every 15 minutes or so to check their progress.

Remove from the heat, remove and discard the bay leaf, and stir in the salt, white pepper, butter, lemon juice, and hot sauce. Serve right from the pan.

PRESSURE-COOKER GRITS

SERVES 4 AS A SIDE

One 1-liter bottle (4¼ cups) spring water

1 cup Anson Mills Rosebank Gold Grits (see Resources, page 368)

1 fresh bay leaf

1 tablespoon kosher salt

½ teaspoon freshly ground white pepper

2 tablespoons unsalted butter

1 tablespoon fresh lemon juice

1½ teaspoons Hot Sauce (page 260) or Red Clay Original Hot Sauce (see Resources, page 369)

EQUIPMENT

Electric pressure cooker (see Note, page 43)

Using an electric pressure cooker is my favorite way to cook grits at home. You get perfect results every time. Think of it like using a rice cooker to cook rice. The pressure cooker also doesn't take up any valuable stove space. The grits need to soak for at least 8 hours, so the high temperature and shorter cooking time result in a more aromatic and delicious plate of grits.

NOTE: You'll need to plan ahead to soak the grits.

Combine the water and grits in a container, cover, and refrigerate for at least 8 hours or up to overnight.

Use a fine-mesh sieve to skim off any hulls or chaff from the surface of the water, being careful not to disturb the water too much so that none of the bits sink back into the grits. Transfer the grits and soaking water to the pressure cooker, add the bay leaf, salt, and white pepper, and stir to combine. Lock on the lid, bring the cooker up to high pressure, and cook for 15 minutes.

Carefully release the steam from the pressure cooker. Remove the lid and stir in the butter, lemon juice, and hot sauce. Transfer the grits to a serving bowl, removing the bay leaf, and serve immediately.

CORNMEAL PORRIDGE

SERVES 4 AS A SIDE

1½ cups water

1½ cups whole milk

1 fresh bay leaf

¾ cup fine white cornmeal, preferably Weisenberger (see Resources, page 369)

1 tablespoon kosher salt

½ teaspoon freshly ground white pepper

Think of this as the South's version of polenta.

Combine the water, milk, and bay leaf in a medium heavy-bottomed saucepan and bring to a simmer over medium-high heat. Slowly sprinkle in the cornmeal, whisking constantly to prevent lumps. Reduce the heat to low and cook, whisking frequently, until the porridge has thickened and no grittiness remains, 6 to 8 minutes. Remove from the heat and remove and discard the bay leaf.

Stir in the salt and white pepper and serve right from the pan.

BISCUITS

MAKES 14 BISCUITS

8 tablespoons (1 stick) unsalted butter

3⅓ cups self-rising flour, preferably White Lily, plus more for rolling out the dough

½ teaspoon kosher salt

1½ teaspoons freshly ground black pepper

1½ cups very cold full-fat buttermilk (see Note, page 27)

GOES WELL WITH:

Country ham (see page 82)
Homemade butter (see page 225)
Fruit Preserves (page 283)
Watermelon Molasses (page 284)

My biscuit recipe is a combination of techniques I learned from my mother and grandmother and from working in the kitchen of Bob Carter, the longtime chef of Charleston's Peninsula Grill. I took the mixing method from him, and the texture and cooking technique are from the ladies. Biscuits can be extremely personal. This is how I like them: with a lot of crunch and a little bit of fluff.

NOTES: For best results, bake the biscuits in two 10-inch cast-iron skillets as directed in the recipe. If necessary, you can bake the biscuits on a heavy baking sheet. Although the biscuits are best served immediately, they can be made up to 6 hours ahead. Cool to room temperature, place in an airtight container, and cover. Reheat briefly in a 350°F oven before serving.

Freeze the butter for 20 minutes, or until it is solid enough to grate on the large holes of a box grater. Grate the butter into a container, cover, and return to the freezer.

Preheat the oven to 475°F. Line a rimmed baking sheet with parchment paper.

Combine the flour, salt, and pepper in a large bowl and mix well. Work the frozen butter into the flour with your fingertips until the pieces of butter are about the size of peas. Add the buttermilk and stir until the dough just comes together.

Turn the dough out onto a lightly floured surface. Lightly sprinkle the dough with flour and, using a lightly floured rolling pin, roll the dough out to a rectangle about ½ inch thick. Fold one-third of the dough over the center third, then fold the opposite side over that like you're folding a letter. Fold the other side over, and roll the dough out again to a ½-inch-thick rectangle. Repeat the folding and rolling process one more time.

Cut out the biscuits with a 3-inch round cutter, flouring it between cuts if necessary, and place them on the prepared baking sheet. Gently gather the scraps of dough together, pat them into a disk, and repeat the rolling and cutting process. Refrigerate the biscuits for 5 minutes to rest the dough.

Transfer the biscuits to two cast-iron skillets, 7 to a pan. The biscuits should just barely touch one another. Bake the biscuits for 10 to 12 minutes, until risen and golden brown. Serve immediately.

HOW TO MAKE BUTTER

Butter is a staple ingredient in Southern cuisine. It's ubiquitous in home cooking and in most restaurants, but people never give it a second thought, and store-bought is the norm. I was the same until I tried my hand at making my own butter. When I worked with Travis Grimes at Husk, we became obsessed with collecting antique churns and paddles and making butter ourselves. I was blown away by the result. The taste of freshly cultured and churned butter is easily worth the effort of making it.

I began experimenting with making butter using the incredible raw milk produced by Celeste Albers's herd of Jersey cattle on her farm on Wadmalaw Island, South Carolina, not far from Charleston. The milk is full of flavor, which varies with the seasons. Over time, I perfected the butter-making process, learning to allow the rich cream to culture just enough and then churning, working, and seasoning the butter until it was ready to be slathered on hot fresh biscuits or served alongside spicy, crunchy raw radishes.

The process couldn't be simpler, and it doesn't require much in the way of specialized equipment. But it does take patience, attention to cleanliness, and high-quality ingredients. Here's how, if you want to try it for yourself.

You will need a butter churn to make the butter. Sure, you can "churn" the cream in the bowl of a stand mixer, but I promise that using a traditional hand-cranked churn makes the experience so much more tactile and enjoyable. Online sources include Amazon and New England Cheese Making Supply Co.; see Resources, page 369.

You will also need butter muslin, a very fine mesh cheesecloth used for making cheeses with soft curds that would press through normal cheesecloth as well as for making butter (see Resources, page 369). You could use multiple layers of regular cheesecloth, but butter muslin really is the best option. (The muslin is reusable. Before the first use and after subsequent uses, wash it in hot water with an unscented detergent and hang to dry.)

EQUIPMENT

Two 1-quart canning jars, sterilized (see page 246)

2 clean kitchen towels

Butter churn

Colander

Butter muslin

2 wooden butter paddles

INGREDIENTS
(TO MAKE ABOUT 12 OUNCES BUTTER)

4 cups raw cream or non–ultra-pasteurized heavy cream from pastured cows

¼ cup full-fat buttermilk (see Note, page 27)

8 cups cold distilled water, or as needed

Coarse finishing salt, like J.Q. Dickinson's, or Bulls Bay Saltworks's Charleston Flake Sea Salt (see Resources, page 368)

Divide the cream and buttermilk evenly between the sterilized jars. (Cleanliness is crucial here, so don't skip the sterilization part!) Give the jars a swirl to combine the ingredients and cover each jar with a clean kitchen towel, securing it tightly with butcher's twine. Place the jars in a cool part of the kitchen where the temperature won't exceed 75°F and let the cream mixture sit for 2 days. The lactic bacteria in the buttermilk will start to ferment the cream, giving it a tangy, complex flavor that will make the finished butter that much more special.

After 2 days, it's time to churn. Make sure the butter churn is completely clean and well rinsed. The butterfat in the cream will readily pick up the flavors and aromas of other ingredients, and making sure you start with clean equipment is the best way to keep off flavors from ruining your butter.

When you open the jars, the cultured cream should have a sharp, sour note on the nose and have thickened considerably. Pour it into your churn, using a rubber spatula to get every last drop out of the jars. The cream that sticks to the sides of the jars is usually the fattiest, so be sure not to leave any behind. Crank the churn at a comfortable pace; not too slow, not too fast. The butterfat is held in suspension in the cream, and as you churn, these little molecules of fat bounce around, hitting and sticking to one another until they form clumps large enough to literally snap out of suspension. At this point, there will be a visible and audible change, letting you know that the butter has separated from the buttermilk you've just made. Depending on your churn and how fast you're churning, this usually takes between 5 and 10 minutes.

The next step is to drain off the buttermilk from the solids. Line a colander with butter muslin. Set the lined colander over a bowl big enough to hold the drained buttermilk and pour in the contents of the churn, making sure to get every last bit. Cover the whole setup with plastic wrap, transfer it to the refrigerator, and let stand for a few hours to drain off as much of the buttermilk as possible. (While the butter is draining, take the time to thoroughly clean your churn so it's ready for the next batch you make.)

After it's drained, the butter is ready to be rinsed. First, transfer the buttermilk collected in the draining process to a clean 1-quart canning jar, cover, and refrigerate. *(The buttermilk will keep for up to 3 weeks in the refrigerator.)* You can use this "by-product" in any recipe calling for buttermilk or to start your next batch of cultured butter; or season the buttermilk with a pinch of salt and enjoy it as a tangy drink with some fresh cornbread.

Rinsing the butter is the most important step you can take to preserve the flavor you've worked so hard to create. Even though you've drained off most of the buttermilk, some will still remain on the surface and inside the butter. If left on the butter, it will continue to ferment and will cause the butter to taste off and eventually go rancid. Divide the cold distilled water among three shallow containers. Using very clean and well rinsed hands, lift the butter out of the colander and place it in the first container of water. Massage the butter in the water to rinse off the remaining buttermilk. Transfer the butter to the next container of water when the previous one gets fairly cloudy, then repeat once this container of water gets cloudy. By the third rinse, the water should remain clear. If it is at all murky, rinse the butter once more in another container of fresh water; usually, though, three changes of water will do the trick.

To finish the process, gather your lump of butter from the water, letting it drain and then squeezing out as much moisture as you can, and transfer it to the ridged part of one of the butter paddles. Using the other paddle, lightly hit the butter to work off and wick away any remaining surface moisture, occasionally folding the butter back on itself, until no more moisture is pulled out of the butter into the grooves of the paddles.

The last step is seasoning the butter. The amount of salt you add will be based on personal taste and can vary depending on the time of year. The different forage that cows graze on throughout the year can change the flavor of the cream and the resulting butter. Taste the butter unseasoned, then add a little bit of salt, working it in with the paddles, and taste the butter again. Add salt little by little until the butter is just right for you. (To clean the butter paddles, rinse with hot water, dry thoroughly, rub with some kosher salt, and wrap tightly in plastic wrap for storage. Rinse with water and dry before each use.)

That's it! You've made butter. You can press it into a butter mold, if you like, or simply shape it into a log and wrap it first in a layer of parchment paper and then in plastic wrap. Well-wrapped, the butter will keep for up to 1 month in the refrigerator or up to 3 months in the freezer.

JOHN EGERTON'S BEATEN BISCUITS

MAKES 30 BISCUITS

3½ cups all-purpose flour,
  preferably White Lily
  (see Resources, page 369),
  plus more for rolling and cutting
  out the dough

¾ teaspoon kosher salt

½ teaspoon baking powder

2½ tablespoons sugar

½ cup Rendered Fresh Lard
  (page 343), chilled

¾ cup half-and-half

¼ cup heavy cream

EQUIPMENT

Pasta machine

GOES WELL WITH:

Country ham (see page 82)
Pickled Green Tomatoes
  (page 249)

I cherish this recipe given to me by John Egerton, one of the South's most important cultural observers. His seminal work, *Southern Food*, first published in 1987, is required reading for anyone serious about learning about the cuisine. This recipe differs from the one in his cookbook, as he adapted it over the years to use a pasta roller instead of the traditional biscuit brake. When John gave me the recipe, he said, "Roll the cold dough through five hundred times for family, a thousand for the president." This version cuts down on that by just a little bit.

Sift the flour, salt, baking powder, and sugar into a large bowl and stir to combine. Work the lard into the dry ingredients with your fingertips until the mixture has the texture of coarse cornmeal. Stirring with a wooden spoon, slowly add the half-and-half and then the cream a little at a time and mix until the dough barely holds together. Wrap the dough in plastic wrap and refrigerate for 3 hours.

Preheat the oven to 350°F. Line a rimmed baking sheet with parchment paper.

Remove the dough from the refrigerator and divide it into 4 equal pieces. (While you are rolling one piece, keep the others lightly covered with plastic wrap.) Set the rollers of the pasta machine to the widest setting and roll each piece of cold dough through them about 30 times, folding the dough in half after each roll and turning it a quarter turn before rolling it out again. The dough should be completely smooth and spring back when stretched. Transfer the sheets of dough to the prepared baking sheet as you go and keep them loosely covered with a kitchen towel until you've rolled out all the dough.

Place one piece of dough on a lightly floured work surface. Using a rolling pin, roll the dough out to a ½-inch thickness. Cut out biscuits using a 1½-inch round cutter, flouring it between cuts if necessary, and place them on the baking sheet; do not let them touch. Gently gather the scraps together into a disk, roll it once through the pasta machine, and cut. Repeat with the remaining 3 pieces of dough. Using a fork, pierce each biscuit clean through three times.

Bake for 25 minutes, or until cream colored, not browned. Place the baking sheet on a wire rack and let cool.

Serve the biscuits at room temperature. They can be stored in an airtight container at room temperature for up to 3 days.

BUTTERMILK ROLLS

MAKES 22 ROLLS

2 tablespoons sugar

2 tablespoons honey, preferably local

½ teaspoon kosher salt

1¾ cups unbleached bread flour

¾ cup all-purpose flour, plus more for the work surface

2 tablespoons finely crumbled cake yeast

1 cup full-fat buttermilk (see Note, page 27)

Nonstick cooking spray

1 large egg, lightly beaten with 1 tablespoon water to make an egg wash

Coarse finishing salt, preferably J.Q. Dickinson's (see Resources, page 368)

GOES WELL WITH:

Pimento Cheese (page 361)
Homemade butter (see page 225)
Creamed Ramps (page 158)

Buttermilk rolls were a classic from day one during my time at Husk. I'm far from the best baker in the world; in fact, baking (especially bread) tends to scare me a little. But this recipe isn't intimidating at all. And the way you can just tear the rolls out of the skillet, their sweet aroma, and their soft chew will make them your go-to dinner roll.

Stir together the sugar, honey, and salt in a bowl to make a paste. Add both flours and stir them in with a wooden spoon.

Mix the yeast with the buttermilk in a small bowl, add it to the flour mixture all at once, and stir to incorporate. Turn the dough out onto a lightly floured work surface and knead it until smooth, 5 to 6 minutes.

Lightly spray a large bowl with nonstick cooking spray and place the dough in the bowl. Cover the bowl with a kitchen towel, put it in a warm place, and let the dough rise until it has doubled in size, about 1 hour.

Remove the towel and gently punch the dough down. Cover the bowl with the kitchen towel and let the dough rise again until doubled in size, about 45 minutes.

Spray a 9-inch cast-iron skillet with nonstick cooking spray. Divide the dough in half, then divide each half into 11 pieces (1 ounce each). Roll each piece into a ball; the balls won't be completely smooth. Carefully place them in the prepared skillet; they should fit snugly. Cover the skillet lightly with a kitchen towel, put it in a warm place, and let the rolls rise until they have doubled in size, about 1 hour.

About 20 minutes before the rolls have finished rising, preheat the oven to 400°F.

Just before baking, use a pastry brush to lightly brush the tops of the rolls with the egg wash. Lightly sprinkle the rolls with finishing salt. Bake the rolls for about 25 minutes, rotating the skillet once halfway through. Test the rolls using an instant-read thermometer: The internal temperature should read 195°F.

Cool the rolls in the skillet on a rack and serve when they've cooled enough to handle. Store leftover rolls, covered, for up to 1 day at room temperature and reheat in a 350°F oven for 3 minutes before serving.

APPALACHIAN FRY BREAD

MAKES 12 FRY BREADS

2 cups all-purpose flour, plus more for the work surface

1 tablespoon baking powder

½ teaspoon kosher salt

1 cup whole milk

Canola oil for the bowl

½ cup plus 2 tablespoons Rendered Fresh Lard (page 343)

2 tablespoons coarse finishing salt, preferably J.Q. Dickinson's (see Resources, page 368)

GOES WELL WITH:

Sea Island Red Pea Spread (page 49)

Chilled Summer Squash Soup with Buttermilk and Sunflower Seeds (page 66)

This fry bread, a quick bread by category, is part of the culinary tradition of Appalachia. Try it with Sea Island Red Pea Spread (page 49) or alongside a hearty soup.

Pictured on page 48

Sift the flour, baking powder, and salt together into a large bowl. Slowly add the milk, stirring until incorporated. Knead just until the dough comes together and forms a ball, taking care not to overwork it. Place the ball of dough in a lightly greased bowl, cover with a kitchen towel, and let rest at room temperature for about 1 hour to relax the gluten.

Preheat the oven to 200°F. Line two rimmed baking sheets with parchment paper and two more with paper towels.

Divide the dough into 12 equal pieces and roll them into balls. On a floured surface, use your palms to flatten each ball of dough, then gently stretch it into a round about 4 inches in diameter. Place the rounds of dough on the parchment-lined baking sheets and pierce each one completely through three times with a fork.

Heat the lard in a large cast-iron skillet over medium heat to 350°F. Working in four batches of 3, fry the bread until golden brown, about 2 minutes. Turn and fry on the other side until golden brown, about 1 minute more. Transfer the cooked breads to the paper towel–lined baking sheets, sprinkle with a few grains of finishing salt, and keep warm in the oven while you fry the remaining breads. Serve hot.

NOTE: The fry breads are best served hot, but they can be cooled and stored in an airtight container for up to 1 day at room temperature. Reheat in a 350°F oven for 3 minutes before serving.

SORGHUM SEED CRACKERS

MAKES ABOUT FORTY 3-BY-3-INCH CRACKERS

SORGHUM SEEDS

¼ cup sorghum seeds (see Resources, page 368), rinsed, drained, and picked through for stones and black seeds

¾ cup water

1 teaspoon kosher salt

CRACKERS

1½ cups all-purpose flour

½ cup sorghum flour (see Resources, page 368)

1 teaspoon baking powder

1 teaspoon paprika

½ teaspoon kosher salt

½ teaspoon freshly ground black pepper

½ teaspoon garlic powder

½ teaspoon onion powder

½ cup water

2½ tablespoons extra-virgin olive oil

1 large egg plus 1 tablespoon water, lightly beaten to make an egg wash

Coarse finishing salt, preferably J.Q. Dickinson's (see Resources, page 368)

EQUIPMENT

Pasta machine

GOES WELL WITH:

Smoked Trout Dip (page 45)

Sorghum is an underused but totally delicious grain. The combination of cooked whole seeds and sorghum flour gives this cracker a unique texture and appearance. Serve these with Smoked Trout Dip or some fine Southern cheese—they're great with just about anything.

FOR THE SORGHUM SEEDS: Combine the seeds, water, and salt in a small saucepan and bring to a boil over high heat. Reduce the heat to low, cover, and simmer until the seeds are tender, about 1 hour. Drain the seeds and transfer to a container. Cool to room temperature and set aside.

FOR THE CRACKERS: Sift the all-purpose flour, sorghum flour, baking powder, paprika, salt, pepper, garlic powder, and onion powder into the bowl of a food processor.

Combine the water and olive oil in a small bowl. With the food processor running, slowly pour in the oil mixture and process for 30 seconds. Scrape down the sides and process until the dough comes together and forms a ball, about 30 seconds. Remove the dough from the processor, wrap in plastic wrap, and refrigerate until completely cold, at least 2 hours.

Meanwhile, place a rack in the center of the oven and preheat the oven to 425°F. Line three baking sheets with parchment paper.

Remove the dough from the refrigerator and divide it into 8 pieces. Shape them into balls and roll each ball through the pasta machine, starting with the widest setting and working down to a thickness of about 2 millimeters. Transfer the sheets of dough to the prepared baking sheets, making sure they don't overlap, and lightly brush them with the egg wash. Sprinkle with the sorghum seeds and press down on them lightly to make sure they stick, then sprinkle each sheet with a few grains of finishing salt.

Bake the crackers for 7 to 8 minutes, until golden brown and crispy. Transfer to wire racks and cool completely.

TO SERVE: Break the sheets of baked crackers into approximately forty 3-by-3-inch pieces.

NOTE: Although the crackers are best eaten the same day, they will keep in an airtight container at room temperature for up to 3 days.

NO-PEEK RICE

SERVES 4 AS A SIDE

1 tablespoon unsalted butter

1 cup Anson Mills Carolina Gold
Rice (see Resources, page 368)

2 teaspoons kosher salt

1½ cups water

This is my preferred quick rice preparation. The fluffy texture makes the rice a great side dish for almost anything.

Melt the butter in a medium saucepan over medium-high heat. Add the rice and salt and stir to coat the rice with the butter. Increase the heat to high, add the water, and bring to a boil. Reduce the heat to low, cover, and simmer until the rice is tender and all of the water has been absorbed, about 12 minutes. Remove from the heat and fluff gently with a fork. Transfer to a serving dish and serve.

CREAMED RICE

SERVES 6 AS A SIDE

1½ cups Anson Mills Carolina Gold Rice Grits (see Resources, page 368)

6 cups whole milk

1 fresh bay leaf

2½ teaspoons kosher salt

¼ ounce firm sheep's-milk cheese, grated

1 tablespoon fresh lemon juice

When the temperature drops outside, I crave creamed rice. It sticks to your ribs and really warms you up. I rarely add this much dairy to rice for any dish, but it's fun to take it to the limit with richness every so often.

Put the rice and milk in a large saucepan, add the bay leaf and salt, and bring to a simmer over medium heat, stirring. Reduce the heat to low and cook the rice, stirring frequently to prevent sticking, until it is completely tender, about 20 minutes. Remove and discard the bay leaf and stir in the cheese and lemon juice. Transfer to a serving bowl and serve.

CHARLESTON ICE CREAM

SERVES 4 AS A SIDE

4 cups water

2 teaspoons kosher salt

¼ teaspoon freshly ground white pepper

1 fresh bay leaf

1 cup Anson Mills Carolina Gold Rice (see Resources, page 368)

4 tablespoons unsalted butter, diced

If you're looking for the most luxurious way to cook rice, this is it. The recipe uses an age-old Lowcountry method that yields rice that is almost risotto-like: creamy, rich, and incredibly aromatic. It got its name just how you might think: The best way to eat a scoop of this rice is on its own in a bowl, the way you would enjoy a scoop of ice cream.

Preheat the oven to 300°F.

Combine the water, salt, white pepper, and bay leaf in a medium saucepan, bring to a boil over medium-high heat, and stir to be sure the salt has dissolved completely. Reduce the heat to medium, add the rice, stir once, and bring to a simmer. Simmer gently, uncovered, stirring occasionally, until the rice is al dente, about 10 minutes. Drain.

Drain the rice and spread it out on a rimmed baking sheet, discarding the bay leaf. Place the rice in the oven to dry for 10 minutes, stirring it occasionally. Scatter the butter evenly over the rice and return it to the oven for 5 minutes more, stirring it twice during that time, until the rice is dry. All the excess moisture should have evaporated and the grains should be separate.

Transfer the rice to a serving dish and serve immediately.

DIRTY RICE

SERVES 4 AS A SIDE

4 cups water

1 tablespoon kosher salt

¼ teaspoon freshly ground white
   pepper

1 fresh bay leaf

1 cup Anson Mills Carolina Gold
   Rice (see Resources, page 368)

2 tablespoons canola oil

½ cup small dice andouille sausage
   (about one 3-ounce link)

5 ounces chicken livers, drained,
   rinsed under cold water, patted
   dry with paper towels, and cut
   into small dice

¼ cup thinly sliced scallions

2 tablespoons unsalted butter,
   diced

1 teaspoon Bourbon Barrel Bourbon
   Smoked Paprika (see Resources,
   page 368)

½ teaspoon freshly ground black
   pepper

2 tablespoons finely chopped
   flat-leaf parsley

GOES WELL WITH:

Fried Chicken (page 127)

Dirty rice is a traditional Creole dish that gets its special flavor from the addition of chicken livers and andouille sausage. For me, it's the perfect example of confronting preconceived notions about a dish. You might think you won't like the chicken liver flavor, but once all the ingredients are combined, you will change your mind.

Combine the water, 2 teaspoons of the salt, the white pepper, and the bay leaf in a medium saucepan and bring to a boil over medium-high heat; stir to make sure the salt has completely dissolved. Reduce the heat to medium, add the rice, stir once, and bring to a simmer. Simmer gently, uncovered, stirring occasionally, until the rice is al dente, about 10 minutes. Drain in a sieve, remove and discard the bay leaf, and set aside.

Heat the canola oil in a medium pot over medium-high heat until it shimmers. Add the sausage, livers, and scallions and cook, stirring frequently, until the livers are cooked through and the scallions are softened, about 4 minutes. Add the rice, butter, paprika, the remaining teaspoon of salt, and the pepper and cook, stirring often, until the butter has melted and the rice is hot, about 4 minutes.

Stir in the parsley, transfer to a serving dish, and serve.

DIRTY FARRO

SERVES 4 AS A SIDE

2½ cups Vegetable Stock
(page 348)

1 tablespoon kosher salt

1 cup Anson Mills Slow-Roasted
Farro (see Resources, page 368)

6 ounces Red Russian kale

1 teaspoon extra-virgin olive oil

¼ teaspoon freshly ground black
pepper

1 tablespoon canola oil

½ cup fine dice sweet onion

4 ounces chicken livers, drained,
rinsed under cold water, patted
dry with paper towels, and cut
into small dice

2 ounces chicken hearts, cut in half,
trimmed of any sinew, and cut
into fine dice

2 tablespoons unsalted butter

2 tablespoons finely chopped
chives

EQUIPMENT

Round 15-inch open-top fine-mesh
wire grill basket

GOES WELL WITH:

*Grilled Quail with Red-Eye Gravy
(page 133)*

Anson Mills slow-roasted farro has a subtle smokiness that can be addictive. I use the farro here for a spin on that Southern classic, dirty rice (see page 235). It's emblematic of my approach to cooking Southern cuisine using the best products you can find on a given day. Try the farro with grilled quail.

Pictured on page 132

Prepare a hot fire in a charcoal grill (see page 96), removing the grill rack and distributing the hot coals in an even layer in the bottom of the grill.

Meanwhile, combine the vegetable stock and 1 teaspoon of the salt in a small saucepan and bring to a boil over high heat. Add the farro, stir, reduce the heat to low, cover, and simmer until the grains are tender, about 25 minutes. Drain the farro in a colander and set aside.

While the farro is simmering, prepare the kale: Remove the stems and ribs from the leaves. Make stacks of the leaves, roll them into cylinders, and cut them into ribbons about ½ inch wide. Wash the kale in the sink or a large bowl of cold water, changing the water several times, to remove any sand. Drain and dry with paper towels.

Combine the kale, olive oil, 1 teaspoon of the salt, and the pepper in a bowl and toss. Transfer the kale to the grill basket and place the basket directly on the coals. Grill the kale, stirring it frequently with long-handled tongs so it cooks evenly, until it has wilted and lightly charred, about 2 minutes. Transfer to a bowl and set aside.

Heat the canola oil in a medium pot over medium-high heat until it shimmers. Add the onion, livers, and hearts and cook, stirring frequently, until the livers and hearts are cooked through and the onion has softened, about 3 minutes. Add the farro, grilled kale, the remaining teaspoon of salt, and the butter and cook, stirring often, until the butter has melted and the farro is hot, about 3 minutes.

Stir in the chives, transfer to a serving dish, and serve.

RYE AND MOREL PORRIDGE

SERVES 4 AS A SIDE

¾ cup Anson Mills Abruzzi Rye Berries (see Resources, page 368)

4 cups water

2 teaspoons culinary lime (see box, page 213, and Resources, page 368)

½ cup Cream of Morel Soup (page 70)

1 teaspoon kosher salt

¼ teaspoon freshly ground white pepper

1 ounce Asiago cheese, preferably Kenny's Farmhouse Dry Fork Reserve (see Resources, page 369), grated

1 tablespoon thinly sliced chives

GOES WELL WITH:

Spring Lamb with Rhubarb Butter (page 148)

Rye berries were one of the first grains other than corn that I experimented with nixtamalizing (see box, page 213). Their outer hulls soften, but they retain a subtle, toothsome texture and chew. The rye berries combined with a little cream of morel soup create a porridge that is both comforting and decadent.

Combine the rye berries, water, and culinary lime in a medium nonreactive saucepan and bring to a boil over high heat, stirring occasionally. Reduce the heat to low and simmer the rye berries until their outer hulls have softened and they are tender, about 1½ hours.

Drain the rye berries and rinse well under cold running water. *(The rye berries can be prepared ahead. Tightly covered once cooled, they will keep for up to 3 days in the refrigerator.)*

Transfer the rye berries to a small saucepan. Add the cream of morel soup, salt, and white pepper and heat over medium heat until hot throughout, about 3 minutes. Add the cheese and chives and stir to combine. Transfer to a serving dish and serve.

PANTRY

DILLY BEANS

MAKES 3 QUARTS

3½ cups distilled white vinegar

3½ cups water

½ cup sugar

¼ cup kosher salt

3 tablespoons ⅛-inch dice sweet onion

6 fresh bay leaves

1 tablespoon crushed red pepper flakes

1¼ teaspoons ground turmeric

1 teaspoon celery seeds

2 tablespoons dill seeds

1½ teaspoons yellow mustard seeds

9 black peppercorns

3 garlic cloves

9 large dill sprigs

3 pounds heirloom beans, such as greasy, cut-short, half-runner, or Turkey Craw, washed, strings removed, and trimmed to fit the jars if necessary

These classic Southern pickled beans are great on their own, but they really shine next to freshly sliced good country ham.

Sterilize three 1-quart canning jars, along with their rings and lids (see page 246), and put them on a clean dish towel or a wire rack (not directly on the countertop).

Combine the vinegar, water, sugar, salt, onion, bay leaves, red pepper flakes, turmeric, and celery seeds in a large nonreactive saucepan and bring to a boil over high heat, stirring to dissolve the sugar and salt. Turn off the heat.

Put 2 teaspoons of the dill seeds, ½ teaspoon of the mustard seeds, 3 peppercorns, 1 garlic clove, and 3 dill sprigs in each sterilized jar. Fill the jars with the beans, standing them up vertically, and ladle over the hot pickling liquid, leaving a ½-inch headspace. Wipe the rims and threads clean. Place the lids and rings on the jars and finger-tighten the rings.

Process the jars in a boiling-water bath for 13 minutes according to the canning instructions on pages 246–47. It is important that the jars seal properly and a vacuum forms. If any jars did not seal, you must store them in the refrigerator. Allow the beans to cure for 1 week before eating. Properly sealed, the beans will keep in a cool, dark place for up to 6 months. Refrigerate after opening.

PICKLED OKRA

MAKES 5 QUARTS

5 pounds medium okra pods

7½ cups apple cider vinegar

3 cups water

7 jalapeño peppers, thinly sliced (with seeds)

7 large garlic cloves, thinly sliced

1½ cups kosher salt

¼ cup plus 2 tablespoons sugar

1½ tablespoons ground turmeric

1½ tablespoons yellow mustard seeds

GOES WELL WITH:

Smoked Trout Dip (page 45)

I learned how to make pickled okra at the Peninsula Grill, cooking under chef Bob Carter. It was my first job at a well-known restaurant. I've used the same technique and flavors ever since. Pickled okra is excellent fried or sliced very thin and served over roasted fish. You could also add some to some cooked Carolina Gold rice to make a new version of Limpin' Susan (page 184).

Sterilize five 1-quart canning jars, along with their rings and lids (see page 246), and put them on a clean dish towel or a wire rack (not directly on the countertop).

Make a small slit under the cap of each okra pod so that the pickling liquid can enter the pods. Pack the okra tightly into the jars.

Combine the vinegar, water, jalapeños, garlic, salt, sugar, turmeric, and mustard seeds in a large nonreactive saucepan and bring to a boil over high heat, stirring to completely dissolve the salt and sugar.

Ladle the mixture over the okra, leaving a ½-inch headspace. Wipe the rims and threads clean. Put the lids and rings on the jars and finger-tighten the rings.

Process the jars in a boiling-water bath for 15 minutes according to the canning instructions on pages 246–47. It is important that the jars seal properly and a vacuum forms. If any jars did not seal, you must store them in the refrigerator. Allow the okra to cure for 1 week before eating. Properly sealed, the okra will keep in a cool, dark place for up to 6 months. Refrigerate after opening.

NOTE: This recipe also works as a quick pickle. Halve the recipe and store the jars in the refrigerator. Allow the okra to cure for 1 week before eating.

BREAD-AND-BUTTER PICKLES

MAKES 3 QUARTS

2 pounds Kirby cucumbers

2 cups small dice sweet onions
(about 8 ounces)

¼ cup kosher salt

1 pound crushed ice

2 cups sugar

1 tablespoon yellow mustard seeds

1 teaspoon ground turmeric

½ teaspoon celery seeds

2 cups apple cider vinegar

1 fresh bay leaf, torn into pieces

3 whole cloves

½ jalapeño pepper, sliced paper-
thin (with seeds)

GOES WELL WITH:

Cheeseburgers (page 138)
*Pit-Cooked-Chicken Sandwiches
(page 130)*

Bread-and-butter pickles are one of my favorite treats. This recipe makes a quick pickle that keeps for up to 2 months in the refrigerator. If you like, you can process the jars in a boiling-water bath for 10 minutes to store them for longer (see pages 246–47).

Cut the blossom ends off the cucumbers and slice the cucumbers into ⅛-inch-thick slices. To draw out the excess liquid and increase the crunch, layer the cucumber slices with the onions, salt, and ice in a glass or stainless steel container and weight with a plate large enough to cover the cucumbers and keep them submerged when the ice melts. Cover and refrigerate overnight.

The next day, sterilize three 1-quart canning jars, along with their rings and lids (see page 246), and put them on a clean dish towel or a wire rack (not directly on the countertop).

Drain the cucumbers and onions, put them in a large non-reactive pot, and add the sugar, mustard seeds, turmeric, celery seeds, vinegar, bay leaf, cloves, and jalapeño. Bring to a simmer over high heat, stirring to completely dissolve the sugar. Using an instant-read thermometer to check, make sure the internal temperature of the cucumbers reaches 180°F and stays there for 90 seconds. Skim off any foam that has risen to the top.

Divide the hot cucumbers among the sterilized jars. Ladle the hot vinegar mixture over the cucumbers, leaving a ¼-inch headspace. Wipe the rims and threads clean, put the lids and rings on the jars, and tighten the rings. Cool the jars to room temperature.

Refrigerate the jars and let the pickles cure for at least 1 week before eating. Unopened, the pickles will keep for up to 2 months in the refrigerator.

PRESERVING AND CANNING

Preserving is not just the practical act of saving that year's crops; in many cases, it's also about protecting a practice that has been a part of Southern culture and identity for centuries. To me, the continued tradition of conserving food for later use is an important one to keep alive at a time when almost everything we want is available year-round at the local supermarket.

The kitchen was always buzzing at my grandmother's home in Pound, Virginia. There was rarely a time when some sort of food preparation wasn't going on. If you were watching television, you were snapping beans. If you were porch sitting, you were shucking corn or grating cabbage. Growing up, I thought that's what every family did. I wasn't allowed to sit back and watch my family painfully cracking walnuts (and occasionally a thumb); I had to grab a hammer and crack walnuts too. But it was always great to catch up with my cousins or aunts and uncles and listen to stories from the old-timers. I miss those days, and I look forward to when I'll be the old-timer, sitting there in my overalls and peeling apples with a pocketknife.

I was in my teens when I realized that much of this work was done to feed my family during rougher times, so preserving took on a whole new meaning for me. It was also around the same time that my grandmother's basement stopped being a scary place and became a delicious place. When I eventually moved away from southwest Virginia and started cooking in professional kitchens, I began to understand how special the food in my grandmother's basement was.

Why should we still go through all the trouble of picking, cleaning, chopping, curing, drying, boiling, sealing, smoking, or salting? The act of preservation is also one of transformation. A frugal Southerner will try to preserve just about anything. But just as often, ingredients are preserved to make them taste even better. If you have ever sat down to a lunch of leather britches (dried pole beans, an Appalachian specialty), some mixed pickles, and a hunk of good cornbread, you know what I mean. Those beans were no doubt delicious fresh in the field and would be amazing canned, but drying them, traditionally by stringing them up and hanging them over the hearth or a wood-burning stove, turned them into something special. After some time spent relaxing in a crock in the pantry, the vegetables in the pickle mix, which were picked at their prime, now act as a salty/sour/funky foil to the savory beans and cornbread.

Thoughtful preserving is also the best way to support your local agriculture. You wouldn't believe how much perfectly good food goes into the compost pile at great farms everywhere because they simply can't sell all their harvest. If we all took the time to live a little more like our grandparents did, we could really make a big difference in the livelihood of our local producers.

As a Southerner, I'm serious about preserving the things I love and am proud of. The history and traditions of these techniques are the roots of my idea of Southern cooking.

GUIDELINES FOR PRESERVING

Most of the recipes in this chapter are examples of pickling with vinegar, using lactic fermentation, or cooking fruits with sugar. Each technique is different, but they share the goal of making a flavorful product that is more shelf-stable than the fresh ingredients that went into it.

Here are some practical guidelines for preserving and canning that will help to ensure that you safely and successfully put up whatever beautiful produce you might have. I also recommend taking the time to study the detailed instructions provided by the National Center for Home Food Preservation and by the Ball Corporation (see Resources, page 368).

- First, the importance of cleanliness and freshness can't be overstated. The ingredients you are preserving, as well as your work surface and kitchen tools, need to be impeccably clean. Choose fruits and vegetables that don't have any sign of rot or mold.

- For pickling, distilled white vinegar and apple cider vinegar are the acids of choice. You can experiment with vinegars for quick pickles, because they will be kept refrigerated, but for preserving or canning safely, you must use a vinegar with an acidity of 5 percent or higher. The acidity acts both to preserve the food and to prevent the growth of bacteria.

- Use kosher salt or pickling salt for pickles. Iodized table salt or sea salts with other minerals will change the flavor of whatever you are preserving.

For Lactic Fermentation

- Invest in a stoneware pickling crock, or use one that's been passed down in your family through the generations. Make sure there are no cracks in the glazing or through the crock itself. Those little nooks and crannies are the perfect hiding places for microbes that can ruin all your hard work. The size depends on what sort of quantities you intend to put up. Most of the recipes in this book call for a 1-gallon crock.

- Traditionally I've used layers of cheesecloth to cover ferments, and that certainly gets the job done, but recently I've found that a nylon-mesh filter bag, specifically one of those used for straining nut milks, makes an excellent, breathable barrier for my crocks. These are widely available online and in health food stores. Buy one and cut it into squares large enough to cover your ferment. You only need to use one layer, and these are reusable, good for many projects.

For Preserving and Canning

The jars you use must be sterilized. Here's how.

- Fill a large canning pot fitted with a rack three-quarters full with water. Place your canning jars and rings in the pot and bring the water to a boil over high heat.

When the water has come to a boil, set a timer for 5 minutes. Remove from the heat and cover the pot.

- Meanwhile, put the lids in a saucepan of hot water and heat until the water reaches 180°F. (Never boil the lids, because the sealant material may get damaged and then won't produce a safe seal.) Remove from the heat and cover the pan.

- Lay a clean kitchen towel out on the counter or set out a wire rack. When you are ready to fill the jars, using canning tongs, remove them from the pot and invert them onto the towel or rack. Leave them there for 1 minute, then turn them right side up and fill them. You want the jars to be hot when you put the food into them. Use tongs to remove the lids and rings and shake off the water before putting them on the jars.

It is important that the jars seal properly and a vacuum forms. When this occurs, the lids become concave in the center and you can't pop the button up and down. The lids usually ping when this happens, but since sealing may take several hours, you should always check the lids before you store the jars, not just rely on hearing a ping. If the jars have sealed properly, it is safe to store them in a pantry or other cool, dark place for up to 6 months. If not, store the jars in the refrigerator. Unopened, most pickles and preserves will keep for up to 2 months in the refrigerator.

BOILING-WATER-BATH CANNING

A boiling-water-bath canning pot has a fitted lid and a removable rack to hold the jars, preferably one with handles so that you can load all the jars onto the rack and lift them into and out of the canning pot all at once. If you have an electric or induction stovetop, the bottom of the pot must sit flat, and the pot should be no more than 4 inches wider in diameter than the burner or heating element, no matter what type of stove you have. The pot must be deep enough that the jars will always be covered with at least 1 inch of boiling water during processing.

Tips to Ensure Safety and Consistency

- Ladle the food into the sterilized jars through a widemouthed funnel, making sure to leave the specified headspace.

- Before putting the lids on, run a clean thin-bladed knife around the inside of each jar to release any air bubbles. Wipe the rims and threads clean. Attach the lids and rings. Screw the rings on firmly but not tight ("finger-tighten").

- Have the water in the canning pot at a high boil. Lower the jars into the boiling water. If using canning tongs, hold the jars below the rings, and be careful not to tilt them. The jars must be covered by at least 1 inch of boiling water at all times during processing; add more boiling water if needed. Cover the pot and return the water to a boil. Process the food for the time specified.

- Lift the jars out using the rack or canning tongs. Set them at least an inch apart on a clean dish towel or a wire rack (not directly on the countertop). Cool to room temperature and make sure the jars have sealed before tightening the rings again and storing.

PICKLED CHILIES

MAKES 1 QUART

1 pound mild chili peppers, such
  as ají dulce or shishito, slit
  lengthwise down one side and
  stems trimmed to ¼ inch

1 large garlic clove, peeled

1 fresh bay leaf

2 cups rice vinegar

1⅓ cups water

⅔ cup sugar

2 teaspoons kosher salt

GOES WELL WITH:

---

*Grilled Chicken Wings with West
  African BBQ Sauce (page 46)*
*Grilled Oysters with Green Garlic
  Butter (page 28)*
Deviled Eggs (page 23)

I can find room for these simple pickles on any dish, but
they are especially good with pimento cheese or grilled fish.

Sterilize a 1-quart canning jar, along with its ring and lid
(see page 246), and put it on a clean dish towel or a wire
rack (not directly on the countertop). Put the peppers, garlic, and bay leaf in the jar.

Combine the vinegar, water, sugar, and salt in a medium
nonreactive saucepan and bring to a boil over high heat, stirring to completely dissolve the sugar and salt. Ladle the liquid over the peppers. Wipe the rim and threads clean, place
the lid and ring on the jar, and tighten the ring. Cool the jar to
room temperature, then refrigerate the peppers for at least
1 week before eating to allow them to cure. Tightly sealed,
the peppers will keep for up to 2 months in the refrigerator.

NOTE: For longer storage, the peppers can be processed
according to the instructions for boiling-water canning on
pages 246–47. Process for 10 minutes. Properly sealed,
the peppers will keep in a cool, dark place for up to 6
months; refrigerate after opening.

PICKLED GREEN TOMATOES

MAKES 3 QUARTS

3½ pounds green heirloom tomatoes, sliced into ½-inch-thick rounds

¼ cup ½-inch-thick slices jalapeño peppers (with seeds)

1½ teaspoons coriander seeds

¾ teaspoon fennel seeds

¾ teaspoon yellow mustard seeds

¾ teaspoon black peppercorns

1¼ cups apple cider vinegar

1¼ cups rice vinegar

1¼ cups water

1 cup sugar

1½ star anise pods

1 green cardamom pod, cracked

1 fresh bay leaf

GOES WELL WITH:

Crispy Pig's Ears with Pimento Ranch (page 43)
Fried Bologna with Pickled Peach Mustard (page 52)
John Egerton's Beaten Biscuits (page 228)

This super-simple recipe is perfect for preserving those fall green tomatoes that probably aren't going to make it all the way to ripe. You can dredge the pickled tomatoes in cornmeal and panfry them (see page 50). They also make a great base for delicious relish on the fly, especially with a nice piece of fish—just add some thinly sliced sweet onions. This pickling brine will work with just about anything.

Sterilize three 1-quart canning jars, along with their rings and lids (see page 246), and put them on a clean dish towel or a wire rack (not directly on the countertop).

Divide the tomato slices, jalapeño slices, coriander seeds, fennel seeds, mustard seeds, and peppercorns among the jars, packing them in tightly.

Combine the vinegars, water, sugar, star anise, cardamom pod, and bay leaf in a large nonreactive saucepan and bring to a boil over high heat, stirring to completely dissolve the sugar. Strain the mixture into the jars; discard the solids. Wipe the rims and threads clean, place the lids and rings on the jars, and tighten the rings. Cool the jars to room temperature, then refrigerate the jars and allow the tomatoes to cure for 1 week before eating. Tightly sealed, the tomatoes will keep for up to 2 months in the refrigerator.

NOTE: For longer storage, the tomatoes can be processed according to the instructions for boiling-water canning on pages 246–47. Process for 10 minutes. Properly sealed, the jars will keep in a cool, dark place for up to 6 months; refrigerate after opening.

PICKLED PEACHES

MAKES 12 PICKLED PEACHES

12 large ripe peaches

3½ cups distilled white vinegar

3 cups water

2½ cups sugar

1 stalk lemongrass, bruised by beating with the back of a chef's knife, then chopped

1 tablespoon grated fresh ginger

15 black peppercorns

10 allspice berries

2 whole cloves

1 cinnamon stick

Pinch of ground mace

GOES WELL WITH:

*Spring Lamb with Rhubarb Butter
(page 148)*

*Hand-Churned Peach Sherbet
(page 337)*

Pickled peaches straddle the line between savory and sweet. They're equally at home incorporated into a tangy barbecue sauce or finely chopped as a tart topping for good vanilla ice cream. Taste them, and you'll think of a hundred things to eat them with.

Bring a large pot of water to a boil over high heat. Make an ice bath with equal parts ice and water in a large bowl. Submerge the peaches in the boiling water for 1 minute. Remove and submerge them in the ice bath to cool them and stop the cooking. Peel the peaches and place them in a nonreactive heatproof container.

Combine all the remaining ingredients in a nonreactive saucepan and bring to a boil over medium-high heat, stirring to completely dissolve the sugar. Reduce the heat to low and simmer for 5 minutes.

Pour the hot pickling liquid over the peaches. Cool to room temperature, cover, and refrigerate for at least 1 week before eating to allow the peaches to cure. Tightly sealed, the peaches will keep for up to 2 months in the refrigerator.

PICKLED RAMPS

MAKES 3 QUARTS

2½ pounds ramps, cleaned and leaves and hairy root ends removed

¼ cup ½-inch-thick slices jalapeño peppers (with seeds)

1¼ cups apple cider vinegar

1¼ cups rice vinegar

1¼ cups water

1¼ cups sugar

1½ teaspoons coriander seeds

¾ teaspoon fennel seeds

¾ teaspoon black peppercorns

3 whole cloves

1½ star anise pods

1 cinnamon stick

1 green cardamom pod, cracked

1 fresh bay leaf

GOES WELL WITH:

Smoked Trout Dip (page 45)
Deviled Eggs (page 23)
Grilled Trout with Cornbread
  Puree (page 103)

Ramp season is never long, and some years it's fleetingly quick. Pickling these iconic foraged bulbs is a way to enjoy their unique flavor all year until it's time to dig some more.

Sterilize three 1-quart canning jars, along with their rings and lids (see page 246), and put them on a clean dish towel or a wire rack (not directly on the countertop).

Combine all the ingredients in a large nonreactive pot and bring to a boil over high heat, stirring to completely dissolve the sugar. Remove the pot from the heat.

Divide the ramp mixture among the canning jars. Wipe the rims and threads clean, place the lids and rings on the jars, and tighten the rings. Cool the jars to room temperature, then refrigerate the jars and allow the ramps to cure for 1 week before eating. Tightly sealed, the ramps will keep for up to 2 months in the refrigerator.

NOTE: For longer storage, the ramps can be processed according to the instructions for boiling-water canning on pages 246–47. Process for 10 minutes. Properly sealed, the jars will keep in a cool, dark place for up to 6 months; refrigerate after opening.

PICKLED FENNEL

MAKES 3 QUARTS

4 cups apple cider vinegar

1 cup white wine vinegar

1 cup water

1 cup sugar

2 tablespoons yellow mustard
    seeds

1 tablespoon crushed red pepper
    flakes

1 teaspoon mustard powder

1 teaspoon ground turmeric

1 teaspoon kosher salt

¼ teaspoon ground cloves

1 bay leaf

3 large fennel bulbs (about
    3 pounds), stalks removed and
    discarded, bottoms trimmed, and
    bulbs cut into large dice

GOES WELL WITH:

*Grilled Catfish with Barely
    Cooked Tomatoes (page 94)*
*Pork Shoulder Steak with Grilled
    Mushrooms (page 141)*

Try these fennel pickles as an accompaniment to smoky grilled pork.

Sterilize three 1-quart canning jars, along with their rings and lids (see page 246), and put them on a clean dish towel or a wire rack (not directly on the countertop).

Combine all the ingredients except the fennel in a large nonreactive pot and bring to a boil over high heat, stirring to completely dissolve the sugar. Remove the pot from the heat and cool to room temperature.

Add the diced fennel to the pickling mixture and bring to a simmer over high heat. Reduce the heat to medium-low and simmer for 10 minutes. Remove from the stove.

Divide the fennel mixture among the canning jars. Wipe the rims and threads clean, place the lids and rings on the jars, and tighten the rings. Cool the jars to room temperature, then refrigerate the jars and allow the fennel to cure for 1 week before eating. Tightly sealed, the fennel will keep for up to 2 months in the refrigerator.

NOTE: For longer storage, the fennel can be processed according to the instructions for boiling-water canning on pages 246–47. Process for 10 minutes. Properly sealed, the jars will keep in a cool, dark place for up to 6 months; refrigerate after opening.

PICKLED EGGS

MAKES 12 PICKLED EGGS

12 large eggs

3 cups apple cider vinegar

1 cup distilled white vinegar

2 cups water

½ cup sugar

1 tablespoon plus 1 teaspoon
    kosher salt

3 whole cloves

½ cinnamon stick

GOES WELL WITH:

Killed Lettuces (page 75)

File these pickled eggs under "childhood avoidance turned adult craving." Today I'm always happy to see pickled eggs served as part of a Southern spread.

Using a sewing needle or pushpin, pierce a hole in the shell at the wide end of each egg. Put the eggs in a large saucepan and cover them with room-temperature water. Bring the water to a boil over medium-high heat and boil the eggs for 2 minutes. Remove the saucepan from the stove, cover it, and leave the eggs in the water for 10 minutes.

Carefully drain the eggs in a colander in the sink, then peel them under cold running water. Put the eggs in a container, cover, and refrigerate until ready to use.

Combine the vinegars, 2 cups water, sugar, salt, cloves, and cinnamon stick in a large nonreactive saucepan and bring to a boil over medium-high heat, stirring to dissolve the sugar and salt. Transfer the mixture to a nonreactive container and cool to room temperature, then refrigerate until completely cold.

Add the eggs to the chilled brine, cover, and refrigerate for at least 1 week before eating; stir and turn them occasionally. Tightly covered, the eggs will keep for up to 1 month in the refrigerator.

ASPARAGUS "CAPERS"

MAKES 1 PINT

4 cups water

¼ cup plus 3 tablespoons kosher salt

¾ teaspoon black peppercorns

1¼ teaspoons dried basil

1 large garlic clove, peeled

4 pounds medium asparagus, tough ends cut off

¾ cup white wine vinegar

EQUIPMENT

Juice extractor

GOES WELL WITH:

Grilled Asparagus (page 202)

You can brine and cure every kind of stem or vegetable that you could imagine, just like traditional capers. Asparagus "capers" are a great way to utilize the short Southern growing season and add a delicious salty, sour, funky note to anything from simply prepared vegetables to traditional sauces.

Bring 2 cups of the water to a boil in a small saucepan over high heat. Add ¼ cup of the salt and stir to completely dissolve it. Remove from the stove, add the peppercorns, basil, and garlic, and let them steep in the brine while it cools to room temperature, then drain the brine through a fine-mesh sieve into a large nonreactive container. Discard the solids.

While the brine is cooling, roughly chop 2 pounds of the asparagus and run it through the juice extractor. Remove the pulp and run it through the juice extractor again to extract as much juice as possible. Strain the juice into the brine and stir well to combine.

Slice the remaining asparagus into ¼-inch-thick slices. Add to the brine, cover tightly, and refrigerate for 2 days.

After 2 days, drain the asparagus and discard the brine.

Bring the remaining 2 cups water to a boil in a small saucepan over high heat. Add the remaining 3 tablespoons salt and stir until completely dissolved. Transfer the brine to a nonreactive heatproof container and cool to room temperature.

Add the asparagus to the brine, cover, and leave at room temperature for 24 hours.

Sterilize a 1-pint canning jar, along with its ring and lid (see page 246), and put it on a clean kitchen towel or a wire rack (not directly on the countertop). Drain the asparagus and add it to the jar.

Bring the vinegar to a simmer in a small saucepan and ladle it over the asparagus. Cool to room temperature, then wipe the rim and threads clean, place the lid and ring on the jar, and tighten the ring. Let stand at room temperature for 1 week, then refrigerate. Tightly sealed, the asparagus capers will keep for up to 2 months in the refrigerator.

ONION FLOWER "CAPERS"

MAKES 1 PINT

1 cup water

1 tablespoon kosher salt

2 cups onion flowers

1 tablespoon Lindera Farms
  Ramp Vinegar (see Resources,
  page 369)

EQUIPMENT

Nylon mesh (see page 246) or
  cheesecloth

GOES WELL WITH:

*Grilled Catfish with Hoppin' John
  (page 98)*

At most farms, onion flowers are mowed over and turned under, but if you're lucky, you can catch them before they're gone and get them almost free. If you brine and ferment them, you'll end up with capers with the distinctive flavor of onion that you can use anywhere you might use their more traditional Mediterranean counterparts.

NOTE: Onion flowers grow in huge clusters. Separate them from one another using sharp kitchen shears.

Bring the water to a boil in a small saucepan over high heat. Remove from the stove, add the salt, and stir until completely dissolved. Cool to room temperature.

Put the onion flowers in a clean 1-pint canning jar, add the brine, cover with nylon mesh or a double layer of cheesecloth, and screw on the rim (without the lid). Put the jar in an area with a maximum temperature of 75°F and let the onion flowers ferment until they are quite salty and pleasantly sour, about 10 days.

Remove the rim and mesh (or cheesecloth). Add the vinegar to the jar, wipe the rim and threads clean, place the lid and ring on the jar, and tighten the ring. Refrigerate the jar and allow the onion flower capers to cure for 1 month to develop flavor before eating. Tightly sealed, the onion flower capers will keep for up to 2 months in the refrigerator.

PRESERVED LEMONS

MAKES 12 PRESERVED LEMONS

2 cups sugar

2 cups kosher salt

12 lemons, washed and dried

GOES WELL WITH:

---

*Summer Melon with Country
Ham and Grilled Honey–Black
Pepper Vinaigrette (page 84)*

USE IN:

---

*Grilled Oysters with Green Garlic
Butter (page 28)*
*Baby Collards with Benne Caesar
Dressing and Cornbread
Croutons (page 80)*

The salty-sweet-sour flavor of preserved citrus might not be a staple of the Southern pantry, but I love to replicate flavors from around the globe using the bounty of the South. This recipe uses lemons, but try it with whatever fresh, beautiful citrus you have.

Combine the sugar and salt in a bowl and mix well.

Cut the lemons into quarters, stopping ½ inch from the bottom so they remain intact. Pack some of the sugar-salt mixture into the cuts in each lemon and gently press the pieces back together. Put the lemons in a plastic freezer bag and cover them with the remaining sugar-salt mixture. Seal the bag and freeze for 1 month before using. *(Kept tightly sealed in the sugar-salt mix, the lemons can be frozen for up to 1 year.)*

To use a lemon, rinse it thoroughly to remove all the salt and sugar. Scrape out all the flesh and white pith, leaving only the yellow peel; discard the flesh and pith. Thinly slice or dice the peel as specified in the recipe you are using.

HOW TO MAKE VINEGAR

Making your own vinegar might seem like a step too far for a lot of home cooks, but the truth is, it couldn't be much simpler. More than anything, it is an investment of time; patience is the most challenging ingredient. I use three basic methods for making flavored vinegars at home: infusing alcohol with my desired flavor and then fermenting it into vinegar; using a steam juicer to infuse ingredients in white vinegar; and fermenting an ingredient into alcohol and then into vinegar. The three processes range from months of time and slightly more difficult to just a few hours and easy as can be. Seasoning a vegetable with a vinegar made from that same vegetable creates a depth of flavor and complexity that can take it from ordinary to amazing. Once you've made a vinegar or two using the following methods, you'll be eyeing every possible ingredient, wondering what you can do with it.

How Vinegar Works

Almost every vinegar is the product of a simple chemical reaction. When wine is exposed to oxygen, acetobacters—or acetic acid bacteria—present in the air around us convert ethanol (alcohol) into acetic acid (vinegar) and water. As long as human beings have been fermenting ingredients into alcohol, acetobacters have been turning it into vinegar. Vinegar's ability to deliciously acidify foods played a crucial role in the development of safe, stable ways of preserving foods. We eat pickles because they're delicious, but pickling was traditionally a method of preserving fruits and vegetables.

Infusing an Existing Alcohol with Your Desired Flavor

This method is especially good for leafy ingredients. The recipe below is made with celery leaves, but you can use whatever herbaceous ingredient you like. This vinegar is made with white wine, but grain alcohol can also be used with this technique.

CELERY VINEGAR

Makes about 3 cups

One 750 ml bottle dry white wine

⅔ cup honey, preferably local

½ cup raw apple cider vinegar, such as Bragg Organic Apple Cider Vinegar

3 cups celery leaves, washed and dried

EQUIPMENT

Nylon mesh (see page 246) or cheesecloth

Sterilize a 2-quart canning jar, along with its ring and lid (see page 246), and put it on a clean dish towel or a wire rack (not directly on the countertop).

Combine the wine, honey, and vinegar in a bowl and whisk to dissolve the honey. Put the celery leaves in the bottom of the canning jar and cover with the wine mixture. Cover the jar with nylon mesh or a double layer of cheesecloth and secure it with butcher's twine, tying a tight knot.

Put the jar in a dark area with a temperature of between 70°F and 75°F and let it ferment for about 2 months. Depending on the specific conditions, the vinegar may be ready sooner or later, so I recommend tasting the mixture after about a month. If it is still alcoholic, cover again and continue to ferment. You might notice a thin, almost gelatinous layer floating on top of your vinegar; this is the "mother" and is a great sign. It indicates that a happy, healthy colony of acetobacters is hard at work on your vinegar.

When your vinegar tastes pleasantly acidic with no alcohol flavor, it's time to strain it. Remove the mother and put it in an airtight nonreactive container. Add just enough of the new vinegar to cover the mother. Seal the container tightly and store the mother in a cool, dark place. (*Tightly covered, the mother will keep for at least a year.*)

Strain the finished vinegar into a clean quart-size canning jar; discard the solids. Wipe the rim and threads clean. Place the lid and ring on the jar and tighten the ring. Tightly sealed, the celery vinegar will stay bright and flavorful for up to 1 year at room temperature.

STEAM JUICER VINEGAR

Makes about 2½ cups

The quickest and easiest method of making a flavored vinegar uses what I think is one of the coolest pieces of cooking equipment around, a steam juicer. A steam juicer is traditionally used to make jelly from fruits like grapes or apples. It works by steaming the ingredient of choice from below and collecting the concentrated juices that are released in a separate chamber of the pot. But why not use vinegar to make the steam?

3½ cups water, or as needed

2¾ cups Surig 25% Vinegar (see Resources, page 368)

3 pounds vegetables or fruits, such as cabbage or turnips, thinly sliced or chopped, depending on the ingredient

EQUIPMENT
Steam juicer

Combine the water and vinegar in the bottom of the steam juicer. Put the vegetables or fruit in the top of the juicer. Cover and bring the liquid to a boil over high heat. Reduce the heat to low and steam until most of the water and vinegar are gone, 50 to 60 minutes. Check the level of water and vinegar often to avoid scorching the bottom of the juicer, and add ½ cup more water if the level becomes very low. Remove the entire juicer from the stove and set aside to cool to room temperature. This allows for as much extraction as possible.

Drain the vinegar through the attached hose into a nonreactive container; discard the solids. Cover and store at room temperature. Tightly covered, the vinegar will keep for up to 1 year.

Making Your Own Booze and Fermenting It into Vinegar

Making vinegar from alcohol is the most traditional method, but it's also the most complicated and time-consuming one. I use the technique to make my favorite honey vinegar. The process starts with anaerobically fermenting honey and water in the presence of yeast into a honey wine, or mead. This can take up to a few months, depending on factors like temperature and whether you use commercial yeast or rely on the natural ones in the air around us.

After I make the honey wine, I ferment it into vinegar by exposing it to oxygen and, usually, adding a small amount of unpasteurized or "living" vinegar, which contains a colony of acetobacters. This vinegar mother is a floating cellulose-based structure made by the bacteria during acetic fermentation and is the best way to seed a new vinegar.

HOT SAUCE

MAKES 2 QUARTS

2½ pounds Charleston Hots or cayenne peppers, washed

5½ tablespoons coarse finishing salt, preferably J.Q. Dickinson's (see Resources, page 368)

1 tablespoon dried rice koji (see Resources, page 369)

8 cups distilled white vinegar

EQUIPMENT

1-gallon stoneware pickling crock

Cheesecloth

Nylon mesh (see page 246; optional)

GOES WELL WITH:

Everything

I use this method most summers to make a batch of hot sauce with rice koji. Koji is a grain, traditionally rice, that has been inoculated with the fungus *Aspergillus orzyae*. It is the ingredient that makes possible many traditional Japanese ingredients, from soy sauce to miso. The koji speeds up the fermentation process and helps to ensure against spoilage. It also acts like a natural thickener, creating a nicely textured hot sauce without the use of a modified starch like xanthan gum.

Remove the stems from the peppers and discard. Roughly chop the peppers. Put them in a large bowl and toss them with 3½ tablespoons of the salt.

Working in batches, transfer the peppers to a food processor and pulse until they are finely chopped but not pureed, about 10 times. Transfer the resulting mash to the pickling crock and fold in the rice. Place a square of cheesecloth on top and sprinkle the remaining 2 tablespoons salt evenly over the cheesecloth. Cover the crock with nylon mesh or a double layer of cheesecloth and secure with butcher's twine, tying a tight knot.

Put the mash in a cool area with a maximum temperature of 75°F and let it ferment for 1 month.

After 1 month, remove the mesh and lift away and discard the cheesecloth. There should be a beautiful bright red pepper mash underneath. Carefully pour the vinegar over the mash. Replace the mesh, secure it with butcher's twine, and put the hot sauce in the same cool spot to age for 2 months.

Working in batches, transfer the mash to a blender and blend on high until smooth, about 2 minutes. Strain through a fine-mesh sieve set over a container; discard the solids.

Ladle the hot sauce into two clean 1-quart canning jars. Wipe the rims and threads clean, place the lids and rings on the jars, and tighten the rings, then refrigerate. Tightly sealed, the hot sauce will keep for up to 6 months in the refrigerator.

PEPPER VINEGAR

MAKES ABOUT 1 QUART

10 ounces chili peppers, such as green or red jalapeño, cayenne, or Charleston Hot, washed

1 tablespoon plus 2¼ teaspoons coarse finishing salt, preferably J.Q. Dickinson's (see Resources, page 368)

4 cups distilled white vinegar

EQUIPMENT

Cheesecloth

Nylon mesh (see page 246; optional)

USE IN:

Cheeseburgers (page 138)
Limpin' Susan (page 184)
Bloody Mary Mix (see page 335)

Here's another way to make vinegar at home (see How to Make Vinegar, page 258). Somewhere between a traditional vinegar and hot sauce, this piquant vinegar pairs brilliantly with Southern barbecue or anything you want to add a tangy kick to.

Remove the stems from the peppers and discard. Roughly chop the peppers. Put them in a large bowl and toss them with 1 tablespoon of the salt.

Transfer the peppers to a food processor and pulse until they are finely chopped but not pureed, about 10 times. Transfer the resulting mash to a clean 2-quart canning jar. Place a square of cheesecloth on top and sprinkle the remaining 2¼ teaspoons salt evenly over the cheesecloth. Cover the jar with nylon mesh or a double layer of cheesecloth and secure with butcher's twine, tying a tight knot.

Put the mash in a cool area with a maximum temperature of 75°F and let it ferment for 1 month.

After 1 month, remove the mesh and lift away and discard the cheesecloth. There should be a beautiful bright pepper mash underneath. Carefully pour the vinegar over the mash. Cover the jar with the mesh, secure it with butcher's twine, and put the pepper vinegar in the same cool spot to age for 2 months.

Strain the vinegar through a fine-mesh sieve set over a container; discard the solids. Ladle the pepper vinegar into a clean 1-quart canning jar. Wipe the rim and threads clean, place the lid and ring on the jar, and tighten the ring, then refrigerate. Tightly sealed, the pepper vinegar will keep for up to 6 months in the refrigerator.

PEPPER MASH

MAKES 3½ CUPS

2 pounds red jalapeño or cayenne
  peppers, washed, dried, and
  stems removed

2 tablespoons kosher salt

EQUIPMENT

Round 15-inch open-top fine-mesh
  wire grill basket

Cheesecloth

Nylon mesh (see page 246;
  optional)

USE IN:

Alabama White Sauce (page 353)
Pepper Sauce (page 353)

What could be more delicious than a funky, fermented pepper mash flavored with char from the hearth? The mash can be used in a thousand and one things, from Alabama White Sauce (page 353) to Traditional Shrimp and Grits (page 61). After the fermentation, you could even pour over some distilled vinegar, age it a little longer, and make a charred hot sauce. How great does that sound?

Prepare a hot fire in a charcoal grill (see page 96), removing the grill rack and distributing the hot coals in an even layer in the bottom of the grill.

Working in batches, place the peppers in a single layer in the grill basket, place the basket directly on the coals, and char the peppers on all sides, turning them with long-handled tongs, until blackened uniformly, about 10 minutes. Remove from the grill basket and cool to room temperature.

Roughly chop the peppers and put them in a food processor. Add 1 tablespoon of the salt and pulse until the peppers are finely chopped but not pureed, about 10 times.

Transfer the mash to a clean 1-quart canning jar. Place a square cheesecloth on top of the jar and sprinkle the remaining tablespoon of salt evenly over the cheesecloth. Cover the jar with nylon mesh or a double layer of cheesecloth and secure it with butcher's twine, tying a tight knot.

Put the mash in a cool area with a maximum temperature of 75°F and let it ferment for 1 month.

After 1 month, remove the nylon mesh and lift off the cheesecloth, revealing the bright red pepper mash underneath. Transfer the mash to a clean 1-quart jar. Wipe the rim and threads clean, place the lid and ring on the jar, and tighten the ring, then refrigerate. Tightly sealed, the pepper mash will keep for up to 1 month in the refrigerator.

HOMINY MISO

MAKES 2 CUPS

1⅓ cups Anson Mills Yellow Hominy Corn (see Resources, page 368)

10½ cups water

1 teaspoon culinary lime (see box, page 213, and Resources, page 368)

1¼ cups dried rice koji (see Resources, page 369)

¼ cup plus 1 tablespoon coarse finishing salt, preferably J.Q. Dickinson's (see Resources, page 368)

Bottled spring water

EQUIPMENT

Gallon freezer bag

1-gallon stoneware pickling crock

USE IN:

Deviled Crab (page 40)
Spring Lamb with Rhubarb Butter (page 148)
Pepper Sauce (page 353)

I started playing around with making various misos and soy sauces using Southern ingredients in 2011. It was about a year after Husk had opened in Charleston, and I was starting to branch out creatively, tapping into the cuisines of other places and cultures for inspiration. I made miso out of various grains and legumes, from Sea Island red peas to green peanuts, but this hominy miso stood out. I find it so exciting to combine two of the cuisines I love the most: Southern and Japanese. Making miso at home takes some time and commitment, but it is totally worth it.

Combine the corn, 2½ cups of the water, and the culinary lime in a medium nonreactive saucepan and bring to a boil over high heat, stirring occasionally. Reduce the heat to medium and simmer, stirring occasionally, until the outer hulls of the hominy begin to soften, about 35 minutes.

Drain the hominy in a colander and rinse it very well under cold running water. Transfer to a large nonreactive saucepan, add the remaining 8 cups water, and bring to a boil over high heat. Reduce the heat to medium-low and simmer, stirring occasionally, until the hominy is soft, about 1½ hours. Drain, reserving the cooking liquid.

Working in batches if necessary, transfer the hominy to a food processor and process until smooth, about 1½ minutes, adding just enough of the reserved cooking liquid so that it processes freely. Transfer to a bowl and cool to room temperature.

Combine the koji and ¼ cup of the finishing salt in a glass bowl and gently massage together with your fingertips until well mixed. Fold the mixture into the hominy and stir to combine completely. If the mixture is too dry and crumbly, add bottled water 1 tablespoon at a time until the mixture is pasty and releases a small amount of clear liquid when pressed.

Place the mixture in the freezer bag, pushing it all the way down to the bottom to eliminate as much air as possible. Sprinkle the remaining tablespoon of finishing salt over the top of the mixture and fold the top of the bag over it, but don't seal the bag. Place the bag in the stoneware crock. Put at least 2 pounds of weight on top (a 1-quart canning jar filled with water works well). Put the crock in a dark area where the temperature will stay between 75°F and 85°F. After about 1 month, taste the miso; it should taste salty, sweet, and pleasantly savory, like a nice aged cheese.

Remove the clear liquid that has formed on top of the miso. (There will be only about 2 tablespoons of it, but you can refrigerate it for up to 6 months use as a salty seasoning, if you like.)

Working in two batches, transfer the miso to a food processor and process until smooth, about 2 minutes. Transfer to a nonreactive container with a lid. Place a piece of wax paper directly on top of the miso, to help prevent a skin from forming, then place the lid on the container and refrigerate. Tightly covered, the miso will keep for up to 6 months in the refrigerator. Check the wax paper occasionally and replace it if it has absorbed some of the liquid and become soggy.

MIXED PICKLES

MAKES 4 QUARTS

8 cups water

⅓ cup pickling salt (see Note, page 272)

1½ pounds fresh heirloom pole beans, such as greasy, cut-short, half-runner, or Turkey Craw, washed, strings removed, and broken into 1½-inch-long pieces

8 ears sweet corn, husks and silks removed

1 pound green cabbage, outer leaves removed, cored and finely chopped

1½ pounds green tomatoes, cored and cut into small dice

8 ounces banana peppers, cut into ½-inch-thick rings

EQUIPMENT

2-gallon stoneware pickling crock

Nylon mesh (see page 246) or cheesecloth

GOES WELL WITH:

Basic Cornbread (page 216)
Grilled Trout with Cornbread Puree (page 103)

The idea of mixed pickles might seem strange to a lot of people. When you hear the word *pickle*, the first thing that comes to mind is vinegar and acidity, not necessarily the funky sourness of lactic-fermented vegetables. If you read through the ingredients, they're not all that dissimilar to those for a traditional chowchow, except for the vinegar and sugar you'd expect. I love that it's a completely different way to preserve the same vegetables from the summer's bounty. It's a simple fermentation project worth every bit of the time and effort.

Put the water in a large saucepan and bring to a boil over high heat. Remove from the stove, add the pickling salt, and stir until completely dissolved. Cool to room temperature.

While the brine is cooling, put the beans in a large pot with enough water to cover and bring to a boil over high heat. Reduce the heat to maintain a simmer and cook until just tender, about 10 minutes. Drain the beans and cool to room temperature.

Bring a large pot of water to a boil over high heat. Add the corn and return to a boil, then reduce the heat to medium and cook until the corn just starts to soften, about 10 minutes. Transfer the corn to a rimmed baking sheet and cool to room temperature, then cut the kernels from the cobs.

Combine the green beans, corn kernels, cabbage, green tomatoes, and banana peppers in a large bowl and mix well, then transfer to the crock. Pour the brine over them. Weight the vegetables down with an inverted plate to help keep them submerged. Cover the crock with nylon mesh or a double layer of cheesecloth, securing it with butcher's twine, then cover with a large plate.

Put the crock in a cool area with a maximum temperature of 75°F and let it ferment until pleasantly sour, 2 to 3 weeks. Twice a week, remove the plate and mesh (or cheesecloth) and skim the top of the vegetables to remove any white scum, then replace the mesh and plate.

Drain the pickles, reserving the brine. Divide the pickles among four clean 1-quart canning jars and ladle in enough brine to fill them. Discard any extra brine. Wipe the rims and threads clean, place the lids and rings on the jars, and tighten the rings, then refrigerate. Tightly sealed, the pickles will keep for up to 3 months in the refrigerator.

BOILED PEANUT MISO

MAKES ABOUT 2 CUPS

5 pounds boiled peanuts, from
  your favorite roadside stand
  or homemade (see page 22),
  drained of any liquid

¾ cup plus 1 tablespoon dried rice
  koji (see Resources, page 369)

¼ cup plus 1 teaspoon coarse
  finishing salt, preferably J.Q.
  Dickinson's (see Resources,
  page 368)

Bottled spring water, if needed

EQUIPMENT

Gallon freezer bag

1-gallon stoneware pickling crock

USE IN:

*West African BBQ Sauce
  (see page 46)*
Groundnut Soup (page 69)

You can make this recipe with homemade or purchased boiled peanuts. If you're going to be making your own, omit the bacon from that recipe. If you're buying them from your favorite road stand, make sure they're vegetarian. The slab bacon or other animal fat sometimes used in cooking them can go rancid, ruining the miso.

Shell the boiled peanuts. Weigh out 1¼ pounds shelled peanuts and snack on any extra.

Working in batches if necessary, transfer the peanuts to a food processor and process until smooth, about 1½ minutes. Transfer to a bowl.

Combine the koji and 3 tablespoons plus 1 teaspoon of the finishing salt in a glass bowl and gently massage together with your fingertips until well mixed. Fold the mixture into the peanuts and stir to combine completely. If the mixture is too dry and crumbly, add bottled water 1 tablespoon at a time until the mixture is pasty and releases a small amount of clear liquid when pressed.

Place the mixture in the freezer bag, pushing it all the way down to the bottom to eliminate as much air as possible. Sprinkle the remaining tablespoon of finishing salt over the top of the mixture and fold the top of the bag over it, but don't seal the bag. Place the bag in the stoneware crock and put at least 2 pounds of weight on top (a 1-quart canning jar filled with water works well). Put the crock in a cool, dark area where the temperature won't exceed 75°F and let ferment for about 6 months. Taste the miso to see if it's ready; it should taste quite salty, a little sweet, and pleasantly savory, like a nice aged cheese.

Remove the clear liquid that has formed on top of the miso. (There will be only about 2 tablespoons, but you can refrigerate it for up to 6 months to use as a salty seasoning, if you like.)

Working in two batches, transfer the miso to a food processor and process until smooth, about 2 minutes. Transfer the miso to a nonreactive container with a lid. Place a piece of wax paper directly on top of the miso to help prevent a skin from forming, then place the lid on the container and refrigerate. Tightly covered, the miso will keep for up to 6 months in the refrigerator. Check the wax paper occasionally and replace it if it has absorbed some of the liquid and become soggy.

RAMP SAUERKRAUT

MAKES 1 PINT

1 pound ramps, cleaned, dried, and hairy root ends removed

1½ teaspoons coarse finishing salt, preferably J.Q. Dickinson's (see Resources, page 368)

EQUIPMENT

Disposable nitrile gloves

USE IN:

Creamed Ramps (page 158)

These funky fermented ramps are the base for the Creamed Ramps on page 158. Or roughly chop them and fold into the Potato and Ramp Puree (page 156), or try them as an unexpected addition to succotash.

Roughly chop the ramp bulbs and leaves. Combine with the salt in a nonreactive container and toss well. Transfer the mixture to a clean 1-pint canning jar, packing it in as tightly as possible. Put a nitrile glove over the mouth of the jar (or use plastic wrap) and secure it with a rubber band.

Let the ramps sit in a cool, dark place for at least 7 days to ferment. As the ramps ferment, the glove will inflate with the released gases. If after 4 days the ramps aren't completely submerged in the liquid they have released, put on nitrile gloves and push them down into the liquid. Replace the original glove on the top of the jar. When properly fermented, the ramps will be completely submerged in their own liquid and have a pleasantly sour smell.

Transfer the ramp sauerkraut to a clean 1-pint canning jar. Wipe the rim and threads clean, place the lid and ring on the jar, and tighten the ring, then refrigerate. Tightly sealed, the sauerkraut will keep for at least 2 weeks in the refrigerator.

SOUR CABBAGE

MAKES 4 QUARTS

3 medium heads green cabbage
(about 2 pounds each), with dark
green outer leaves

3 tablespoons kosher salt

EQUIPMENT

1-gallon stoneware pickling crock

Nylon mesh (see page 246) or
cheesecloth

USE IN:

*Pit-Cooked-Chicken Sandwiches
(page 130)*

There is almost always a crock of this straightforward, classic ferment going at my house. I never want to run out.

Wash and dry the cabbage. Pull off the outer leaves. Stack the leaves a few at a time, roll them into cylinders, cut them into large ribbons, and transfer to a very large bowl. Cut the heads of cabbage into quarters and remove the cores. Slice the quarters crosswise into strips about ¼ inch wide and transfer to the bowl.

Add the salt to the cabbage and toss to coat thoroughly. Transfer the mixture to the pickling crock, pressing down to get all the cabbage in. Weight the cabbage down with an inverted plate to help keep it submerged in the liquid that will be released. Cover the crock with nylon mesh or a double layer of cheesecloth, securing it with butcher's twine. Then cover the crock with a large plate.

Put the cabbage in a cool area with a maximum temperature of 75°F and let it ferment until pleasantly sour, about 2 weeks. Twice a week, remove the plate and mesh (or cheesecloth) and skim the top of the cabbage to remove any white scum, then replace the mesh and plate.

Drain the pickled cabbage, reserving the brine. Divide the cabbage among four clean 1-quart canning jars and add enough of the brine to fill them. Discard any extra brine. Wipe the rims and threads clean, place the lids and rings on the jars, and tighten the rings, then refrigerate. Tightly sealed, the cabbage will keep for up to 1 month in the refrigerator.

TURNIP FERMENT

MAKES 2 CUPS

2½ pounds purple-top turnips,
   peeled and chopped

1¾ teaspoons kosher salt

EQUIPMENT

Juice extractor

Nylon mesh (see page 246) or
   cheesecloth

USE IN:

Turnip Condiment (page 364)

Fermented juices are part of my never-ending quest to layer the flavors of my favorite vegetables all in one dish. Turnip juice was one of the first I made, but the technique works with almost any vegetable. A little juice added to a pan of braising vegetables gives them some depth and an acidic kick.

Run the turnips through the juicer. Discard the pulp and transfer 2 cups of the juice to a clean 1-quart canning jar (discard any extra juice). Add the salt and stir until completely dissolved. Cover the jar with nylon mesh or a double layer of cheesecloth and secure with butcher's twine.

Put the jar in a cool area with a maximum temperature of 75°F and let ferment until pleasantly sour, about 1 week. Remove the mesh (or cheesecloth), wipe the rim and threads clean, place the lid and ring on the jar, and tighten the ring, then refrigerate. Tightly sealed, the turnip ferment will keep for up to 1 month in the refrigerator.

SOUR CORN

MAKES 2 QUARTS

10 ears sweet corn, husks and silks removed

8 cups water

⅓ cup pickling salt (see Note)

EQUIPMENT

1-gallon stoneware pickling crock

Nylon mesh (see page 246) or cheesecloth

GOES WELL WITH:

Beeliner Snapper with Fried Peppers (page 108)

USE IN:

Sour Corn Chowchow (page 274)

Sour corn could always be found in one of those mysterious crocks that sat in the dark and musky basement at my grandma's house. I would look at it and think, "What on earth could be in there that I'd want to eat?" But when the contents of that crock hit the frying pan, I was the most eager one there.

These sour little corn kernels can be a part of many meals throughout the year. They're essentially a sauerkraut of corn, which came into Southern cuisine by way of German immigrants to the Appalachian Mountains. They used what they had on hand—in this case, corn—to get the sour flavor that reminded them of the food they had left across the ocean.

Bring a large pot of water to a boil over high heat. Add the corn and return to a boil, then reduce the heat to medium and cook until the corn just starts to soften, about 10 minutes. Transfer the corn to a rimmed baking sheet and cool to room temperature.

While the corn is cooling, combine the water and pickling salt in a bowl, stirring to completely dissolve the salt.

Cut the corn kernels off the cobs and put them in the crock, discarding the cobs. Pour the brine over the kernels and cover the crock with nylon mesh or a double layer of cheesecloth, securing it with butcher's twine. Cover the crock with a large plate.

Put the corn in a cool area with a maximum temperature of 75°F and let it ferment until pleasantly sour, about 1 week. Twice during the week, remove the plate and mesh (or cheesecloth) and skim the top of the corn to remove any white scum, then replace the mesh and plate.

Drain the sour corn, reserving the brine. Divide the corn between two clean 1-quart canning jars and add enough brine to fill them. Discard any extra brine. Wipe the rims and threads clean, place the lids and rings on the jars, and tighten the rings, then refrigerate. Tightly sealed, the corn will keep for up to 3 months in the refrigerator.

NOTE: Pickling salt is much finer than kosher salt and sea salt and is used because no heat is needed for it to dissolve quickly in water.

SOUR CORN CHOWCHOW

MAKES 3 PINTS

3 cups apple cider vinegar

¾ cup packed light brown sugar

1 tablespoon kosher salt

1½ teaspoons ground turmeric

1½ teaspoons yellow mustard seeds

¾ teaspoon celery seeds

¾ teaspoon crushed red pepper flakes

½ medium sweet onion (about 3 ounces), cut into small dice

1 red bell pepper (about 6 ounces), cored, seeded, and cut into small dice

½ hot banana pepper, cut into ½-inch pieces

½ small head green cabbage (about 12 ounces), outer leaves removed, cored and finely chopped

1½ cups small dice Pickled Green Tomatoes (page 249)

1 cup Sour Corn (page 272), drained

¼ cup yellow mustard

GOES WELL WITH:

Hominy and Pokeweed Griddle Cakes (page 211)
Fried Green Tomatoes (page 50)

Adding sour corn to a fairly traditional chowchow takes this familiar condiment in a different, delicious direction.

Sterilize three 1-quart canning jars, along with their rings and lids (see page 246), and put them on a clean dish towel or a wire rack (not directly on the countertop).

Combine the vinegar, brown sugar, and salt in a medium nonreactive pot and bring to a boil over high heat, stirring to completely dissolve the sugar and salt. Reduce the heat to medium-high and briskly simmer the mixture until reduced by half, about 20 minutes.

Add the turmeric, mustard seeds, celery seeds, and red pepper flakes and stir well. Add the onion, bell pepper, banana pepper, cabbage, and green tomatoes and cook, stirring occasionally, until the cabbage is tender, about 15 minutes. Fold in the sour corn and mustard, remove the pot from the heat, and cool completely.

Divide the chowchow among the canning jars. Wipe the rims and threads clean, place the lids and rings on the jars, and tighten the rings. Refrigerate for at least 3 days to develop the flavors before eating. Tightly sealed, the chowchow will keep for up to 2 months in the refrigerator.

NOTE: For longer storage, the chowchow can be processed according to the instructions for boiling-water canning on pages 246–47. Process for 15 minutes. Properly sealed, the jars will keep in a cool, dark place for up to 6 months; refrigerate after opening.

SCUPPERNONG VERJUS

MAKES ABOUT 1½ QUARTS

5 pounds small, tart, underripe
scuppernong grapes

½ Campden tablet (see Note and
Resources, page 369), crushed
and dissolved in 2 tablespoons
water

The best grapes for making verjus are the tart, underripe
ones you find early in the season. They are considerably
firmer than their ripe counterparts. The result is an almost
tropical flavored liquid that can be used for seasoning just
the way you would use lemon juice.

NOTE: Campden tablets, which are metabisulfites, either
sodium metabisulfite or potassium metabisulfite, are commonly used as a preservative in the winemaking process.

Working in batches, place the grapes in a blender and blend
on low to extract as much juice as possible without breaking
up the seeds or pureeing the skins. Transfer to a fine-mesh
sieve set over a bowl and press the grape mash to extract as
much juice as possible. Discard the skins and seeds.

Line a fine-mesh sieve with three layers of cheesecloth and
strain the juice into a nonreactive container. Stir the dissolved Campden tablet into the juice, cover, and leave at
room temperature for 12 hours. The juice will separate into
a clear liquid and a layer of sediment on the bottom.

Carefully ladle the clear verjus into one clean 1-quart canning jar and one clean 1-pint jar, making sure not to disturb
the layer of sediment at the bottom of the container. Wipe
the rims and threads, place the lids and rings on the jars,
and tighten the rings, then refrigerate. Tightly sealed, the
verjus will keep for up to 3 months in the refrigerator.

CANNED GREASY BEANS

MAKES 3 QUARTS

3 pounds greasy beans or cut-short, half-runner, or Turkey Craw beans, washed, strings removed, and broken into pieces about 1½ inches long

1½ teaspoons kosher salt

3 quarts water

EQUIPMENT

Pressure canner

GOES WELL WITH:

Basic Cornbread (page 216)
Strip Steak with Worcestershire (page 142)
Chicken Breasts with Black Pepper and Peanut Butter Gravy (page 120)

Picking, stringing, washing, and canning my family's haul of greasy beans each summer is one of my strongest food memories. Greasy beans are a type of pole bean so named because of their smooth, shiny pods. Pole beans epitomize the food heritage of the South, from the effort to develop and preserve special bean varieties to the necessity of putting up food. My pantry is empty if it doesn't hold at least a few jars.

Sterilize three 1-quart canning jars, along with their rings and lids (see page 246), and put them on a clean dish towel or a wire rack (not directly on the countertop).

Divide the beans among the sterilized jars and sprinkle ½ teaspoon of the salt over each of them.

Bring the water to a boil in a large saucepan over high heat. Pour boiling water into each jar, leaving a 1-inch headspace; you won't use all the water. Wipe the rims and threads clean, place the lids and rings on the jars, and finger-tighten the rings.

Set up the pressure canner according to the manufacturer's directions. At altitudes of 2,000 feet or less, process the jars at 11 pounds of pressure for 25 minutes. At above 2,000 feet, consult the canner manual for guidelines for high-altitude processing pressure and time.

When the processing is complete, turn off the heat and transfer the canner to one of the stove's turned-off burners. Let the pressure completely dissipate on its own. The pressure has dissipated only when the pressure plug has dropped and no steam is released when the pressure regulator is lifted. Wait 10 minutes after the pressure dissipates before carefully opening the canner.

Carefully remove the jars from the canner and set them on a clean dish towel or a wire rack (not directly on the countertop) to cool to room temperature.

It is important that the jars seal properly and a vacuum forms (see page 246). If any jars did not seal, store them in the refrigerator. Properly sealed, the beans will keep in a cool, dark place for up to 6 months; refrigerate after opening.

PRESERVED TOMATOES

MAKES 2 QUARTS PLUS 1 PINT

5 pounds heirloom Roma (plum) tomatoes

½ cup tomato juice or water

2 tablespoons fresh lemon juice

1½ teaspoons kosher salt

1½ teaspoons Hot Sauce (page 260) or Red Clay Original Hot Sauce (see Resources, page 369)

There are 101 uses for these tomatoes, from Lowcountry Fish-Head Stew (page 115) to a smoky, beef fat–infused condiment (see page 367). They're one of the most versatile ingredients you can stock your pantry with.

Sterilize two 1-quart canning jars and one 1-pint canning jar, along with their rings and lids (see page 246), and put them on a clean dish towel or a wire rack (not directly on the countertop).

Bring a large pot of water to a boil over high heat. Make an ice bath with equal parts ice and water in a large bowl. Working in batches, lightly score the skin on the bottom of each tomato with an X and submerge the tomatoes in the boiling water for 20 seconds. Remove and submerge them in the ice bath to cool; do not leave them in the ice bath for longer than 5 minutes. Drain. Peel the tomatoes and place in a large nonreactive pot.

Add the tomato juice, lemon juice, salt, and hot sauce to the tomatoes, cover, and heat over medium-low heat, gently stirring occasionally, until the tomatoes register an internal temperature of 180°F on an instant-read thermometer, about 20 minutes.

Using a slotted spoon, divide the tomatoes among the jars and then ladle the liquid into the jars, leaving a ½-inch headspace. Wipe the rims and threads clean, place the lids and rings on the jars, and finger-tighten the rings.

Process the jars in a boiling-water bath for 40 minutes according to the canning instructions on pages 246–47. It is important that the jars seal properly and a vacuum forms. If any jars did not seal, store them in the refrigerator. Properly sealed, the tomatoes will keep in a cool, dark place for up to 6 months; refrigerate after opening.

RHUBARB-TOMATO CONSERVE

MAKES 4 PINTS

4 pounds heirloom tomatoes

½ cup dry white wine

½ cup white wine vinegar

½ cup sugar

¼ cup minced shallots

1½ teaspoons grated fresh ginger

1 cinnamon stick

½ star anise pod

6 cups diced peeled rhubarb
(about 2 pounds stalks)

1½ teaspoons tomato vinegar
(see Resources, page 368)

1 tablespoon kosher salt

GOES WELL WITH:

---

*Cured Duck Breasts with Rice
Porridge (page 136)*
Grilled Asparagus (page 202)

Serve this condiment alongside roasted or grilled poultry, but do try it as a foil to some good sharp cheese too.

Bring a large pot of water to a boil over high heat. Make an ice bath with equal parts ice and water in a large bowl. Working in batches, lightly score the skin on the bottom of each tomato with an X and submerge the tomatoes in the boiling water for 20 seconds. Remove and submerge them in the ice bath to cool; do not leave them in the ice bath for longer than 5 minutes. Drain. Peel, halve, and seed the tomatoes and cut them into ¼-inch dice.

Combine the wine, wine vinegar, sugar, shallots, ginger, cinnamon stick, and star anise in a nonreactive pot and bring to a boil over high heat. Reduce the heat to medium and simmer until the liquid has reduced by one-third, about 5 minutes.

Increase the heat to high, gently stir in the tomatoes and rhubarb, and bring the mixture back to a boil. Continue to cook for 30 seconds, then remove from the heat. Transfer the conserve to a glass or nonreactive container and cool to room temperature, then stir in the tomato vinegar and salt.

Divide the conserve among four clean 1-pint canning jars. Wipe the rims and threads clean, place the lids and rings on the jars, and tighten the rings, then refrigerate. Tightly sealed, the conserve will keep for up to 1 month in the refrigerator.

TOMATO JAM

MAKES ABOUT 1½ PINTS

3 pounds ripe heirloom tomatoes

2 cups apple cider vinegar

1 cup packed light brown sugar

½ cup Worcestershire sauce,
   preferably Bourbon Barrel
   (see Resources, page 368)

2½ tablespoons extra-virgin
   olive oil

½ teaspoon kosher salt

¼ teaspoon ground cardamom

GOES WELL WITH:

Fried Okra (page 181)
Cheeseburgers (page 138)

USE IN:

---

*Rice-and-Shrimp Croquettes with
   Tomato Chili Sauce (page 24)*
Ol' Fuskie Crab Rice (page 58)

Just as with using bruised fruit to make a fruit butter, this tomato jam is a good way to use tomatoes that aren't perfect looking. You can get them for a great price, and cooking them down with all these sweet and sour flavors gives you an incredible result. Try the jam with a burger and fries for a change of pace.

Bring a large pot of water to a boil over high heat. Make an ice bath with equal parts ice and water in a large bowl. Working in batches, lightly score the skin on the bottom of each tomato with an X and submerge the tomatoes in the boiling water for 20 seconds. Remove and submerge them in the ice bath to cool; do not leave them in there for longer than 5 minutes. Drain the tomatoes, then peel, halve, seed, and chop them.

Combine the vinegar and brown sugar in a large non-reactive saucepan, bring to a boil over high heat, and stir to be sure the sugar has completely dissolved. Boil until reduced by half, about 7 minutes. Add the tomatoes and Worcestershire sauce and bring back to a boil. Reduce the heat to medium-low and simmer, stirring frequently, until the mixture is a dark color and very thick, about 1½ hours. Remove from the heat and cool to room temperature.

Transfer the jam to a cutting board and finely chop it. Transfer to a bowl and add the olive oil, salt, and cardamom. Stir to combine well.

Transfer the jam to two clean 1-pint canning jars. Wipe the rims and threads clean, place the lids and rings on the jars, and tighten the rings, then refrigerate. Tightly sealed, the jam will keep for up to 3 weeks in the refrigerator.

FRUIT PRESERVES

MAKES 1 PINT

1 pound fruit of your choice, such as strawberries, washed, hulled, and cut into small dice, or blueberries, washed and dried (for peach preserves, see box)

¼ cup plus 2 tablespoons sugar

¼ cup sorghum syrup, preferably Muddy Pond (see Resources, page 369)

2 tablespoons dry white wine

1 tablespoon grated lemon zest

1 tablespoon fresh lemon juice

EQUIPMENT

Candy thermometer

GOES WELL WITH:

Biscuits (page 223)

USE IN:

Fruit Preserves Hand Pies (page 316)

Most of my favorite fruits have pretty short seasons, and so I never really get my fill. Putting them up in a preserve with the rich flavor of sorghum syrup is my preferred way to enjoy them longer.

NOTE: You'll need to start this recipe a day ahead of time to macerate the fruit.

Combine all the ingredients in a nonreactive container and stir to mix well. Cover and macerate in the refrigerator for 24 hours.

Transfer the macerated fruit mixture to a small nonreactive saucepan. Place the saucepan over low heat, attach a candy thermometer to the side, and cook, stirring occasionally, until the mixture is very thick and a rich, deep color and registers 220°F on the candy thermometer, about 1 hour. Remove from the stove and cool slightly.

Meanwhile, sterilize a 1-pint canning jar, along with its ring and lid (see page 246), and put it on a clean dish towel or a wire rack (not directly on the countertop).

Ladle the hot fruit preserves into the sterilized jar, leaving a ¼-inch headspace. Wipe the rim and threads clean, place the lid and ring on the jar, and tighten the ring. Cool to room temperature, then transfer the jar to the refrigerator. Tightly sealed, the preserves will keep for up to 2 months in the refrigerator.

HOW TO MAKE PEACH PRESERVES

To make peach preserves, start with 2½ pounds large ripe peaches. Bring a large pot of water to a boil over high heat. Make an ice bath with equal parts ice and water in a large bowl. Working in batches, lightly score the skin on the bottom of each peach with an X and submerge the peaches in the boiling water for 10 seconds. Remove and submerge them in the ice bath to cool them and stop the cooking; do not leave them in the ice bath for longer than 5 minutes. Peel the peaches, cut the flesh away from the pits, and roughly chop. Proceed as directed.

WATERMELON MOLASSES

MAKES ABOUT 1 PINT

1 large ripe watermelon
(about 20 pounds)

GOES WELL WITH:

Biscuits (page 223)

USE IN:

*Heirloom Tomato and
Watermelon Salad (page 78)*

After tasting the famous Bradford watermelon (see page 78), I started experimenting with methods for making watermelon molasses, a by-product of (ultimately unsuccessful) nineteenth-century attempts to make table sugar from watermelons. After hundreds of pounds of watermelons, I came up with this recipe.

A word to the wise: This recipe is messy and requires quite an investment of time, but the result is worth it.

Cut the watermelon into manageable chunks and remove the rind, then remove any seeds (don't worry about keeping the fruit intact). Working in batches, put the watermelon in a food processor and pulse several times to extract as much liquid as you can without breaking the melon up completely.

Drain the watermelon in a large fine-mesh sieve set over a large stainless steel pot or other container, pressing lightly on the pulp. You should have about 5½ quarts juice.

Put the watermelon juice in a large saucepan and bring to a simmer over medium heat, frequently skimming off any foam that forms on the surface. Keep the juice at a gentle simmer, adjusting the heat accordingly and stirring occasionally to prevent scorching, until it has reduced by about two-thirds. Transfer the juice to a medium saucepan and continue to gently simmer, stirring occasionally, until it has reduced to about 2 cups. (Transferring it to a smaller clean saucepan at this point helps ensure that the molasses won't scorch; if you notice any browning around the edges of the saucepan, immediately transfer the molasses to another saucepan to prevent any burnt flavors.) The whole process will take 4 to 6 hours. When it's done, the watermelon molasses should be a deep crimson color and have the consistency of real maple syrup. Remove from the stove and cool for 30 minutes.

Set a clean 1-pint canning jar on a clean dish towel or a wire rack (not directly on the countertop). Transfer the watermelon molasses to the jar, wipe the rim and threads clean, place the lid and ring on the jar, and tighten the ring. Cool to room temperature, then refrigerate. Tightly sealed, the watermelon molasses will keep for up to 1 year in the refrigerator.

MUSCADINE MOLASSES

MAKES ABOUT 1 PINT

4 pounds muscadine grapes

Use grape molasses to glaze meat on the grill.

Working in batches, place the grapes in a blender and blend on low speed to extract the juice without breaking up the seeds or pureeing the skins. Transfer to a fine-mesh sieve set over a bowl and press on the grape mash to extract as much juice as possible. Discard the skins and seeds.

Transfer the juice to a large heavy-bottomed saucepan and slowly reduce it over low heat, skimming off any foam and stirring it occasionally, until it is a deep red color and as thick as maple syrup, 1½ to 2 hours. If the sides of the pan start to brown, transfer the juice to a clean saucepan and continue to reduce. Let cool for 30 minutes.

Set a clean 1-pint canning jar on a dish towel or a wire rack. Transfer the molasses to the jar, wipe the rim and threads clean, place the lid and ring on the jar, and tighten the ring. Cool to room temperature, then refrigerate. Tightly sealed, the molasses will keep for up to 2 months in the refrigerator.

RHUBARB BUTTER

MAKES 2 PINTS

2½ pounds rhubarb, trimmed and chopped

½ cup water

1⅔ cups sugar

1 teaspoon ground sumac (see Resources, page 369)

¼ teaspoon ground cinnamon

¼ teaspoon ground nutmeg

Use this method to preserve any fruit.

Combine the rhubarb and water in a large nonreactive pot, cover, and cook over medium-low heat, stirring occasionally, until the rhubarb is very soft, about 1½ hours.

Add the sugar and spices, cover, and cook over medium-low heat, stirring frequently, until very thick, about 2 hours. Remove from the heat, uncover, and cool.

Transfer the rhubarb butter to a blender and blend on high until completely smooth, about 1 minute. Transfer the rhubarb butter to two clean 1-pint canning jars. Wipe the rims and threads clean, place the lids and rings on the jars, and tighten the rings, then refrigerate. Tightly sealed, the rhubarb butter will keep for up to 2 months in the refrigerator.

BOUDIN

MAKES 3 CUPS

RICE

½ cup Anson Mills Carolina Gold Rice (see Resources, page 368)

1 cup water

½ teaspoon kosher salt

BOUDIN

10 ounces boneless, skinless chicken breasts, cut into 1-inch cubes

1½ cups Chicken Stock (page 344)

2 tablespoons Rendered Fresh Chicken Fat (page 342)

4 ounces chicken livers, drained, rinsed, and cut into small dice

¼ cup fine dice sweet onion

¼ cup fine dice celery

½ jalapeño pepper, seeded and diced

1 teaspoon minced garlic

¼ cup chopped scallions

¼ cup chopped flat-leaf parsley

2¼ teaspoons kosher salt

1 teaspoon Aleppo pepper (see Resources, page 369)

¾ teaspoon freshly ground black pepper

¾ teaspoon freshly ground white pepper

⅛ teaspoon TCM (see box, page 293, and Resources, page 368)

⅛ teaspoon chili powder

1 tablespoon Hot Sauce (page 260) or Red Clay Original Hot Sauce (see Resources, page 369)

EQUIPMENT

Meat grinder

This boudin is a riff on the Cajun classic, made with chicken instead of pork. Eat boudin by itself on crackers, or stuff it into a casing, grill, and serve with some spicy mustard or hot sauce. Any boudin left over from dinner can be shaped into patties and fried up like breakfast sausage the next morning. It also makes an excellent stuffing for grilled quail.

FOR THE RICE: Combine the rice, water, and salt in a small saucepan and bring to a boil over medium-high heat. Reduce the heat to low, cover, and simmer the rice until it is soft and all the water has been absorbed, about 12 minutes. Transfer the rice to a rimmed baking sheet, spread it out, and cool to room temperature, then transfer 1½ cups of the rice to a large bowl (refrigerate any extra rice for another use).

FOR THE BOUDIN: Combine the chicken breasts and stock in a saucepan, cover, and simmer over medium heat until the chicken is just cooked through, about 10 minutes. Transfer the chicken to a small bowl and refrigerate until completely cold. Reserve the stock in the saucepan.

Heat the chicken fat in a large heavy-bottomed skillet over medium heat until it shimmers. Add the chicken livers, onion, celery, jalapeño, garlic, scallions, and parsley and cook, stirring frequently, until the livers are cooked through and the vegetables are translucent, about 5 minutes. Spread the mixture out on a plate and refrigerate until cold.

Reheat the reserved chicken stock over low heat.

Grind the chicken breast and liver mixture together through the large die of the meat grinder and add it to the rice. Add the salt, Aleppo pepper, black pepper, white pepper, TCM, chili powder, and hot sauce and mix well. Slowly add about ¼ cup of the warm stock, mixing in just enough stock to give the boudin a stuffing-like consistency.

Cool the boudin to room temperature, cover, and refrigerate until ready to serve. Tightly covered, the sausage will keep for up to 3 days in the refrigerator.

BOLOGNA

MAKES TWO 1½-POUND SAUSAGES

¼ cup plus 1½ teaspoons nonfat
   dry milk powder

1 tablespoon kosher salt

1¼ teaspoons phosphate
   (see Resources, page 368)

1¾ teaspoons Bourbon Barrel
   Bourbon Smoked Paprika
   (see Resources, page 368)

½ teaspoon plus ⅛ teaspoon
   Cure #2 (see Resources,
   page 368)

1 teaspoon monosodium glutamate
   (see Resources, page 368)

1¼ teaspoons onion powder

1¼ teaspoons freshly ground white
   pepper

1 teaspoon mustard powder

⅛ teaspoon sodium erythorbate
   (see Resources, page 368)

Scant ½ teaspoon ground nutmeg

¼ teaspoon ground mace

1½ pounds lean beef

1 pound pork shoulder

1¾ ounces bacon, preferably
   Benton's (see Resources,
   page 368)

⅓ cup plus 2 teaspoons ice water

2 summer sausage casings (2.9 by
   20 inches: see Resources, page
   368), soaked in lukewarm water
   for 30 minutes

EQUIPMENT

Meat grinder

Stand mixer with sausage stuffer
   attachment

I'm not going to sugarcoat this: It takes a lot of effort to make bologna. It takes a lot of practice, too, and you're probably going to mess up the first few, but saying that you make your own bologna can be an incredible source of pride. Once you get it right, you'll never want to buy bologna again.

Combine the milk powder, salt, phosphate, paprika, Cure #2, monosodium glutamate, onion powder, white pepper, mustard powder, sodium erythorbate, nutmeg, and mace in a bowl and mix thoroughly. Set aside.

Grind the beef, pork, and bacon separately through the large die of the meat grinder into a bowl. Then combine the meats and run them through the grinder again into another bowl. Cover and refrigerate while you clean the grinder of any sinew and wash it under cold water.

Grind the meat mixture once more through the large die. Transfer the mixture to the bowl of the stand mixer fitted with the paddle attachment. Add the spice mixture and mix on low speed until combined, about 1 minute. With the mixer running, slowly add the ice water to form a smooth paste. Scraping down the sides as needed, mix the bologna until the friction from mixing causes the temperature of the meat mixture to rise and it registers 57°F on an instant-read thermometer, about 1 minute.

Preheat the oven to 300°F. Fill a 12-by-20-by-3-inch roasting pan with enough water to completely submerge the bologna and place the pan in the oven.

Divide the meat mixture in half. Using the sausage stuffer attachment, stuff half the meat mixture into each of the casings, then remove as much air as possible and tie off the ends with a double knot of butcher's twine.

Put the bologna in the roasting pan, making sure it is completely submerged in the water; add more hot water if needed. Cook the bologna for about 1 hour, until it registers an internal temperature of 165°F on an instant-read thermometer.

Just before the bologna has finished cooking, make an ice bath with equal parts water and ice in a bowl large enough to hold both sausages. Submerge the cooked bologna in the ice bath until completely cold.

Remove the bologna from the ice bath, pat dry, place on a rimmed baking sheet, and refrigerate until cold before serving. The bologna can be sliced and served as soon as it is cold, but it is better after being refrigerated overnight. Uncut in the casings or tightly wrapped after cutting, the bologna will keep for up to 1 week in the refrigerator.

VENISON SUMMER SAUSAGE

MAKES TWO 1½-POUND SAUSAGES

½ cup nonfat dry milk powder

1 tablespoon plus 1¼ teaspoons kosher salt

1 tablespoon corn syrup solids (see Resources, page 368)

2¾ teaspoons dextrose (see Resources, page 368)

2 teaspoons Bourbon Barrel Bourbon Smoked Paprika (see Resources, page 368)

1¾ teaspoons phosphate (see Resources, page 368)

1½ teaspoons mustard seeds, crushed

1¼ teaspoons freshly ground white pepper

¾ teaspoon TCM (see box and Resources, page 368)

½ teaspoon ascorbic acid (see Resources, page 369)

¼ teaspoon celery seeds

¼ teaspoon ground coriander

⅛ teaspoon ground nutmeg

2½ pounds boneless lean venison, very cold

1 pound pork fat, cut into ½-inch pieces, very cold

Scant ½ teaspoon minced garlic

2 summer sausage casings (2.9 by 20 inches: see Resources, page 368), soaked in lukewarm water for 30 minutes

EQUIPMENT

Meat grinder

Stand mixer with sausage stuffer attachment

Smoker

Venison sausage is an homage to my childhood, when the arrival of whitetail season each year always meant this smoky sausage wasn't far off.

Combine the milk powder, salt, corn syrup solids, dextrose, paprika, phosphate, mustard seeds, white pepper, TCM, ascorbic acid, celery seeds, coriander, and nutmeg in a bowl and mix thoroughly. Set aside.

Combine the venison and pork fat and run the mixture through the large die of the meat grinder into a bowl. Cover and refrigerate while you clean the grinder of any sinew and wash it in cold water.

Grind the meat mixture once more through the large die. Transfer the mixture to the bowl of the stand mixer fitted with the paddle attachment. Add the spice mixture and mix on low speed until combined, about 1 minute. With the mixer running, add the garlic and combine. Transfer the meat mixture to a container, cover with plastic wrap, pressing it directly against the mixture, and refrigerate for 24 hours.

About 30 minutes before you're ready to cook the sausage, preheat the oven to 300°F. Fill a 12-by-20-by-3-inch roasting pan with enough hot water to completely submerge the sausages and place the pan in the oven.

Divide the meat mixture in half. Using the sausage stuffer attachment, stuff half the mixture into each of the casings, then remove as much air as possible and tie off the ends with a double knot of butcher's twine.

Put the sausages in the roasting pan, making sure they are completely submerged in the water; add additional hot water if needed. Cook them for about 1 hour, until they register an internal temperature of 165°F on an instant-read thermometer.

Just before the sausages have finished cooking, make an ice bath with equal parts water and ice in a bowl large enough to hold both of them. Submerge the cooked sausages in the ice bath until completely cold. Drain, pat them dry, place on a rimmed baking sheet, and refrigerate for at least 2 hours and up to 4 hours.

Prepare the smoker for cold smoking with hardwood charcoal and hickory (see page 57); maintain a temperature of between 75°F and 90°F.

Smoke the sausages for 4 hours. Remove the sausages from the smoker, transfer to a rimmed baking sheet, and cool to room temperature; wrap with plastic wrap and refrigerate for 24 hours before slicing. Uncut in the casing or tightly wrapped after cutting, the summer sausage will keep for up to 2 weeks in the refrigerator.

TCM

TCM, or pink curing salt, is a preservative that keeps meat from oxidizing. It's 94 percent salt and 6 percent sodium nitrite. The nitrite helps prevent the growth of botulinum toxin. It's important to follow the amounts specified precisely; an accidental overdose of TCM would not be good for you. In fact, it's colored pink so it won't be mistaken for table salt.

PICKLED PIG'S FEET

MAKES 3 PICKLED PIG'S FEET

PIG'S FEET

Kosher salt

3 pig's feet (about 1 pound each), split lengthwise in half and rinsed under cold running water

1 fresh bay leaf

3 thyme sprigs

PICKLING LIQUID

4 cups distilled white vinegar

2 cups water

1 cup sugar

3 tablespoons kosher salt

2 tablespoons crushed red pepper flakes

1 tablespoon cayenne pepper

1 tablespoon Bourbon Barrel Bourbon Smoked Black Peppercorns (see Resources, page 368)

1 tablespoon yellow mustard seeds

1½ teaspoons Bourbon Barrel Bourbon Smoked Paprika (see Resources, page 368)

1 teaspoon celery seeds

1 teaspoon minced garlic

3 fresh bay leaves

½ sweet onion (about 3 ounces), thinly sliced

Let's face it: You may feel that eating one of those pickled pig's feet from a jar perched on the counter of an out-there convenience store seems like a high-risk venture. But make them yourself with high-quality ingredients, and the risk becomes reward. I love to finely dice the meat and fold it into a pot of beans or slow-cooked greens.

Sterilize three 1-quart canning jars, along with their rings and lids (see page 246), and put them on a clean dish towel or a wire rack (not directly on the countertop).

FOR THE PIG'S FEET: Bring a large pot of salted water to a boil over high heat. Add the pig's feet, bay leaf, and thyme, reduce the heat to medium-low, and simmer until the pig's feet are tender and offer no resistance when pierced with a knife in the meatiest part of the foot, about 2 hours. Drain the feet in a colander and rinse under cool running water to remove any fat and impurities. Discard the bay leaf and thyme.

While the feet are still slightly warm, use your hands to remove any bones that pull away easily. Get as many as you can, but do not cut into the feet with a knife, because you want to maintain their shape. Transfer the feet to the canning jars, putting 2 halves in each jar.

FOR THE PICKLING LIQUID: Combine all the ingredients in a large nonreactive saucepan and bring to a simmer over medium heat, stirring to completely dissolve the sugar and salt. Reduce the heat to medium-low and simmer for 20 minutes to develop the flavors.

Divide the hot pickling liquid among the jars, leaving a ½-inch headspace. Wipe the rims and threads clean and cool to room temperature.

Place the lids and rings on the jars, tighten the rings, and refrigerate for 1 week to allow the pig's feet to cure before serving. Tightly sealed, the pig's feet will keep for up to 1 month in the refrigerator.

CRAB ROE BOTTARGA

MAKES ONE 12-OUNCE PIECE

8 ounces blue crab roe, carefully picked over for shells and cartilage

12 large egg yolks

1 summer sausage casing (2.9 by 20 inches; see Resources, page 368)

4 cups kosher salt, plus more as needed

USE IN:

Grilled Oysters with Green Garlic Butter (page 28)
Ol' Fuskie Crab Rice (page 58)
She-Crab Soup (page 73)

Crab roe bottarga lets you push the fresh blue crab roe season out a little longer. This recipe came about because I wanted to grate a little cured egg yolk over a she-crab soup to get an added layer of richness. Then I realized I could combine the egg yolk with the sweet crab roe and preserve that flavor for use throughout the year, until the next roe season came around.

NOTE: Blue crab roe is available in some seafood markets and from online sources (including Charleston Seafood; see Resources, page 368).

Pictured on the following page

Combine the roe and egg yolks in a food processor and process until completely combined, about 1 minute.

Using a funnel, slowly pour the roe mixture into the casing. Lightly tap the side of the casing to remove air bubbles. Cut off any excess casing about 3 inches above the mixture and tie the end off tightly with a double knot of butcher's twine.

Pour 2 cups of the salt into the bottom of an 8-by-6-by-4-inch glass loaf pan or other nonreactive container. Add the bottarga and cover with the remaining 2 cups salt. Refrigerate, uncovered, for 3 days.

Remove the bottarga from the salt and wipe away any salt from its surface. Attach a length of butcher's twine to the bottarga just below the knot at the top of the casing and hang the bottarga in the refrigerator, making sure it hangs freely and doesn't touch anything; it's important to have good air circulation around it. Place a bowl filled with kosher salt underneath the bottarga to catch any drippings and absorb odors. Let the bottarga hang for 7 to 10 days, making sure the temperature stays below 40°F. The bottarga will lose moisture and the texture will become firmer.

Transfer the bottarga to a container, cover, and refrigerate for up to 1 month.

DRIED OYSTERS

MAKES 12 DRIED OYSTERS

1¼ cups water

1 tablespoon kosher salt

12 fresh oysters

EQUIPMENT

Dehydrator

USE IN:

*Potlikker-Steamed Sea Bass with
Corn Dodgers (page 112)
Cooked greens (see page 177)*

Dried oysters are traditionally used in West African meat dishes such as lamb stew. They can be found everywhere in the market stalls of Dakar, sold alongside a huge variety of salted and dried seafood from the coastal waters, like sea snails, conch, catfish, shrimp, and clams. This simple technique for drying gives the oyster an umami blast along with the deep, oceanic flavor of a roasted oyster. Add them to flavor any sort of potlikker or broth or grate them over a dish for an intense, in-your-face seafood taste.

Pictured on the preceding page

Bring the water to a boil in a small saucepan over high heat, then remove it from the stove, add the salt, and stir until completely dissolved. Pour the brine into a nonreactive heat-proof container large enough to hold the oysters and cool to room temperature, then refrigerate until completely cold.

When the brine is cold, shuck the oysters (discard the liquor and shells). Add the oysters to the cold brine, cover, and refrigerate for 12 hours.

Transfer the oysters to the dehydrator tray and dehydrate at 145°F until they are completely dried out and have turned a deep brown color, about 12 hours. Transfer to an airtight container, cover, and store in a cool, dry place for up to 1 month.

CURED EGG YOLKS

MAKES 12 CURED YOLKS

1¾ cups plus 2 tablespoons
    kosher salt

½ cup plus 2 tablespoons sugar

12 large eggs yolks

Curing egg yolks is a simple way to use up an abundance of farm-fresh eggs and put a savory, rich flavor into your pantry. Grate them over anything from salads and egg dishes to creamy grits.

Mix the salt and sugar together in a bowl. Spread half the mixture in the bottom of a 9-by-12-inch glass baking dish. Make 12 equal indentations in the mixture to hold the yolks. Carefully place a yolk in each indentation and then carefully cover them with the remaining salt-sugar mixture. Cover and refrigerate for 7 days.

After 7 days, brush as much of the salt mixture off the yolks as possible. Lay a 26-by-8-inch double layer of cheesecloth out on a clean work surface. Arrange the yolks on it in a line, leaving space between them. Roll up the yolks in the cheesecloth. Using butcher's twine, knot the cheesecloth between the yolks as if you were tying off sausage links and knot the ends.

Tie a length of butcher's twine to one end of the roll and hang it in your pantry or another cool, enclosed area for 1 week.

After 1 week, remove the yolks from the cheesecloth and place them in an airtight container between layers of parchment paper. Cover tightly and store at room temperature or in a cool, dry place for up to 2 months.

DESSERTS

BLACKBERRY COBBLER

SERVES 8

FILLING

¼ cup plus 2 tablespoons sugar

2 tablespoons all-purpose flour

¼ teaspoon ground cinnamon

¼ teaspoon ground ginger

2 pounds (4 cups) cultivated or wild blackberries (see Note), washed and dried

1 tablespoon fresh lemon juice

¼ teaspoon vanilla extract

TOPPING

1 cup plus 2 tablespoons all-purpose flour, plus more for rolling out the dough

3 tablespoons granulated sugar

½ teaspoon baking powder

Scant ½ teaspoon kosher salt

4 tablespoons unsalted butter, diced and refrigerated

½ large egg, lightly beaten

¼ cup plus 1 tablespoon full-fat buttermilk (see Note, page 27)

1 tablespoon Demerara sugar

1 recipe Hickory-Smoked Ice Cream (page 339)

GOES WELL WITH:

Beeliner Snapper with Fried Peppers (page 108)

Blackberry cobbler was *the* summer dessert in my grandma's kitchen. She used to pay us by the gallon to pick wild blackberries, so we'd jump in the car and drive to the secret patches only we knew about. We could pick blackberries just a couple of times each year, so we cherished the cobbler when she whipped one up—there's a real luxury in having enough ripe wild blackberries to make a big cobbler.

This is a flexible dessert. You can substitute an equal weight of your favorite berry, or a mix. And I love it with the Hickory-Smoked Ice Cream, but you could serve it with high-quality vanilla ice cream or just heavy cream for drizzling.

NOTE: Wild blackberries will require a little extra sugar. Taste the fruit mixture and adjust as necessary.

FOR THE FILLING: Combine the sugar, flour, cinnamon, and ginger in a small bowl and mix well.

Combine the blackberries, lemon juice, and vanilla in a large saucepan and stir well. Stir in the dry ingredients and cook the mixture over medium-low heat, stirring occasionally, until the blackberries release their juices, 12 to 15 minutes. Pour the blackberries into a 3-inch-deep 9-inch round baking dish and set aside to cool while you make the topping.

FOR THE TOPPING: Preheat the oven to 350°F.

Combine the flour, granulated sugar, baking powder, and salt in a large bowl. Add the butter and cut it in with your fingertips until the mixture resembles coarse cornmeal. Add the egg and ¼ cup of the buttermilk and stir just until a dough begins to form. Turn the dough out onto a lightly floured surface. Using a lightly floured rolling pin, roll the dough out to a 9-inch circle about ¼ inch thick. Carefully roll the dough up around the rolling pin and unroll it over the blackberry mixture in the baking dish.

Lightly brush the topping with the remaining tablespoon of buttermilk and sprinkle with the Demerara sugar.

Bake the cobbler for 40 to 45 minutes, rotating it halfway through, until the filling is bubbling and the topping is crisp and golden brown. Remove the cobbler from the oven, cool for 5 minutes, and serve with scoops of hickory-smoked ice cream. Any leftover cobbler can be cooled, tightly covered, and stored for up to 3 days in the refrigerator. Before serving, uncover the cobbler and reheat it at 350°F.

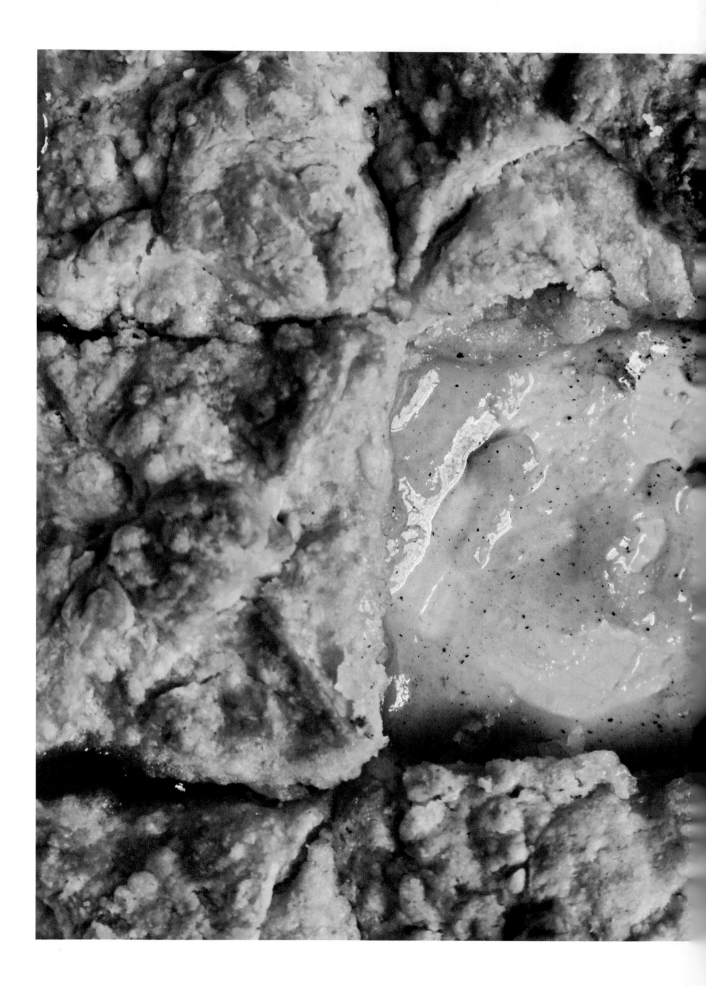

ELDERBERRY DUMPLINGS

with Grapefruit Crème Anglaise

MAKES 9 DUMPLINGS

SYRUP

2 cups sugar

2 cups water

¼ teaspoon ground cinnamon

¼ teaspoon ground nutmeg

4 tablespoons unsalted butter, diced

2 tablespoons fresh lemon juice

DUMPLINGS

2 tablespoons unsalted butter, finely diced and refrigerated, plus more for the pan

2 teaspoons sugar

1 tablespoon grated lemon zest

1½ cups elderberries, washed and dried

2 cups all-purpose flour, plus more for rolling out the dough

2 teaspoons baking powder

1 teaspoon kosher salt

¾ cup Rendered Fresh Lard (page 343)

½ cup whole milk

¼ cup fresh elderflowers, washed and dried (optional)

1 recipe Grapefruit Crème Anglaise (recipe follows)

GOES WELL WITH:

Pork Shoulder Steak with Grilled Mushrooms (page 141)

The original recipe for these tender, flavorful dumplings, filled with fruit and baked in a spiced syrup, hails from West Virginia. That recipe used Spry, a vegetable shortening, and the dumplings were filled with sliced June apples or ripe peaches. I've tweaked the recipe a bit, replacing the shortening with lard and the apples with foraged elderberries. You can use any fruit you'd like, from the original apples or peaches to blueberries, in lieu of the elderberries, which are very seasonal and can be tough to track down. Serve the dumplings with the rich but bright grapefruit anglaise sauce, or simply with scoops of vanilla ice cream.

FOR THE SYRUP: Combine the sugar, water, cinnamon, and nutmeg in a medium saucepan and bring to a simmer over medium heat, stirring to dissolve the sugar completely. Remove from the stove, stir in the butter and lemon juice, and set aside at room temperature.

FOR THE DUMPLINGS: Preheat the oven to 375°F. Butter an 8-inch-square baking dish.

Combine the sugar and lemon zest in a large bowl, add the elderberries, and gently toss to coat. Set aside to macerate while you make the dough.

Sift the flour, baking powder, and salt into a large bowl and mix well. Cut in the lard with two forks (or your grandma's pastry cutter) until the pieces are the size of peas. Add the milk all at once and stir until the dough is moistened and just starting to come together.

Turn the dough out onto a lightly floured work surface. Lightly flour a rolling pin and roll the dough into a 7½-inch square about ¼ inch thick. Cut the dough into nine 2½-inch squares. Dot the squares with the diced butter and divide the elderberries among them, spooning them into the center of each square. Moisten the edges of the squares with water and bring the dough up around the elderberries to form square packets, crimping the edges together with your fingers to seal.

Arrange the dumplings in the prepared baking dish and pour the syrup over them. Bake for 35 to 45 minutes, until the dumplings have puffed and the exposed tops are evenly golden brown. Remove from the oven and cool for 10 minutes before serving.

Sprinkle the dumplings with the elderflowers, if using, and offer the grapefruit crème anglaise on the side. Any leftover dumplings can be cooled to room temperature; transferred to a container, along with their syrup; covered; and refrigerated for up to 4 days. Reheat in a 350°F oven before serving.

NOTE: You can make the dumplings ahead so they are easy to enjoy anytime. Assemble them as directed (wait to make the syrup). Chill the uncooked dumplings on a baking sheet until firm, then transfer to a covered container and freeze them. When you're ready to serve them, simply make the syrup, pull out as many dumplings as you want to bake, arrange them in a buttered baking dish, and pour the syrup over them. Bake at 375°F as directed. Your guests will think you've been toiling away all day.

GRAPEFRUIT CRÈME ANGLAISE

MAKES ABOUT 3 CUPS

6 large egg yolks

½ cup sugar

2 cups whole milk

2 tablespoons grated grapefruit zest

Whisk the egg yolks and sugar together in a medium bowl until completely combined. Set aside.

Heat the milk in a small saucepan over medium heat, stirring often so that it doesn't scorch, for 3 to 5 minutes, until the temperature registers 150°F on an instant-read thermometer. Remove the saucepan from the heat. While whisking constantly, slowly stream ½ cup of the hot milk into the egg-sugar mixture to temper the yolks. Whisk in the remaining ½ cup milk. Transfer the tempered yolk mixture back to the saucepan and heat over medium heat, stirring often so that it doesn't scorch, until it registers 180°F, 2 to 3 minutes.

Strain the crème anglaise through a fine-mesh sieve into a heatproof container. Stir in the grapefruit zest.

Make an ice bath with equal parts ice and water in a large bowl. Put the container of crème anglaise in the ice bath to chill and stir occasionally, being careful not to let any water get into the crème anglaise, until it is completely cold. Cover and refrigerate overnight before serving. Tightly covered, the crème anglaise will keep for up to 3 days in the refrigerator.

MAGNOLIA VINEGAR AND BROWN BUTTER PIE

SERVES 8

1 recipe Flaky Piecrust dough (recipe follows), chilled

2 tablespoons all-purpose flour, plus more for rolling out the dough

8 tablespoons (1 stick) unsalted butter

1 cup sugar

¾ cup water

3 large eggs

3 tablespoons Lindera Farms Magnolia Vinegar (see Resources, page 369) or apple cider vinegar

1 tablespoon grated lemon zest

Vinegar and butter pie is a really old tradition in the South. You hardly ever see the pie served in restaurants, but it is certainly a favorite in many a grandmother's kitchen. It's a perfect dessert for the winter when good fresh fruits are hard to find.

This is my spin on the classic. Browning the butter and using magnolia vinegar give the simple pie an unexpected floral taste. Substitute a good-quality apple cider vinegar if you can't get magnolia vinegar.

Preheat the oven to 350°F.

If the dough has been refrigerated overnight, let it soften a little at room temperature before rolling it out. Place the dough on a lightly floured work surface. Lightly flour your rolling pin and start rolling the dough gently from the center out. Do this a few times, then pick up the dough, rotate it a quarter turn, and roll again. Continue to roll, rotating the dough and flouring the work surface and the dough as needed, until you have a 12-inch circle approximately ⅛ inch thick.

Loosely fold the dough into quarters and unfold it in a 9-inch pie pan. Gently fit it into the bottom and up the sides of the pan. Trim the dough, leaving an overhang of about ½ inch around the edges. Fold the excess under and crimp the edges: With one hand on the inside of the rim and the other hand on the outside, use the index finger of your inside hand to push the dough between the thumb and index finger of your outside hand to form a V shape. Repeat all around the rim. Refrigerate the crust for 10 minutes.

Line the crust with parchment paper and fill it with an even layer of dried beans or pie weights. Place the crust on a rimmed baking sheet and bake for 15 minutes. Remove the crust from the oven and remove the beans or weights and the parchment. Prick the bottom of the crust a few times with a fork. Return it to the oven and bake for about 20 minutes more, until it is golden brown and appears baked. Cool completely before filling.

Heat the butter in a small saucepan over medium heat, stirring, until it is golden brown and starts to smell slightly nutty, about 9 minutes. Strain the butter through a fine-mesh

sieve into a small bowl and set aside. Discard the solids. You'll need 2 tablespoons of brown butter for this recipe. (It's difficult to make a smaller amount of brown butter successfully; the extra butter can be used for a simple dish of pasta with butter, drizzled over eggs, served with seared fish, or employed in myriad other ways.) Transfer the rest to a container, cool to room temperature, cover, and refrigerate. (Tightly covered, the brown butter will keep for up to 2 weeks in the refrigerator.)

Combine the sugar, water, eggs, vinegar, and flour in the top of a double boiler and whisk to mix well. Fill the bottom of the double boiler with water, set over low heat, and insert the top. The water should not touch the bottom of the top and should never be hotter than a simmer. Cook the mixture, whisking frequently, until it is thickened and smooth and registers 180°F on an instant-read thermometer, about 45 minutes. Remove from the stove and stir in the 2 tablespoons brown butter and the lemon zest.

Pour the filling into the prepared piecrust and refrigerate for at least 6 hours or up to overnight to set before serving.

Slice the pie and serve chilled. Tightly cover any leftovers and refrigerate for up to 3 days.

FLAKY PIECRUST

**MAKES ENOUGH DOUGH FOR
1 SINGLE-CRUST 9-INCH PIE OR
10-INCH DEEP-DISH PIE**

1¼ cups all-purpose flour,
  plus more for the work surface

1 teaspoon kosher salt

10 tablespoons (1¼ sticks)
  unsalted butter, diced and
  refrigerated

¼ cup ice water

Combine the flour and salt in a medium bowl. Add the butter and, using your fingers, cut the butter into the flour mixture until the pieces are about the size of small peas. Drizzle in the ice water, mixing it in with your hands until the dough just comes together.

Turn the dough out onto a lightly floured work surface and gather it into a ball. You should still see pieces of butter, and you want to work quickly to keep the butter cold. Flatten the dough into a disk about 1 inch thick, wrap in plastic wrap, and let rest in the refrigerator for at least 1 hour or up to overnight before using. Wrapped in plastic wrap, the dough will keep for up to 3 days in the refrigerator. Stored in a freezer bag, the wrapped disk of dough can be frozen for up to 3 months. Thaw it in the refrigerator and let it soften a little before rolling it out.

BUTTERMILK PIE

SERVES 8

1 recipe Flaky Piecrust dough
  (page 309), chilled

¼ cup all-purpose flour, plus more
  for rolling out the dough

1½ cups sugar

½ teaspoon kosher salt

3 large eggs, at room temperature

4 tablespoons unsalted butter,
  melted

¼ teaspoon grated lemon zest

2 teaspoons fresh lemon juice

¾ cup full-fat buttermilk (see Note,
  page 27)

1 vanilla bean

GOES WELL WITH:

*Chicken Breasts with Black
  Pepper and Peanut Butter
  Gravy (page 120)*

Buttermilk ranks right up there with sorghum as one of my favorite Southern ingredients. Whether as a drink, as part of cornbread, or as the star of this pie, I can never get my fill. I've made a lot of chess pies, shoo-fly pies, and vinegar pies, but when I finally worked out this recipe, I knew I'd found the perfect buttermilk pie. I love how easy it is to make the filling: no precooking, just mix it together and into the pie shell it goes.

NOTE: Scraped vanilla bean pods can have a second life. Submerge them in a jar of sugar or salt to flavor it, or steep in syrups or poaching liquids.

Preheat the oven to 350°F.

If the dough has been refrigerated overnight, let it soften a little at room temperature before rolling it out. Place the dough on a lightly floured work surface. Lightly flour your rolling pin and start rolling the dough gently from the center out. Do this a few times, then pick up the dough, rotate it a quarter turn, and roll again. Continue to roll, rotating the dough and flouring the work surface and the dough as needed, until you have a 12-inch circle approximately ⅛ inch thick.

Loosely fold the dough into quarters and unfold it in a 10-inch pie pan. Gently fit it into the bottom and up the sides of the pan. Trim the dough, leaving an overhang of about ½ inch around the edges. Fold the excess under and crimp the edges: With one hand on the inside of the rim and the other hand on the outside, use the index finger of your inside hand to push the dough between the thumb and index finger of your outside hand to form a V shape. Repeat all around the rim. Refrigerate the crust for 10 minutes.

Line the crust with parchment paper and fill it with an even layer of dried beans, uncooked rice, or pie weights. Place the crust on a rimmed baking sheet and bake for 15 minutes. Remove the crust from the oven and remove the beans, rice, or weights and the parchment. Prick the bottom of the crust a few times with a fork. Return it to the oven and bake for about 20 minutes, until it is golden brown and appears fully baked. Cool completely before filling.

Put the flour, sugar, and salt in a small bowl and whisk to combine. Whisk the eggs in a medium bowl until blended.

Add the flour mixture and whisk to combine. Add the butter, lemon zest, and lemon juice and whisk well. Add the buttermilk and whisk well.

Split the vanilla bean lengthwise in half and, using the back of a paring knife, scrape out the seeds (see Note). Add the seeds to the filling and whisk to combine.

Place the crust on a rimmed baking sheet. Gently pour the filling into the crust. Bake for 40 to 45 minutes, until the custard is set and no longer jiggles in the center when the pan is gently shaken. Let the pie cool to room temperature on a baking rack, then refrigerate it for at least 2 hours before serving.

Bring the pie to room temperature, slice, and serve. Any leftover pie can be tightly wrapped and stored for up to 3 days in the refrigerator.

PEANUT BUTTER CHESS PIE

SERVES 8

CRUST

1 recipe Chocolate Cornmeal Crust dough (recipe follows), chilled, plus flour for rolling it out

FILLING

2 tablespoons unsalted butter, diced, at room temperature

½ cup creamy peanut butter

2¼ cups sugar

1 tablespoon unsweetened cocoa powder

¾ teaspoon kosher salt

¾ cup whole milk

4 large eggs, lightly beaten

1 teaspoon vanilla extract

CHOCOLATE GANACHE

6 ounces 60% bittersweet chocolate, finely chopped

⅔ cup heavy cream

If you love the taste of a classic Reese's peanut butter cup, this is the pie for you. I've taken my favorite childhood treat and re-created it with delicious "grown-up" ingredients like high-quality vanilla in the filling and good bittersweet chocolate in the ganache topping. In the South, we're all about peanut butter, but you can make this pie with any nut or seed butter.

It's important to let the pie cool completely before topping it with the ganache. If you don't, you'll be left with tiny bubbles on the surface of the ganache. It'll still taste delicious, but it won't look quite as refined.

FOR THE CRUST: Place the dough on a lightly floured work surface. Let the dough soften a little before rolling it out if you refrigerated it overnight. Lightly flour your rolling pin and start rolling the dough gently from the center out. Do this a few times, then gently pick up the dough, rotate it a quarter turn, and roll again. Continue to roll, rotating the dough and flouring the work surface and the dough as needed, until you have a 12-inch circle approximately ⅛ inch thick.

Loosely fold the dough into quarters and unfold it in a 10-inch deep-dish pie pan. Gently fit it into the bottom and up the sides of the pan. You should have an overhang of about ½ inch around the edges. Fold the excess under and crimp the edges: With one hand on the inside of the rim and the other hand on the outside, use the index finger of your inside hand to push the dough between the thumb and index finger of your outside hand to form a V shape. Repeat all around the rim. Place the pie shell in the refrigerator while you make the filling.

FOR THE FILLING: Preheat the oven to 325°F.

Combine the butter and peanut butter in the top of a double boiler. Fill the bottom of the double boiler with water, set over low heat, and insert the top. The water should not touch the bottom of the insert and should never be hotter than a simmer. Stir the mixture with a silicone spatula until the butter has melted and the mixture is completely combined, scraping down the sides as necessary and being careful not to incorporate air. Remove the top of the double boiler and set aside.

Combine the sugar, cocoa powder, and salt in a large bowl and whisk to combine. Whisk in the milk, then whisk in the eggs and vanilla. Stir in the peanut butter mixture.

Place the piecrust on a rimmed baking sheet. Gently pour the filling into the crust and bake for 30 minutes. Rotate the baking sheet and bake for 30 minutes more, or until the filling is set and no longer jiggles in the center when the pan is gently shaken. Transfer the pie to a wire rack and cool to room temperature.

WHEN THE PIE IS COMPLETELY COOL, MAKE THE GANACHE: Put the chocolate in a heatproof container. Put the cream in a small saucepan and bring to a simmer over medium heat. Pour the cream over the chocolate, cover, and let stand for 3 minutes. Stir to completely combine the melted chocolate and cream.

Pour the ganache over the top of the pie, rotating the pie if necessary to ensure that the ganache topping is even. Cool for 5 minutes, then refrigerate the pie for at least 2 hours to allow the topping to set before serving.

Serve the pie chilled. Tightly cover any leftovers and refrigerate for up to 3 days.

CHOCOLATE CORNMEAL CRUST

MAKES ENOUGH DOUGH FOR 1 SINGLE-CRUST 10-INCH DEEP-DISH PIE

¾ cup plus 2 tablespoons all-purpose flour, plus more for the work surface

⅓ cup fine cornmeal, preferably Geechie Boy Jimmy Red (see Resources, page 368)

1½ tablespoons unsweetened cocoa powder

½ teaspoon kosher salt

8 tablespoons (1 stick) unsalted butter, diced and refrigerated

¼ cup ice water

Chill the bowl, lid, and steel blade of a food processor and all the ingredients for the crust in the freezer for 1 hour.

Put the flour, cornmeal, cocoa powder, and salt in the food processor and pulse to combine. Add the butter and pulse 4 or 5 times, until it is in pieces the size of peas. Slowly add the water through the feed tube, pulsing 4 or 5 times to incorporate it.

Turn the dough out onto a lightly floured work surface and gather it into a ball. You should still see bits of butter, and you want to work quickly to keep the butter cold. Flatten the dough into a disk about 1 inch thick, wrap in plastic wrap, and let rest in the refrigerator for at least 1 hour or up to overnight before using. Wrapped in plastic wrap, the disk of dough will keep for up to 3 days in the refrigerator. Stored in a freezer bag, the wrapped disk of dough can be frozen for up to 3 months. Thaw it in the refrigerator and let it soften a little at room temperature before rolling it out.

SWEET POTATO PIE

SERVES 8

1¾ pounds large sweet potatoes,
scrubbed and patted dry

1 recipe Flaky Piecrust dough
(page 309), chilled

2½ teaspoons all-purpose flour,
plus more for rolling out the
dough

1 cup heavy cream

3 large eggs, lightly beaten

1 tablespoon sorghum syrup,
preferably Muddy Pond
(see Resources, page 369)

½ cup granulated sugar

½ cup packed light brown sugar

¾ teaspoon ground ginger

¼ teaspoon ground cardamom

¼ teaspoon ground cloves

⅛ teaspoon ground nutmeg

⅛ teaspoon kosher salt

GOES WELL WITH:

*Homemade Whipped Topping
(page 331)*
*Pork Prime Rib with Mustard
Onions (page 144)*

Sweet potato pie is about as Southern a dessert as you can find. Many great country songs have been written about it, and rightfully so. The dough for this pie is just one among the many great things I learned from my time working alongside Lisa Donovan. Husk's former pastry chef, she is the Jedi master of flaky piecrust. She taught me so many tricks about working with dough. Once, I would have worried if I saw flecks of butter in the finished dough; now I know that's a good sign.

Preheat the oven to 375°F.

Place the sweet potatoes in a baking dish and bake for 1 hour and 15 minutes, or until tender. Remove from the oven and let cool completely. Lower the oven temperature to 350°F.

Place the dough on a lightly floured work surface. If the dough has been refrigerated overnight, let it soften a little at room temperature before rolling it out. Lightly flour your rolling pin and start rolling the dough gently from the center out. Do this a few times, then gently pick up the dough, rotate it a quarter turn, and roll again. Continue to roll, rotating the dough and flouring the work surface and the dough as needed, until you have a 12-inch circle approximately ⅛ inch thick.

Loosely fold the dough into quarters and unfold it into a 10-inch deep-dish pie pan. Gently fit it into the bottom and up the sides of the pan; you should have an overhang of about ½ inch around the edges. Fold the excess under and crimp the edges of the dough: With one hand on the inside of the rim and the other hand on the outside, use the index finger of your inside hand to push the dough between the thumb and index finger of your outside hand to form a V shape. Repeat all around the rim. Refrigerate the piecrust while you make the filling.

Cut the sweet potatoes in half, scoop the flesh into a large bowl, and discard the skins. Mash the sweet potatoes with a potato masher or the back of a fork until smooth. You need 2 cups mashed sweet potatoes for the filling.

Combine the 2 cups mashed sweet potatoes, cream, eggs, and sorghum syrup in the bowl of a stand mixer fitted with the paddle attachment (or use a large bowl and a hand mixer) and beat on medium speed until blended. Combine

the granulated sugar, light brown sugar, flour, ginger, cardamom, cloves, nutmeg, and salt in a medium bowl. With the mixer on low, slowly add the dry ingredients to the sweet potato mixture and beat until completely incorporated.

Pour the filling into the piecrust and place the pie on a rimmed baking sheet. Bake for about 1 hour, rotating the baking sheet halfway through, until the filling is set and no longer jiggles in the center when the pan is gently shaken. Let the pie cool to room temperature on a wire rack.

Slice the pie into 8 wedges and serve. Cover any leftovers and refrigerate for up to 3 days. Remove from the refrigerator 30 minutes before serving.

FRUIT PRESERVES HAND PIES

MAKES 16 HAND PIES

CRUST

2 recipes Flaky Piecrust dough
(page 309), chilled, plus flour for
rolling it out

STRAWBERRY FILLING

½ cup Fruit Preserves (page 283)
made with strawberries

1½ teaspoons finely chopped basil

½ teaspoon grated fresh ginger

½ teaspoon Lindera Farms Ginger
Vinegar (see Resources, page
369)

BLUEBERRY FILLING

½ cup Fruit Preserves (page 283)
made with blueberries

1½ teaspoons finely chopped
cilantro

¾ teaspoon raspberry vinegar

½ teaspoon ground coriander

1 large egg, lightly beaten with
1 tablespoon water to make an
egg wash

2 teaspoons turbinado sugar

These little gems are another pastry I credit to my time working with Lisa Donovan. I remember how happy I was when I tasted one of her hand pies for the first time. You can fill them with the homemade preserves called for in this recipe or with any store-bought fruit preserves you love (you'll need 1 cup total preserves for the fillings).

FOR THE CRUST: Line a rimmed baking sheet with parchment paper.

If the dough has been refrigerated overnight, let it soften a little at room temperature before rolling it out. Place one piece of the dough on a lightly floured work surface and, using a lightly floured rolling pin, roll it out to a ⅛-inch-thick round. Using a 4-inch round cookie cutter, cut out 6 rounds and transfer them to the prepared baking sheet, arranging them so that they do not touch. Top with a sheet of parchment paper. Gather up the scraps of dough, pat them into a disk, and roll the dough out again. Cut out 2 more rounds and transfer them to the second sheet of parchment paper on the baking sheet. Repeat the process with the second piece of dough, covering the second layer of rounds with another sheet of parchment before adding the final rounds. Refrigerate the rounds while you make the fillings.

FOR THE STRAWBERRY FILLING: Combine the preserves, basil, ginger, and vinegar in a small bowl.

FOR THE BLUEBERRY FILLING: Combine the preserves, cilantro, vinegar, and coriander in a small bowl.

TO ASSEMBLE AND BAKE THE PIES: Preheat the oven to 450°F. Line two rimmed baking sheets with parchment paper.

Fill half the hand pies with strawberry filling and half with blueberry filling: Brush the edges of one round with some of the egg wash and spoon 1 tablespoon of preserves onto the center. Fold the dough over the preserves to form a half-moon shape. Crimp the edges firmly with a fork to seal and transfer the pie to one of the prepared baking sheets. Repeat with the remaining rounds, arranging the hand pies 2 inches apart on the baking sheets.

Brush the tops of the hand pies with egg wash. Using a paring knife, cut 3 small slits in the top of each one. Sprinkle the tops with the turbinado sugar. Bake the pies for 15 to 18 minutes, rotating the baking sheets halfway through, until puffed and golden brown. Transfer the hand pies to a wire rack and cool slightly.

Serve the hand pies warm. Any leftover pies can be stored in an airtight container for up to 3 days at room temperature. Reheat in a 350°F oven until just warm, a few minutes at most, before serving.

PLUM UPSIDE-DOWN CAKE

SERVES 8

PLUM TOPPING

3 tablespoons unsalted butter

⅔ cup packed light brown sugar

⅛ teaspoon kosher salt

1 pound ripe black plums (about 4 ounces each), quartered and pitted

CAKE

1⅔ cups all-purpose flour

1½ teaspoons baking powder

½ teaspoon ground cinnamon

¼ teaspoon ground ginger

¼ teaspoon kosher salt

8 tablespoons (1 stick) unsalted butter, diced, at room temperature

¾ cup sugar

½ vanilla bean

¾ cup whole milk

Pineapple upside-down cake is a classic dessert that registers with people no matter where they're from. There is no such thing as a homegrown pineapple in the South, of course, so I use gorgeous local black plums. The sweet and tart flavor of a good plum is delicious for the same reason a ripe pineapple tastes good, so using plums for this dessert makes perfect sense.

You can substitute an equal amount of peaches for the plums in this recipe. Peel the peaches first (see Pickled Peaches, page 250, for the method).

Position a rack in the middle of the oven and preheat the oven to 350°F.

FOR THE PLUM TOPPING: Combine the butter and brown sugar in a 10-inch cast-iron skillet and cook over medium heat, stirring, until the butter melts and the sugar dissolves. Continue to cook until the mixture boils and turns golden brown, about 2 minutes. Stir in the salt, remove from the stove, and cool for 10 minutes.

Add the plum quarters to the skillet, arranging them in a pinwheel pattern starting in the center and working your way out to the edges. Set aside while you make the cake batter.

FOR THE CAKE: Sift the flour, baking powder, cinnamon, ginger, and salt into a bowl and set aside.

Combine the butter and sugar in the bowl of a stand mixer fitted with the paddle attachment (or use a large bowl and a hand mixer). Split the vanilla bean lengthwise in half and, using the back of a paring knife, scrape out the seeds and add to the butter mixture (reserve the vanilla pod for another use, if desired; see Note, page 310). Cream the butter and sugar on medium speed, scraping down the sides as necessary, until light and fluffy, about 5 minutes. Reduce the speed to low and add the dry ingredients alternately with the milk in 3 increments, starting and ending with the dry ingredients and beating until just incorporated, scraping down the sides after each addition. Do not overmix the batter.

Using the back of a spoon or an offset spatula, carefully spread the batter in an even layer over the plums, taking care not to disturb the pattern you made. Bake the cake for 30 to 35 minutes, until the top is golden brown and a cake tester inserted in the center comes out clean; rotate the skillet halfway through baking for even cooking. Remove the

cake from the oven and cool in the skillet on a baking rack for 20 minutes.

Run a paring knife around the edges of the cake to release it from the skillet and, using pot holders or oven mitts, place a cake plate on top of the skillet, invert the skillet and plate, and gently lift off the skillet, leaving the cake fruit side up.

Cut the cake into 8 slices and serve. Any leftover cake can be tightly covered, once cooled, and refrigerated for up to 1 day. Remove from the refrigerator 30 minutes before serving.

CARAMEL CAKE

SERVES 12

CAKE

½ pound (2 sticks) unsalted butter, diced, at room temperature, plus more for the pans

1½ cups all-purpose flour

1½ cups cake flour

1 tablespoon baking powder

¾ teaspoon kosher salt

¼ teaspoon baking soda

2⅔ cups sugar

4 large eggs

1½ cups full-fat buttermilk (see Note, page 27)

2 teaspoons vanilla extract

CARAMEL ICING

4 cups sugar

2 cups full-fat buttermilk (see Note, page 27)

1 pound (4 sticks) unsalted butter, diced, at room temperature

1 teaspoon baking soda

EQUIPMENT

Candy thermometer

The caramel cake is a perennial favorite in the pantheon of Southern desserts. It always makes any celebration or gathering that much more delicious.

When you make this cake, use a big cast-iron Dutch oven to cook the icing, as there is a dramatic increase in volume that happens during the cooking process. A Dutch oven is also the best bet for providing the even, steady heat you need. Making the icing this way is time-consuming and might feel like a workout, but you'll find it well worth the effort.

FOR THE CAKE: Position a rack in the middle of the oven and preheat the oven to 350°F. Lightly butter two 9-inch round cake pans. Line the bottoms of the pans with rounds of parchment paper cut to fit and butter the parchment.

Sift the two flours, baking powder, salt, and baking soda into a large bowl and set aside.

Combine the butter and sugar in the bowl of a stand mixer fitted with the paddle attachment (or use a large bowl and a hand mixer). Cream the butter and sugar on medium speed, scraping down the sides as necessary, until light and fluffy, about 5 minutes. Add the eggs one at a time, beating until smooth after each addition and scraping down the sides as necessary. Combine the buttermilk and vanilla in a measuring cup with a spout. With the mixer on low speed, add the dry ingredients in 3 increments alternating with the buttermilk mixture, starting and ending with the dry ingredients, beating until incorporated, and scraping down the sides after each addition.

Divide the batter evenly between the prepared cake pans. Tap the pans on the counter to level the batter and remove air bubbles. Bake the cakes for 35 to 40 minutes, until the tops are golden brown and a cake tester inserted in the center of each cake comes out clean. Transfer the pans to wire racks and cool for 10 minutes, then turn the cakes out onto the racks to cool completely. Once they are cool, peel off the parchment paper.

FOR THE ICING: While the cakes are cooling, combine the sugar, buttermilk, butter, and baking soda in a large Dutch oven. Attach the candy thermometer to the side and cook the mixture over medium heat, stirring occasionally with a wooden spoon, until it registers 235°F, about 45 minutes. Remove the pot from the heat and, using a wooden spoon, beat the icing until thickened but still spreadable, 25 to 30 minutes; it should register 110°F on an instant-read thermometer.

TO ASSEMBLE: Cut each layer of cake horizontally in half, making 4 even layers. Place one layer cut side up on a cake plate and, using an icing spatula, spread ¾ cup of the icing on top. Repeat with the remaining layers, placing the second layer cut side down, the third layer cut side up, and the final layer cut side down. Cover the top and sides of the cake with the remaining icing.

Cut the cake into wedges and serve. The cake will keep in a cake keeper or cake box for up to 3 days at room temperature or up to 5 days in the refrigerator. Bring to room temperature before serving.

PECAN AND BLACK WALNUT CHURCH CAKE

SERVES 12

PECAN CAKE

8 tablespoons (1 stick) unsalted butter, diced, at room temperature, plus more for the pans

1¼ cups (4 ounces) raw pecan pieces

2½ cups all-purpose flour

1¼ teaspoons baking soda

¾ teaspoon kosher salt

1½ cups packed light brown sugar

½ cup plus 2 tablespoons granulated sugar

3 large eggs

1 cup plus 3 tablespoons full-fat buttermilk (see Note, page 27)

1 teaspoon vanilla extract

SORGHUM ICING

1¼ pounds cream cheese, at room temperature

¾ pound (3 sticks) unsalted butter, diced, at room temperature

3 cups powdered sugar, sifted

¾ cup sorghum syrup, preferably Muddy Pond (see Resources, page 369)

¾ cup (3½ ounces) chopped black walnuts (see Resources, page 368)

For generations, the South has been known for its layer cakes. This beauty brings back memories of the small country church I attended growing up. Getting up early on Sunday wasn't always easy, but the lineup of Tupperware cake keepers that greeted us after the service made it just fine. This is a simple cake with a couple of sneaky little tricks and touches. The ground pecans in the batter give the cake a nice body and combine well with the aromatic black walnuts that adorn the outside. The icing is made with one of my all-time favorite ingredients, sorghum. The sorghum syrup gives the whole cake a deep, malty sweetness.

FOR THE CAKE: Position a rack in the middle of the oven and preheat the oven to 325°F. Lightly butter four 9-inch round cake pans (or as many as you have—you will need to make a total of 4 layers). Line the bottoms of the pans with rounds of parchment paper cut to fit and butter the parchment.

Put the pecan pieces in a food processor and process, scraping the sides as necessary, until ground into a fine meal, about 1 minute. Transfer to a medium bowl.

Sift the flour, baking soda, and salt into the bowl with the pecan meal, and stir to combine well. Set aside.

Combine the butter, brown sugar, and granulated sugar in the bowl of a stand mixer fitted with the paddle attachment (or use a large bowl and a hand mixer). Cream the butter and sugar on medium speed, scraping down the sides as necessary, until light and fluffy, about 5 minutes.

Add the eggs one at a time, beating until smooth after each addition and scraping down the sides of the bowl as necessary. Combine the buttermilk and vanilla in a measuring cup with a spout. With the mixer on low speed, add the dry ingredients in 3 increments alternating with the buttermilk mixture, beginning and ending with the dry ingredients, beating until incorporated, and scraping down the sides after each addition.

Pour 1⅓ cups of the batter into each prepared cake pan (if you have fewer than four pans, set the remaining batter aside) and use the back of a spoon or a small offset spatula to spread it evenly. Place two of the pans in the oven and bake for 16 to 18 minutes, until the tops of the cakes are golden brown and a cake tester inserted in the center of the cake comes out clean. Transfer the pans to wire racks and cool for 10 minutes, then turn the cakes out onto the racks, using a metal spatula to ease them out of the pans, and cool completely. Bake the remaining layers (if you're reusing any pans, let them cool, then prepare them as you did initially before pouring in the batter). Once the layers are cool, peel off the parchment paper.

FOR THE ICING: While the cakes are cooling, combine the cream cheese and butter in the bowl of a stand mixer fitted with the paddle attachment (or use a large bowl and a hand mixer). Beat the mixture on medium speed until completely combined and smooth, about 3 minutes. Reduce the speed to low and add the powdered sugar 1 cup at a time, scraping down the sides of the bowl as necessary, until the icing is smooth and spreadable, about 3 minutes. With the mixer on low, slowly pour in the sorghum syrup, scraping down the sides as necessary, and mix until completely incorporated. Refrigerate the icing for 10 minutes to firm it.

TO ASSEMBLE: Place one layer on a cake plate and, using an icing spatula, spread 1¼ cups of the icing on top. Repeat with the remaining layers; do not ice the sides of the cake. You also do not need to smooth any icing that comes out between the layers on the outside of the cake.

Sprinkle the black walnut pieces evenly over the top of the cake. Refrigerate for at least 1 hour before serving.

Cut the cake into slices and serve. The cake will keep in a cake keeper or cake box for up to 5 days in the refrigerator. Remove from the refrigerator 15 minutes before serving.

PAWPAW AND BANANA PUDDING

SERVES 8

ROASTED BANANA MILK

3 ripe bananas (about 1 pound)

3 cups whole milk

1 tablespoon sugar

CUSTARD

1 pound ripe pawpaws
(see Resources, page 368)

¾ cup sugar

½ cup cornstarch

¼ teaspoon kosher salt

8 large egg yolks

1 tablespoon vanilla extract

4 tablespoons unsalted butter,
diced and refrigerated

1 recipe Vanilla Wafers
(recipe follows)

½ recipe Homemade Whipped
Topping (recipe follows)

GOES WELL WITH:

Fried Chicken (page 127)

There are hundreds of delicious banana puddings on the menus of barbecue joints, roadside stands, and meat-and-threes throughout the South. While I love the straight-forward original versions, I love this nontraditional rendition even more.

The pawpaw, North America's largest indigenous fruit, grows throughout southern Appalachia. With its incredible, tropical aroma and flavor, the pawpaw is a natural addition to classic banana pudding. In fact, one of its nicknames is poor man's banana. The roasted banana milk, homemade vanilla wafers, and whipped topping take this dessert to the next level. (The topping recipe makes more than you need for the pudding, but the extra can be served alongside most any pie or used to garnish hot chocolate.) Show up to your next potluck or family dinner with this, and you might be dubbed the queen or king of banana pudding.

FOR THE BANANA MILK: Preheat the oven to 350°F.

Put the bananas on a rimmed baking sheet and bake for 15 to 20 minutes, until the peels have darkened and split and the flesh of the bananas begins to bubble out. Remove from the oven and cool to room temperature.

Scoop the roasted banana flesh out of the peels into a medium saucepan. Add the milk and sugar, stir well, and bring to a simmer over medium heat, stirring occasionally to prevent scorching, about 15 minutes.

Working in batches if necessary, transfer the mixture to a blender (set the saucepan aside) and blend on high until completely smooth, about 1 minute. Return the banana milk to the saucepan and bring to a boil over medium heat, stirring to prevent scorching. Turn off the heat and cover to keep hot.

FOR THE CUSTARD: Cut the pawpaws lengthwise in half, scoop the flesh out onto a rimmed baking sheet, and spread it out to make it easier to spot the seeds. Pick out all the large black seeds and discard. Roughly chop the pulp and transfer to a container. You need 1 cup pulp for the pudding; enjoy any extra just the way it is.

CONTINUED

Combine the sugar, cornstarch, and salt in a large bowl and stir to thoroughly mix. Add the egg yolks and whisk vigorously until the mixture has doubled in volume. While whisking constantly, slowly stream 1 cup of the hot banana milk into the egg yolk mixture to temper the eggs. Add the tempered egg yolk mixture to the saucepan of banana milk and cook over medium-low heat, whisking constantly, until it simmers and becomes very thick, 8 to 10 minutes. Then continue to cook the pudding, whisking constantly, for 2 minutes more to completely hydrate the cornstarch and ensure that the pudding is evenly thickened.

Remove from the stove, add the vanilla and butter, and stir until the butter has melted. Fold in the 1 cup pawpaw pulp.

Line the bottom of a large serving bowl with vanilla wafers, starting in the center and working your way up the sides of the bowl; reserve the remaining wafers. Pour the pudding into the bowl. Cool to room temperature, cover, and refrigerate for at least 4 hours or up to overnight. (*Tightly covered, the pudding will keep for up to 3 days in the refrigerator.*)

TO SERVE: Remove the pudding from the refrigerator and spread the whipped topping evenly over the top. Arrange the remaining vanilla wafers around the edges of the pudding.

CONTINUED

VANILLA WAFERS

MAKES 36 COOKIES

2¼ cups all-purpose flour

¾ teaspoon baking powder

¾ teaspoon kosher salt

8 tablespoons (1 stick) unsalted
butter, diced, at room temperature

½ cup Bourbon Barrel Vanilla Sugar
(see Resources, page 368)

1 vanilla bean

1 large egg

1 tablespoon whole milk

1 tablespoon plus 1 teaspoon
vanilla extract

Position the oven racks in the upper and lower thirds of the oven and preheat the oven to 350°F. Line two rimmed baking sheets with parchment paper.

Sift the flour, baking powder, and salt into a medium bowl and set aside.

Combine the butter and sugar in the bowl of a stand mixer fitted with the paddle attachment (or use a large bowl and a hand mixer). Split the vanilla bean lengthwise in half and, using the back of a paring knife, scrape out the seeds and add to the bowl (reserve the vanilla pod for another use, if desired; see Note, page 310). Cream the mixture on medium speed, scraping down the sides as necessary, until light and fluffy, about 4 minutes. Add the egg, beat until smooth, and scrape down the sides of the bowl. Add the milk and vanilla extract and mix just to combine. Add the flour mixture and beat just to combine. Refrigerate the dough for 10 minutes before shaping the cookies.

Using a 1-tablespoon cookie scoop (or tablespoon), scoop a portion of the dough, roll it into a ball, and pat it between your palms into a disk about 1½ inches in diameter. Place it on one of the prepared baking sheets. Repeat with the remaining dough, leaving at least 1 inch between the cookies.

Bake the cookies for 20 to 25 minutes, rotating the pans from top to bottom and front to back halfway through, until the edges are golden brown. Cool the cookies completely on the baking sheets on wire racks.

Transfer the cooled cookies to an airtight container. The cookies will keep for up to 5 days at room temperature.

HOMEMADE WHIPPED TOPPING

MAKES 6 CUPS

3 sheets silver-strength gelatin (see Resources, page 369), broken in half

2 tablespoons cold water

1⅓ cups sugar

¼ cup water

3½ tablespoons light corn syrup

¼ cup whole milk

3 tablespoons dry nonfat milk powder

Scant ¼ teaspoon kosher salt

1¾ cups plus 2 tablespoons heavy cream

EQUIPMENT

Candy thermometer

NOTE: You'll need to start this recipe a day ahead of time to chill the base.

Place the gelatin and the cold water in a shallow bowl, pressing down on the gelatin to make sure it is submerged; set aside to soften.

Combine the sugar, the ¼ cup water, and the corn syrup in a small heavy-bottomed saucepan. Place the saucepan over low heat, attach the candy thermometer to the side, and cook, stirring occasionally, until the mixture registers 248°F on the candy thermometer, 12 to 14 minutes.

Transfer the softened gelatin to the bowl of a stand mixer fitted with the whisk attachment. With the mixer on high speed, slowly and carefully pour the hot sugar mixture into the bowl, streaming it down the side, away from the whisk, and whip until the mixture has cooled, tripled in size, and turned an opaque, matte white, 5 to 6 minutes.

Combine the milk, milk powder, and salt in a small bowl and whisk to blend completely. With the mixer on high, add the milk mixture in 3 increments, stopping to thoroughly scrape down the sides of the bowl after each addition. (The more you scrape the bowl, the less likely it is that the finished topping will have any lumps.) Transfer the topping base to a container, cover tightly with plastic wrap pressed directly against the surface, and refrigerate overnight.

The next day, transfer the topping base to the bowl of the stand mixer fitted with the whisk attachment. Whisk on medium-high speed until smooth, about 4 minutes. Add the cream in 3 increments, thoroughly scraping down the sides of the bowl after each addition. Whip the topping until it holds stiff peaks, scraping down the sides of the bowl at least five times to ensure against lumps in the finished topping, about 3 minutes. Transfer the topping to a container, cover tightly, and refrigerate until ready to use.

Tightly covered, the whipped topping will keep for up to 3 days in the refrigerator.

A FEW SOUTHERN LIBATIONS

No meal in the South is complete without a freshly prepared drink. Something to beat the heat in a sultry Southern summer is always welcome at the table. There are plenty of boozy concoctions that have their roots in the South, but these three recipes are for drinks that everyone can enjoy. (For kids and others who prefer not to indulge in alcohol, just leave out the vodka in the Bloody Mary.)

SWEET TEA

Everyone has his or her personal preference about how sweet sweet tea should be, so keep the tea and the "sweet" separate and let your guests sweeten their own. The tradition of sweet tea in the South is just as important as a skillet of cornbread, in my opinion, so why use inferior tea to make it? This particular blend is unique and adds a level of care and quality to the drink.

For a variation, try a cold-brew version: Combine the tea leaves with all 12 cups of the water and let sit on the counter at room temperature for 8 hours to infuse.

MAKES TWELVE 8-OUNCE GLASSES

SIMPLE SYRUP

1 cup sugar

1 cup water

BREWED TEA

12 cups water

½ cup plus 2 tablespoons Tea Blend (recipe follows)

12 lemon wedges, seeds removed

FOR THE SIMPLE SYRUP: Combine the sugar and water in a small saucepan and bring to a simmer over medium heat, stirring to dissolve the sugar, about 5 minutes. Remove from the stove and cool to room temperature, then transfer to a container, cover, and refrigerate. (*Tightly covered, the syrup will keep for up to 2 weeks in the refrigerator.*)

FOR THE BREWED TEA: Put 8 cups of the water in a large pitcher. Bring the remaining 4 cups water to a boil in a small saucepan over high heat. Remove from the stove and cool for 1 minute. Add the tea blend and let steep for 6 minutes.

Strain the brewed tea through a fine-mesh sieve into the pitcher of water, stirring to combine. Discard the solids. Cover and refrigerate. (*Tightly covered, the brewed tea will keep for up to 1 day in the refrigerator.*)

TO SERVE: For each glass, combine 1 cup of the brewed tea and 2 tablespoons (or as desired) of the simple syrup in an 8-ounce glass and stir to combine. Add ice to fill the glass and garnish with a lemon wedge perched on the rim.

TEA BLEND

MAKES A SCANT 4½ CUPS, ENOUGH FOR 6 BATCHES OF TEA

3 cups plus 2 tablespoons loose-leaf Assam tea (3½ ounces)

½ cup plus 2 tablespoons loose-leaf Ceylon tea (¾ ounce)

½ cup plus 2 tablespoons loose-leaf Darjeeling tea (¾ ounce)

Combine the teas in an airtight container, cover, and shake to mix well. Store in a cool, dry place for up to 3 months.

Herb-Infused Lemonade

This lemonade offers an opportunity to showcase the best herbs and fruits you can find at your local market—no matter what time of year. If you want to simplify the recipe, omit the herbs and fruits, but do leave in the lemon zest. The essential oils in the zest take the drink to another lemon level.

NOTE: You'll need to start this recipe a day ahead of time to infuse the flavors.

MAKES ABOUT 3¾ QUARTS

3 quarts plus 1 cup cold water

2 cups sugar

1¾ cups fresh lemon juice (from 7 to 8 large lemons)

1 teaspoon kosher salt

½ cup strips lemon zest removed with a vegetable peeler (any white pith removed)

1 large lemon (about 4 ounces), cut into ¼-inch-thick rounds

12 ounces blueberries, blackberries, or sliced strawberries, or a mix (about 2 cups)

1 large ripe peach (about 8 ounces), cut away from the pit and then into eighths

1½ mint sprigs

1 rosemary sprig

½ thyme sprig

¼ cup lemon balm leaves

¼ cup lemon verbena leaves

1½ large basil leaves

OPTIONAL GARNISHES

Fresh berries

Lemon balm and basil leaves

Combine the water, sugar, lemon juice, and salt in a container large enough to hold all the ingredients and whisk to dissolve the sugar and salt. Add the lemon zest, lemon rounds, berries, and peach and whisk again to help release the flavors from the lemon zest and fruits. Add the herbs and whisk to combine. Cover and refrigerate overnight, or for up to 3 days for a more intense herbaceous flavor.

Strain the lemonade through a fine-mesh sieve into a pitcher and discard the solids (feel free to snack on the berries). Cover and refrigerate until ready to serve. (Tightly covered, the lemonade will keep for up to 3 days in the refrigerator.)

Pour tall glasses of lemonade and garnish with a few berries and fresh herbs leaves, if desired.

Bloody Mary

A Bloody Mary made with a premade mix might be an easy shortcut, but it won't have the same fresh flavor as one you make from scratch. You can drink this fresh Bloody Mary with or without vodka. These days I enjoy it without any alcohol at all—V8 has nothing on this!

NOTE: This recipe calls for precise measurements for the vegetables and greens to ensure the best results.

MAKES 8 CUPS MIX, ENOUGH FOR 8 DRINKS

BLOODY MARY MIX

6 ounces chopped celery

3½ ounces chopped sweet onion

3½ ounces chopped peeled carrots

1½ ounces chopped peeled red beet

2 ounces chopped romaine lettuce

2 ounces chopped watercress

1 ounce chopped flat-leaf parsley

4¼ cups tomato juice

⅔ cup fresh lemon juice (from 3 to 4 lemons)

½ cup Worcestershire sauce, preferably Bourbon Barrel (see Resources, page 368)

½ cup Preserved Tomatoes (page 278) or canned whole tomatoes, with their juices

⅓ cup Hot Sauce (page 260) or Red Clay Original Hot Sauce (see Resources, page 369)

3 tablespoons agave nectar

2 tablespoons pickling liquid from Pickled Okra (page 242)

2 tablespoons Pepper Vinegar (page 262)

2½ tablespoons prepared horseradish

2 teaspoons kosher salt

1 teaspoon celery seeds

¾ teaspoon freshly ground black pepper

¾ teaspoon Bourbon Barrel Bourbon Smoked Paprika (see Resources, page 368)

½ teaspoon onion powder

OPTIONAL

Vodka

Garnishes such as paper-thin slices of ham and homemade pickles

EQUIPMENT

Juice extractor

FOR THE BLOODY MARY MIX: Combine the celery, onion, carrots, and beet and run through a juice extractor. Transfer the juice to a 3-quart container with a lid. Combine the romaine, watercress, and parsley, run through the juice extractor, and add to the celery juice mixture.

Add the tomato juice, lemon juice, Worcestershire, tomatoes, hot sauce, agave nectar, pickling liquid, vinegar, horseradish, salt, celery seeds, pepper, paprika, and onion powder and blend with an immersion blender until smooth, about 1 minute. (Or blend the mix in a regular blender.) Cover and refrigerate until chilled before serving. *(Tightly covered, the mix will keep for up to 3 days in the refrigerator.)*

TO SERVE: The drink is delicious all on its own poured over ice in a tall glass. To make it boozy, combine 1½ ounces of vodka with 1 cup of the mix in a tall glass filled with ice; stir to mix.

The best garnishes are two of my favorite things: country ham and tangy homemade pickles. Drape a paper-thin slice of country ham over the rim of each glass and garnish with a skewer of your favorite pickles. I especially love pickled ramps and okra here.

HAND-CHURNED PEACH SHERBET

MAKES ABOUT 2½ QUARTS

1½ pounds large ripe peaches

½ cup full-fat buttermilk (see Note, page 27)

1 tablespoon fresh lemon juice

3½ cups whole milk

1 cup heavy cream

1½ cups sugar

1 cup light corn syrup

1 cup Fruit Preserves (page 283) made with peaches

EQUIPMENT

Hand-cranked ice cream maker

(plus ice and ice cream salt or rock salt)

GOES WELL WITH:

Blackberry Cobbler (page 303)
Elderberry Dumplings with
  Grapefruit Crème Anglaise
  (page 305)

I have so many fond memories of sitting on the porch with my family, taking turns cranking the old wooden ice cream churn. It's a process that makes you instantly impatient. You just can't wait to taste the sherbet, but time is an essential ingredient (along with some elbow grease). And all your hard work will make the finished sherbet taste that much better. If you don't have the time to make the peach preserves, don't fret. You can add any delicious fruit preserves you have in your pantry. It's hard to go wrong.

Bring a large pot of water to a boil over high heat. Make an ice bath with equal parts ice and water in a large bowl. Lightly score the skin on the bottom of each peach with an X and submerge the peaches in the boiling water for 10 seconds. Remove and submerge them in the ice bath to cool them and stop the cooking; do not leave them in the ice bath for longer than 5 minutes.

Peel the peaches, cut the flesh away from the pits, and roughly chop. Reserve the pits for the sherbet base. Transfer the chopped peaches to a blender and blend on high until completely smooth, about 1 minute. Measure out 2½ cups of the puree and transfer it to a container. (Any extra peach puree can be enjoyed just as it is.) Stir in the buttermilk and lemon juice, cover, and refrigerate.

Lay the peach pits out on a cutting board, cover with a kitchen towel, and lightly tap with a hammer to crack them and expose the almond-shaped kernels inside. Remove the kernels and discard the cracked pits. Roughly chop the kernels.

Make an ice bath with equal parts ice and water in a large bowl. Combine the milk, cream, sugar, corn syrup, and chopped peach kernels in large heavy-bottomed saucepan and whisk to mix thoroughly. Bring the mixture to a boil over medium heat, whisking frequently to prevent scorching. Reduce the heat to low and simmer, whisking, for 1 minute. Transfer the mixture to a heatproof container large enough to hold it and the peach puree.

Put the container of sherbet base in the ice bath to chill. Stir occasionally, being careful not to let any water get into the sherbet base, until the mixture is completely cold. Stir in the peach puree, cover, and refrigerate overnight.

CONTINUED

The next day, strain the sherbet base through a fine-mesh sieve into the canister of the ice cream maker. Discard the solids. Fill the ice cream maker with ice and ice cream salt or rock salt according to the manufacturer's directions and crank until the sherbet is frozen.

Add the peach preserves and crank just enough to evenly incorporate. Serve right out of the canister for a creamy, soft-serve texture, or transfer the sherbet to a freezer container and freeze until ready to serve. It will keep for up to 1 month.

HICKORY-SMOKED ICE CREAM

MAKES ABOUT 1½ QUARTS

One 5-by-1-by-1-inch piece
    hickory wood

3½ cups heavy cream

½ cup whole milk

1 vanilla bean

½ cup sugar

5 large egg yolks

EQUIPMENT

Candy thermometer

Ice cream maker

GOES WELL WITH:

Blackberry Cobbler (page 303)

I developed this recipe with s'mores on the brain. The way a marshmallow tastes, slightly burnt and crispy from a trip over the campfire, is a flavor memory many of us have. When you hear "smoked ice cream," it may seem odd, but one taste and you'll be transported. If you plan ahead, you can burn the hickory when you have a fire going for grilling.

Prepare a small hot fire in a charcoal grill (see page 96) with no rack. Place the hickory wood directly on the coals and let sit, turning occasionally, until it is burning evenly on all sides.

Combine the cream and milk in a large heatproof bowl. Place the burning hickory in the cream-milk mixture, cover tightly, and steep at room temperature for 20 minutes.

Remove the wood and strain the cream-milk mixture through a fine-mesh sieve into a large saucepan. Split the vanilla bean lengthwise in half and, using the back of a paring knife, scrape out the seeds and add them to the saucepan (reserve the vanilla pod for another use, if desired; see Note, page 310). Stir in 2 tablespoons of the sugar. Attach the candy thermometer to the side of the saucepan and heat the mixture over medium heat, stirring often so that it doesn't scorch, until it registers 180°F on the candy thermometer, about 10 minutes.

Meanwhile, put the egg yolks in a small bowl and whisk in the remaining ¼ cup plus 2 tablespoons sugar. Make an ice bath with equal parts ice and water in a large bowl. Remove the saucepan from the heat. While whisking constantly, slowly stream ½ cup of the hot liquid into the egg-sugar mixture to temper the eggs. Whisk in another ½ cup of the liquid. Transfer the tempered yolk mixture to the saucepan and heat over medium heat, stirring often so that it doesn't scorch, until the custard registers 180°F on the candy thermometer, 2 to 3 minutes. Strain the custard through a fine-mesh sieve into a heatproof container.

Put the container of custard in the ice bath to chill. Stir occasionally (don't let any water get into the custard) until the custard is completely cold. Cover and refrigerate overnight.

The next day, pour the custard into the ice cream maker and freeze it according to the manufacturer's instructions. Transfer the ice cream to a freezer container and freeze until ready to serve. It will keep for up to 1 month.

TURBINADO

AWASE DASHI

BAKING SODA

SHRIMP FLOSS

LOUISIANA
DRIED SHRIMP

BAKING POWDER

USKA ORANGE CUMIN

CHARCOAL FLYING FISH DASHI

GOMASIO

CHILE PLANT

KATSUDASHI

TAKI
UMAMI POWDER

OKINAWA HOKUTO
JAPANESE BROWN SUGAR

BONITO FLAKES

CHOCOLATE
OAXAQUENO

STONE GROUND
KAFFIR LIME LEAVES

YUZU PEEL

BASICS

RENDERED BACON FAT

MAKES ABOUT 1 CUP

1 pound smoked bacon scraps,
preferably Benton's (see
Resources, page 368),
cut into ¼-inch pieces

Put the bacon scraps in a medium heavy-bottomed saucepan and cook over low heat, stirring frequently, until all the fat has rendered, about 1 hour.

Strain the fat through a fine-mesh sieve into a heatproof container. (The browned bits can be saved and used on a salad or sprinkled on your eggs in the morning.) Cool to room temperature, cover, and refrigerate until ready to use. Tightly covered, the bacon fat will keep for up to 3 weeks in the refrigerator.

RENDERED FRESH BEEF FAT

MAKES ABOUT 1½ CUPS

1 pound fresh beef fat, cut into
½-inch pieces

½ cup water

Combine the beef fat and water in a medium heavy-bottomed saucepan and cook over low heat, stirring occasionally, until all the fat has rendered and the water has completely evaporated, about 1½ hours.

Strain through a fine-mesh sieve into a heatproof container. Discard the browned bits in the sieve. Cool to room temperature, cover, and refrigerate until ready to use. Tightly covered, the beef fat will keep for up to 3 weeks in the refrigerator.

RENDERED FRESH CHICKEN FAT

MAKES ABOUT 1 CUP

1½ pounds chicken skins, cut into
½-inch squares

½ cup water

Combine the chicken skins and water in a medium heavy-bottomed saucepan and cook over low heat, stirring frequently, until all the fat has rendered and the water has completely evaporated, about 1½ hours.

Strain the fat through a fine-mesh sieve into a heatproof container. (The chicken skins can be dried on paper towels and seasoned with a little salt and pepper for a snack.) Cool to room temperature, cover, and refrigerate until ready to use. Tightly covered, the chicken fat will keep for up to 3 weeks in the refrigerator.

RENDERED FRESH LARD

MAKES ABOUT 1½ CUPS

1 pound fresh pork fat, cut into
  ½-inch pieces

½ cup water

Combine the pork fat and water in a medium heavy-bottomed saucepan and cook over low heat, stirring occasionally, until all the fat has rendered and the water has completely evaporated, about 1½ hours.

Strain the fat through a fine-mesh sieve into a heatproof container. Discard the browned bits in the sieve. Cool to room temperature, cover, and refrigerate until ready to use. Tightly covered, the lard will keep for up to 3 weeks in the refrigerator.

RENDERED HAM FAT

MAKES ABOUT 1 CUP

1 pound fatty country ham scraps,
  preferably Bob Wood's Country
  Ham Trimmings (see Resources,
  page 368), cut into ½-inch
  pieces

¼ cup water

Combine the ham scraps and water in a medium heavy-bottomed saucepan and cook over low heat, stirring frequently, until all the fat has rendered and the water has completely evaporated, about 1 hour.

Strain the fat through a fine-mesh sieve into a heatproof container. (The browned bits can be saved and used on a salad or sprinkled on your eggs in the morning.) Cool to room temperature, cover, and refrigerate until ready to use. Tightly covered, the ham fat will keep for up to 3 weeks in the refrigerator.

CHICKEN STOCK

MAKES 3½ QUARTS

10 pounds chicken bones
(a combination of necks,
wings, and backs)

1 pound chicken feet

5 quarts cold water, plus more
as needed

8 cups ice cubes

2 cups (8 ounces) 1-inch-thick
slices peeled carrots

3 cups (8 ounces) 1-inch-thick
slices leeks, white and light
green parts only

8 ounces yellow onions, quartered

4 large garlic cloves

2 fresh bay leaves

1 bunch thyme (1½ ounces)

2 rosemary sprigs

NOTE: Keeping the pot on one side of the burner sets up
a convection movement, pulling all the impurities to one
side of the pot.

Rinse the bones and feet very well, being careful to remove
all blood and impurities. Put the bones, feet, and water in a
large stockpot and put the pot on one side of a burner set
to medium-high (see Note). Bring to a simmer, skimming
off any impurities that rise to the top, about 20 minutes.
Turn off the heat and add the ice. Remove and discard the
fat that congeals on the top, along with any impurities that
have risen to the surface.

Add the remaining ingredients to the pot and bring the stock
to a gentle boil over medium heat, skimming off any impurities, about 30 minutes. Reduce the heat to low and simmer
the stock for 5 hours, continuing to skim off any impurities; add more water if necessary to keep the ingredients
covered.

Gently ladle the stock through a fine-mesh sieve into a
heatproof container. Do not press down on the solids, or you
will make the stock cloudy. Discard the solids. Make an ice
bath in the sink with equal parts ice and water, place the
container of stock in the ice bath, and leave it, stirring occasionally, until the stock is chilled, about 1 hour. Cover and
refrigerate until ready to use.

Tightly covered, the stock will keep for up to 3 days in the
refrigerator or up to 3 months in the freezer. Remove any fat
that has solidified on the top before using.

DUCK STOCK

MAKES 8 CUPS

2½ pounds duck bones
  (a combination of necks,
  wings, backs, and legs;
  see box, page 137)

3 quarts cold water, plus more
  as needed

½ cup (2 ounces) 1-inch-thick
  slices peeled carrots

½ cup (2 ounces) ¼-inch-thick
  slices celery

¼ cup (1 ounce) large dice yellow
  onion

3 large garlic cloves

½ bunch flat-leaf parsley
  (2 ounces)

1 tablespoon black peppercorns

1 fresh bay leaf

Preheat the oven to 350°F.

Put the bones in a roasting pan large enough to hold them in one layer. Roast them, turning occasionally, until golden brown and caramelized, 45 minutes to 1 hour.

Transfer the bones to a large stockpot. Discard the fat from the roasting pan. Use a little of the water to deglaze the pan, scraping up the browned bits from the bottom, then pour the bits and liquid into the pot with the bones.

Add the remaining water and the rest of the ingredients to the pot and put the pot on one side of a burner set to medium-high (see Note, opposite). Bring to a gentle boil, skimming off any impurities that rise to the top, about 30 minutes.

Reduce the heat to low and simmer the stock for 5 hours, continuing to skim off any impurities; add more water if necessary to keep the ingredients covered.

Gently ladle the stock through a fine-mesh sieve into a heatproof container. Do not press down on the solids, or you will make the stock cloudy. Discard the solids. Make an ice bath in the sink with equal parts ice and water, place the container of stock in the ice bath, and leave it, stirring occasionally, until the stock is chilled, about 1 hour. Cover and refrigerate until ready to use.

Tightly covered, the stock will keep for up to 3 days in the refrigerator or up to 3 months in the freezer. Remove any fat that has solidified on the top before using.

PORK STOCK

MAKES 4 QUARTS

2 tablespoons canola oil

5 pounds pork bones

2 gallons cold water, plus more
    as needed

1 cup (4 ounces) 1-inch-thick slices
    peeled carrots

1 cup (4 ounces) ¼-inch-thick
    slices celery

4 ounces yellow onions, quartered

5 large garlic cloves

1 large bunch flat-leaf parsley
    (4 ounces)

2 tablespoons black peppercorns

2 fresh bay leaves

Preheat the oven to 350°F. Select a roasting pan large enough to hold the bones in one layer and put it in the oven to heat for 20 minutes. (Or use two pans if necessary.)

Add the canola oil to the pan(s) and heat for about 30 seconds. Add the bones and toss them in the oil to coat. Roast the bones, turning occasionally, for 45 minutes to 1 hour, until golden brown and caramelized.

Transfer the bones to a large stockpot. Discard the fat in the roasting pan(s). Use a little of the water to deglaze the pan(s), scraping up the browned bits from the bottom. Pour the bits and liquid into the pot with the bones. Add the remaining water and the rest of the ingredients to the pot and put the pot on one side of a burner set to medium-high (see Note, page 344). Bring to a gentle boil over medium heat, skimming off any impurities that rise to the top, about 1 hour.

Reduce the heat to low and simmer the stock for 12 hours, continuing to skim off any impurities; add more water if necessary to keep the ingredients covered.

Gently ladle the stock through a fine-mesh sieve into a heatproof container. Do not press down on the solids, or you will make the stock cloudy. Discard the solids. Make an ice bath in the sink with equal parts ice and water, place the container of stock in the ice bath, and leave it, stirring occasionally, until the stock is chilled, about 1 hour. Cover and refrigerate until ready to use.

Tightly covered, the stock will keep for up to 3 days in the refrigerator or up to 3 months in the freezer. Remove any fat that has solidified on the top before using.

VEAL OR BEEF STOCK

MAKES 3 QUARTS

6 pounds veal or beef bones

8 quarts cold water, plus more
as needed

½ calf's foot

1 cup (4 ounces) 1-inch-thick slices
peeled carrots

1½ cups (4 ounces) 1-inch-thick
slices leeks, white and light green
parts only

1 yellow onion, quartered

½ head garlic (cut the head
horizontally in half)

¼ large bunch flat-leaf parsley
(1 ounce)

⅓ bunch thyme (½ ounce)

1 fresh bay leaf

Put the bones in a large stockpot and cover with 4 quarts of the cold water. Slowly bring to a simmer over medium-high heat, skimming off any impurities that rise to the top, about 45 minutes. Drain the bones and discard the liquid. Clean the stockpot.

Rinse off the bones while they are still hot. Place them in the clean stockpot and add the remaining 4 quarts cold water. Put the pot on one side of a burner set to medium (see Note, page 344). Bring to a gentle boil, skimming off any impurities that rise to the top, about 30 minutes. Add the remaining ingredients to the pot and bring to a slow boil, skimming off any impurities, about 5 minutes. Reduce the heat to low and simmer the stock for 7 hours, continuing to skim off any impurities; add more water if necessary to keep the ingredients covered.

Gently ladle the stock through a fine-mesh sieve into a heatproof container. Do not press down on the solids, or you will make the stock cloudy. Discard the solids. Make an ice bath in the sink with equal parts ice and water, place the container of stock in the ice bath, and leave it, stirring occasionally, until the stock is chilled, about 1 hour. Cover and refrigerate until ready to use.

Tightly covered, the stock will keep for up to 3 days in the refrigerator or up to 3 months in the freezer. Remove any fat that has solidified on the top before using.

VEGETABLE STOCK

MAKES 8 CUPS

1½ cups (4 ounces) chopped leeks, white parts only

1½ cups (4 ounces) chopped sweet onions

1 cup (4 ounces) chopped peeled carrots

1 cup (4 ounces) diced celery

1 cup (4 ounces) diced fennel bulb

4 large garlic cloves

2 tablespoons canola oil

8 cups cold water, plus more as needed

1 cup dry white wine

1 large bunch flat-leaf parsley (4 ounces)

3 thyme sprigs

1 star anise pod

1 fresh bay leaf

Working in batches, pulse the leeks, onions, carrots, celery, fennel, and garlic in a food processor until the vegetables are the size of peas.

Heat the canola oil in a medium pot over medium-high heat. Add the vegetables and cook, stirring frequently, until just tender, about 5 minutes.

Add the water, wine, parsley, thyme, star anise, and bay leaf and bring to a simmer, skimming off any impurities that rise to the top. Reduce the heat to medium-low and simmer the stock, continuing to skim off any impurities, for 45 minutes, or until rich in color, deeply flavored, and very fragrant; add more water if necessary to keep the ingredients covered.

Gently ladle the stock through a fine-mesh sieve into a heatproof container. Do not press down on the solids, or you will make the stock cloudy. Discard the solids. Make an ice bath in the sink with equal parts ice and water, place the container of stock in the ice bath, and leave it, stirring occasionally, until the stock is chilled, about 1 hour. Cover and refrigerate until ready to use.

Tightly covered, the stock will keep for up to 3 days in the refrigerator or up to 3 months in the freezer. Remove any fat that has solidified on the top before using.

MUSHROOM STOCK

MAKES 8 CUPS

1 pound button mushrooms,
   washed, dried, and very thinly
   sliced

4 ounces fresh shiitake mushrooms,
   washed, dried, and very thinly
   sliced

8 cups cold water

½ cup (2 ounces) thinly sliced
   sweet onion

¼ cup (1 ounce) thinly sliced
   peeled carrots

¼ cup (1 ounce) thinly sliced celery

1 fresh bay leaf

1 tablespoon white peppercorns

The specific temperature called for in this recipe was inspired by my experience making traditional Japanese dashi. A constant temperature of 140°F is perfect for extracting the rich, savory umami flavor from the mushrooms. That little bit of extra care will make the resulting stock that much more delicious.

Combine the mushrooms and water in a medium pot and heat over medium-low heat until it registers 140°F on an instant-read thermometer. Add the onion, carrots, celery, bay leaf, and white peppercorns and return to 140°F. Maintain this temperature for 1 hour, frequently checking with the thermometer and adjusting the heat accordingly, to extract the flavor from the mushrooms.

Strain the stock through a fine-mesh sieve into a heatproof container. Gently press on the mushrooms to extract all the flavorful liquid. Discard the solids. Make an ice bath in the sink with equal parts ice and water, place the container of stock in the ice bath, and leave it, stirring occasionally, until the stock is chilled, about 1 hour. Cover and refrigerate until ready to use.

Tightly covered, the stock will keep for up to 3 days in the refrigerator or up to 3 months in the freezer.

BASIC MEAT SAUCE

MAKES 1½ CUPS

1 tablespoon canola oil

1¾ cups thinly sliced shallots

1 cup chopped peeled carrots

½ cup chopped celery

1 small garlic clove, smashed and peeled

1 cup dry red wine

1 cup dry Madeira

4 cups Veal or Beef Stock (page 347)

2 cups Chicken Stock (page 344)

1 bouquet garni (a 4-inch piece of leek green, 4 thyme sprigs, 2 fresh bay leaves, and 6 black peppercorns, wrapped in cheesecloth and tied tightly with butcher's twine)

1 teaspoon fresh lemon juice

1 teaspoon soy sauce, preferably Bourbon Barrel Bluegrass Soy Sauce (see Resources, page 368)

½ teaspoon sherry vinegar

1 tablespoon unsalted butter

1 teaspoon kosher salt

Heat the canola oil in a large saucepan over medium-high heat until it shimmers. Add the shallots, carrots, celery, and garlic and cook, stirring frequently, until dark brown, about 7 minutes. Add the wine and Madeira and deglaze the pan, scraping up any brown bits from the bottom. Cook, stirring occasionally, until the wine has almost completely evaporated, about 10 minutes.

Reduce the heat to low, add the veal stock, chicken stock, and bouquet garni, and bring to a simmer. Simmer, stirring occasionally to prevent the vegetables from scorching, until the sauce has reduced to 1½ cups, about 3 hours.

Gently ladle the sauce through a fine-mesh sieve into a heatproof container. Discard the solids. Make an ice bath with equal parts ice and water in a large bowl. Place the container of sauce in the ice bath and leave it, stirring occasionally, until the sauce has chilled, about 30 minutes, then cover and refrigerate. (*The sauce can be made ahead to this point and refrigerated for up to 3 days or frozen for up to 3 months.*)

When ready to serve, heat the sauce in a small saucepan over medium heat until melted and warmed through, about 3 minutes. Add the lemon juice, soy sauce, and sherry vinegar. Remove the saucepan from the stove, stir in the butter and salt, and serve at once.

CHICKEN SAUCE

MAKES 1 CUP

4 cups Chicken Stock (page 344)

2 tablespoons fresh lemon juice

2 teaspoons sorghum, preferably Muddy Pond (see Resources, page 369)

2 teaspoons Rendered Fresh Chicken Fat (page 342), melted

1 teaspoon kosher salt

½ teaspoon freshly ground black pepper

½ teaspoon cayenne pepper sauce powder (see Resources, page 369)

Put the chicken stock in a medium saucepan and bring to a simmer over medium heat. Simmer the stock until it has reduced to 1 cup, about 1 hour.

Remove from the stove and stir in the lemon juice, sorghum syrup, melted chicken fat, salt, black pepper, and cayenne pepper sauce powder. If not using the sauce immediately, transfer to a heatproof container, cool to room temperature, cover, and refrigerate. Tightly covered, the sauce will keep for up to 3 days in the refrigerator.

To reheat the sauce, heat it in a small saucepan over medium heat until melted and warmed through, about 2 minutes. Serve immediately.

DUCK JUS

MAKES 1 CUP

1 tablespoon canola oil

¼ cup chopped sweet onion

2 tablespoons chopped celery

2 tablespoons chopped peeled carrot

1 small garlic clove, thinly sliced

3 black peppercorns

1 small fresh bay leaf

1 small thyme sprig

½ cup dry red wine

4 cups Duck Stock (page 345)

Kosher salt and freshly ground black pepper

Heat the canola oil in a medium saucepan over medium-high heat until it shimmers. Add the onion, celery, and carrot and cook, stirring frequently, until golden brown, about 5 minutes. Add the garlic, peppercorns, bay leaf, and thyme, then add the wine and deglaze the pan, scraping up any brown bits from the bottom. Cook, stirring, until the wine has almost completely evaporated, 6 to 8 minutes.

Add the duck stock and bring to a simmer over medium-high heat. Reduce the heat to medium and simmer, stirring occasionally to prevent the vegetables from scorching, until the liquid has reduced to 1 cup, about 1 hour.

Gently ladle the jus through a fine-mesh sieve into a heatproof container. Do not press down on the solids, or you will make the jus cloudy. Discard the solids. Lightly season the jus with salt and pepper. Make an ice bath with equal parts ice and water in a large bowl. Place the container in the ice bath and leave it, stirring occasionally, until chilled, about 30 minutes, then cover and refrigerate until ready to use.

Tightly covered, the jus will keep for up to 3 days in the refrigerator or up to 3 months in the freezer.

To reheat the jus, heat it in a small saucepan over medium heat until melted and warmed through, about 2 minutes. Serve immediately.

PORK JUS

MAKES 2 CUPS

1 tablespoon Rendered Fresh Lard
(page 343)

¼ cup chopped sweet onion

2 tablespoons chopped celery

2 tablespoons chopped peeled
carrot

1 small garlic clove, thinly sliced

3 black peppercorns

1 small fresh bay leaf

1 small thyme sprig

½ cup dry red wine

4 cups Pork Stock (page 346)

Kosher salt and freshly ground
black pepper

Heat the lard in a medium saucepan over medium-high heat. Add the onion, celery, and carrot and cook, stirring frequently, until golden brown, about 5 minutes. Add the garlic, peppercorns, bay leaf, and thyme, then add the wine and deglaze the pan, scraping up any brown bits from the bottom. Cook, stirring, until the wine has almost completely evaporated, 6 to 8 minutes.

Add the pork stock and bring to a simmer over medium-high heat. Reduce the heat to medium and simmer, stirring occasionally to prevent the vegetables from scorching, until the liquid has reduced to 2 cups, about 30 minutes.

Gently ladle the jus through a fine-mesh sieve into a heat-proof container. Do not press down on the solids, or you will make the jus cloudy. Discard the solids. Lightly season the jus with salt and pepper. Make an ice bath with equal parts ice and water in a large bowl. Place the container in the ice bath and leave it, stirring occasionally, until chilled, about 30 minutes, then cover and refrigerate until ready to use.

Tightly covered, the jus will keep for up to 3 days in the refrigerator or up to 3 months in the freezer.

To reheat the jus, heat it in a small saucepan over medium heat until melted and warmed through, about 2 minutes. Serve immediately.

BBQ SAUCE

MAKES ABOUT 4 CUPS

1 cup Pork Stock (page 346)

5 cups apple cider vinegar

5 tablespoons BBQ Rub (page 363)

1½ cups ketchup

1 tablespoon fresh lemon juice

Combine all the ingredients in a large nonreactive saucepan and bring to a simmer over high heat. Reduce the heat to medium-high and cook, stirring frequently to prevent scorching, until the sauce has reduced by half, about 30 minutes.

Ladle the sauce into two clean 1-pint canning jars. Cool to room temperature, then wipe the rims and threads clean, place the lids and rings on the jars, tighten the rings, and refrigerate. Tightly sealed, the sauce will keep for up to 2 weeks in the refrigerator.

ALABAMA WHITE SAUCE

MAKES 1½ CUPS

1 cup mayonnaise, preferably
    Duke's (see Resources, page 369)

½ cup apple cider vinegar

2 tablespoons Pepper Mash
    (page 263)

1½ teaspoons grated lemon zest

1 tablespoon fresh lemon juice

1 teaspoon freshly ground black
    pepper

¾ teaspoon Worcestershire sauce,
    preferably Bourbon Barrel (see
    Resources, page 368)

½ teaspoon kosher salt

½ teaspoon Espelette pepper

½ teaspoon Aleppo pepper
    (see Resources, page 369)

½ teaspoon celery seeds

¼ teaspoon cayenne pepper

Combine all the ingredients in a bowl and whisk to mix well. Transfer to a container, cover, and refrigerate until ready to use. Tightly covered, the sauce will keep for up to 5 days in the refrigerator.

PEPPER SAUCE

MAKES ABOUT 3¼ CUPS

½ cup Hominy Miso (page 264)

2½ cups Pepper Mash (page 263)

3 tablespoons plus 2 teaspoons
    fish sauce

4 teaspoons soy sauce, preferably
    Bourbon Barrel Bluegrass Soy
    Sauce (see Resources, page 368)

This pepper sauce is a one-stop flavor shop. I created it while I was working on a shrimp and grits recipe, but with its multiple layers of flavor, it has found its way into countless dishes since.

Combine the miso, pepper mash, fish sauce, and soy sauce in a blender and blend on high until completely smooth, about 2 minutes. Transfer to a container, cool to room temperature, cover, and refrigerate until ready to use. Tightly covered, the pepper sauce will keep for up to 1 month in the refrigerator.

WEST AFRICAN PEANUT SAUCE

MAKES 2½ CUPS

½ sweet onion (about 4 ounces), not peeled

1 large garlic clove, not peeled

½ jalapeño pepper (with its seeds)

½ red bell pepper (about 4 ounces), cored and seeded

1 cup Preserved Tomatoes (page 278) or canned whole tomatoes, drained

2 tablespoons organic palm oil

½ teaspoon ground ginger

½ teaspoon Bourbon Barrel Bourbon Smoked Paprika (see Resources, page 368)

½ teaspoon chili powder

⅓ cup creamy peanut butter

1 cup Vegetable Stock (page 348)

1 teaspoon kosher salt

1½ teaspoons soy sauce, preferably Bourbon Barrel Bluegrass Soy Sauce (see Resources, page 368)

1 tablespoon fresh lime juice

Preheat the oven to 425°F.

Spread the onion, garlic, jalapeño, bell pepper, and tomatoes out on a rimmed baking sheet and roast for about 25 minutes, until the vegetables start to brown and their skins can easily be peeled off. Remove from the oven and cool to room temperature.

Carefully peel the cooled vegetables and cut them into ½-inch dice.

Heat the palm oil in a large skillet over high heat until it shimmers. Add the diced vegetables and cook, stirring frequently, until completely softened, about 3 minutes. Add the ginger, paprika, and chili powder and cook for another minute. Stir in the peanut butter, stock, and salt, bring to a boil, and cook for another minute to meld the flavors. Remove from the stove and cool for 5 minutes.

Transfer the mixture to a blender and blend on high until completely smooth, about 1 minute. Blend in the soy sauce and transfer to a container with a lid. If using immediately, stir in the lime juice. Alternatively, cool to room temperature, cover, and refrigerate for 2 up to days. Remove from the refrigerator 1 hour before using and stir in the lime juice just before serving.

PORK RINDS

MAKES 24 SQUARES

One 12-inch square of pork skin

Canola oil for deep-frying

Kosher salt

EQUIPMENT

Immersion circulator

Vacuum bag and sealer

Dehydrator

You will need an immersion circulator for this recipe, but these are increasingly available and affordable. A circulator creates a precise and consistent environment for cooking ingredients sous vide—that is, in a vacuum-sealed bag in a hot-water bath. Cooking ingredients this way lets you maintain exact temperatures over a long period of time. The circulator is the ideal way to cook these pork rinds.

Preheat the water bath in the immersion circulator to 181.4°F.

Place the skin fat side up on a cutting board. Using a thin, flexible knife, slice off as much of the fat as possible. The more fat you remove, the lighter the pork rinds will be. When you have removed the fat, turn the knife over and scrape the skin with the back of the knife. You should be able to see through the skin. Discard the fat.

Place the skin in the vacuum bag and seal it at the highest setting. Cook the skin in the water bath at 181.4°F until it is soft, about 24 hours.

When the skin is cooked, make an ice bath with equal parts ice and water in a large bowl and put the bag in the ice bath. Let sit until the skin is completely chilled. Remove the skin from the bag and scrape the fat side of the skin one more time to make sure all the fat has been removed.

Cut the skin into twenty-four 1-inch squares. Dry the pieces in the dehydrator at 160°F for 24 hours. They should snap when you try to break a piece off.

Transfer the pork skin to an airtight container lined with paper towels, cover, and set aside at room temperature. *(The dehydrated pieces can be stored in an airtight container for up to 1 week at room temperature. Do not refrigerate them.)*

When you're ready to serve the pork skins, fill a deep fryer with canola oil according to the manufacturer's directions and heat the oil to 350°F. Alternatively, fill a deep heavy pot half full with canola oil and heat the oil over medium heat to 350°F. Cover a wire rack with paper towels.

Working in batches, fry the pork rinds until they are fully puffed, about 1 minute. Drain on the prepared rack for at least 1 minute, then season lightly with salt and serve.

BACON JAM

MAKES 2 CUPS

13 ounces bacon, preferably Benton's (see Resources, page 368), cut into ¼-inch dice

2 tablespoons light brown sugar

⅔ cup sorghum syrup, preferably Muddy Pond (see Resources, page 369)

½ cup plus 2 tablespoons Chicken Stock (page 344)

¼ cup sherry vinegar

1 tablespoon soy sauce, preferably Bourbon Barrel Bluegrass Soy Sauce (see Resources, page 368)

Put half the bacon in a skillet large enough to hold it in one layer and cook over medium-low heat, stirring frequently, until the fat has rendered and the pieces of bacon are crispy, 4 to 5 minutes. Using a slotted spoon, transfer the bacon bits to a paper towel to drain. Remove the fat from the skillet and repeat with the remaining bacon. (Reserve the fat for another use, if desired.)

Combine the brown sugar and sorghum syrup in a medium heavy-bottomed saucepan and heat over medium heat, stirring, to dissolve the sugar, then cook, without stirring, gently swirling the pan occasionally to help the mixture cook evenly, until the color darkens and the sugar caramelizes, about 5 minutes.

Remove the saucepan from the heat and carefully add the chicken stock and vinegar; once the intense bubbling has subsided, stir to combine. Return the saucepan to the heat, bring the mixture to a simmer, and cook until it has reduced by half, about 10 minutes.

Add the soy sauce and bacon and bring to a simmer; the mixture should be thick and sticky. Remove from the stove and cool to room temperature. Transfer the bacon jam to a container, cover, and refrigerate until ready to use.

Tightly covered, it will keep for up to 3 days in the refrigerator; remove from the refrigerator 30 minutes before using.

FINES HERBES

MAKES ¼ CUP

1 tablespoon finely chopped flat-leaf parsley

1 tablespoon finely chopped tarragon

1 tablespoon minced chives

1 tablespoon finely chopped chervil

Combine all the herbs in a small bowl and mix well. Line a container with paper towels, transfer the herbs to it, cover, and refrigerate until ready to use. Tightly covered, the herbs will keep for up to 1 day in the refrigerator.

BENNE TAHINI

MAKES ABOUT ⅔ CUP

1 cup Anson Mills Antebellum
Benne Seeds (see Resources,
page 368)

¼ cup canola oil

3 tablespoons benne oil (see
Resources, page 369)

Heat a large skillet over medium heat. Add the benne seeds and cook, stirring constantly, for 2 to 3 minutes, until the seeds toast and start to smell a little nutty. Transfer to a plate and cool to room temperature.

Place the toasted benne seeds, canola oil, and benne oil in a food processor and process until smooth, 4 to 5 minutes. Scrape down the sides as needed and take care to not get the contents too hot. Feel the bowl; it should be barely warm. If the mixture gets too hot, wait for it to cool before continuing.

Transfer the tahini to a container, cover, and refrigerate until ready to use. Tightly covered, the tahini will keep for up to 6 months in the refrigerator.

BUTTERMILK VINAIGRETTE

MAKES ABOUT 2 CUPS

½ cup sour cream

½ cup full-fat buttermilk (see Note,
page 27)

1½ ounces Asiago cheese,
preferably Kenny's Farmhouse
Dry Fork Reserve (see Resources,
page 369), grated

¼ cup mayonnaise, preferably
Duke's (see Resources, page 369)

1 tablespoon apple cider vinegar

1½ teaspoons Worcestershire
sauce, preferably Bourbon Barrel
(see Resources, page 368)

½ cup finely chopped basil

1½ teaspoons finely chopped
flat-leaf parsley

1½ teaspoons finely chopped
chives

1½ teaspoons sugar

1 teaspoon minced garlic

1½ teaspoons kosher salt

1½ teaspoons freshly ground pepper

Combine all the ingredients in a bowl and mix well. Transfer to a container, cover, and refrigerate for at least 4 hours, or preferably overnight, before using to allow the flavors to develop. Tightly covered, the buttermilk vinaigrette will keep for up to 5 days in the refrigerator.

SMOKED TOMATO VINAIGRETTE

MAKES 5½ CUPS

4 cups tomato juice

1½ cups Lindera Farms Hickory
    Vinegar (see Resources,
    page 369)

EQUIPMENT

Smoker

Technically this isn't a true vinaigrette, but the richness of the smoked tomato juice creates a similar effect without adding any fat. Try it drizzled over grilled summer squash and zucchini.

Prepare the smoker with hardwood charcoal and hickory (see page 57); maintain a temperature of between 185°F and 200°F.

Put the tomato juice in a medium saucepan and transfer it to the smoker. Smoke the juice, stirring occasionally, until it has a deep, smoky flavor but hasn't begun to evaporate, about 1 hour.

Remove the juice from the smoker, transfer to a container, and stir in the vinegar. Cool to room temperature, cover, and refrigerate until ready to use. Tightly covered, the vinaigrette will keep for up to 5 days in the refrigerator or up to 3 months in the freezer.

CORNBREAD CROUTONS

MAKES ABOUT 4 CUPS

Canola oil for deep-frying

1 recipe Basic Cornbread (page
    216), made a day ahead, cut into
    ¾-inch dice

Fill a deep fryer with canola oil according to the manufacturer's directions and heat the oil to 350°F. Alternatively, fill a deep heavy pot half full with canola oil and heat the oil over medium heat to 350°F. Line two rimmed baking sheets with paper towels.

Working in three batches, fry the diced cornbread, stirring occasionally to prevent the pieces from sticking to one another, until golden brown and crispy on the outside but still moist on the inside, about 2 minutes. Using a slotted spoon, transfer the fried cornbread to the prepared baking sheets and cool to room temperature. Repeat with the remaining cornbread. Transfer to an airtight container, cover, and set aside at room temperature. Tightly covered, the croutons will keep for up to 1 day at room temperature.

CORNBREAD OYSTER STUFFING

MAKES ABOUT 5 CUPS

1 tablespoon Rendered Bacon Fat (page 342)

½ cup small dice sweet onion

½ cup small dice celery

1 recipe Basic Cornbread (page 216), made a day ahead

1 tablespoon chopped sage

1 tablespoon chopped flat-leaf parsley

1 teaspoon celery seeds

1 teaspoon kosher salt

1 teaspoon freshly ground black pepper

¼ cup Chicken Stock (page 344)

1 large egg, lightly beaten

20 oysters, shucked (liquor reserved) and roughly chopped

Heat the bacon fat in a large skillet over medium heat until it shimmers. Add the onion and celery and cook, stirring occasionally, until softened and translucent, about 5 minutes. Transfer to a bowl and cool to room temperature.

Crumble the cornbread into a large bowl. Add the cooked onion and celery, the sage, parsley, celery seeds, salt, pepper, chicken stock, egg, oysters, and reserved oyster liquor and stir well. The stuffing should be evenly moist. Use immediately.

The stuffing can be baked in a 350°F oven in a greased 9-by-13-inch baking dish for 15 to 20 minutes, until hot throughout and golden brown on the top, or stuffed inside your favorite poultry. This recipe makes enough for one chicken or several quail; double it for a smaller (14- to 15-pound) turkey.

COTTAGE CHEESE

MAKES ABOUT 1 CUP

2 quarts pasteurized skim milk

¼ cup full-fat cultured buttermilk (see Note, page 27), at room temperature

½ teaspoon kosher salt

¼ cup plus 2 tablespoons heavy cream

NOTE: You'll need to start this recipe a day ahead of time to allow the milk to thicken.

Pour the skim milk into a large nonreactive saucepan and heat it over very low heat until it registers 75°F on an instant-read thermometer. Remove from the stove and stir in the buttermilk, then transfer to a heatproof bowl and cover lightly with aluminum foil.

Put the mixture in a place where the temperature remains close to 75°F and let sit for 24 hours. After 24 hours, the buttermilk should have coagulated the mixture, making a delicate layer of thickened milk on the top.

Insert a sharp knife into the thickened milk and pull the knife through it from one side of the bowl to the other. Repeat at 1-inch increments across the surface of the milk mixture. Turn the bowl a quarter turn and repeat to make a crosshatch pattern. This will shape the curds as they form when you heat the milk mixture. Let the mixture rest for 15 minutes.

Meanwhile, select a pot large enough to hold the bowl containing the milk mixture. Add enough water to come up the sides of the bowl up to the level of the milk and heat the water over low heat to 120°F.

Place the bowl in the pot of warm water, making sure not to let any water get into the milk, and heat, occasionally stirring gently, until the milk mixture reaches a temperature of 100°F and begins to separate into curds and whey, 10 to 15 minutes. Increase the heat to medium and heat until the milk mixture reaches a temperature of 120°F, 8 to 10 minutes. Maintain this temperature until the cheese curds are firm and not easily broken, about 5 minutes longer.

Meanwhile, line a fine-mesh strainer with a double layer of cheesecloth, place it over a bowl, and set aside.

Pour the curds and whey into the strainer. Let rest for 5 minutes. *(The whey that drains into the bowl can be used to make bread or cook grits. Transfer it to a container, cover, and refrigerate for up to 5 days or freeze for about 3 months in the freezer.)*

While the curds are resting, make an ice bath with equal parts ice and water in a large bowl.

Keeping the curds in the strainer, run them under room-temperature water to wash away any remaining whey. Gather up the edges of the cheesecloth to make a sack for the curds, secure it with a knot at the top, and submerge the sack in the ice bath until the curds cool to 50°F, about 10 minutes. Return the sack to the strainer, set over another bowl, and drain the curds for 30 minutes at room temperature.

Transfer the curds to a container, stir in the salt and cream, cover, and refrigerate until ready to use. Tightly covered, the cottage cheese will keep for up to 1 week in the refrigerator.

PIMENTO CHEESE

MAKES 2½ TO 3 CUPS

12 ounces pimento peppers

4 ounces cream cheese, at room temperature

½ cup mayonnaise, preferably Duke's (see Resources, page 369)

½ teaspoon Hot Sauce (page 260) or Red Clay Original Hot Sauce (see Resources, page 369)

½ teaspoon kosher salt

¼ teaspoon sugar

⅛ teaspoon cayenne pepper

⅛ teaspoon freshly ground white pepper

⅛ teaspoon Bourbon Barrel Bourbon Smoked Paprika (see Resources, page 368)

¼ cup chopped Pickled Ramps (page 251), plus ½ cup of their pickling liquid

1 pound sharp cheddar cheese, grated on the large holes of a box grater

NOTE: For a creamier pimento cheese, combine all the ingredients in the bowl of a stand mixer fitted with the paddle attachment (or use a hand mixer and a large bowl) and beat on medium speed for 2 minutes.

One at a time, skewer each pepper on the prongs of a carving fork and roast over an open flame on a gas stovetop, turning the peppers to blacken on all sides. Alternatively, place all the peppers on a rimmed baking sheet and roast under a hot broiler, turning occasionally, until blackened on all sides. Transfer the peppers to a bowl and cover the bowl with plastic wrap. Let the peppers steam until cool enough to handle.

Carefully peel the blackened skin off each pepper. Cut the peppers lengthwise in half, open out flat on a cutting board, and scrape away all the seeds and membranes. Dice the peppers.

Put the cream cheese in a medium bowl and beat it with a wooden spoon until softened. Add the mayonnaise and mix well. Add the hot sauce, salt, sugar, cayenne, white pepper, and paprika and stir to blend. Add the ramps, ramp pickling liquid, and cheddar cheese and stir again. Fold in the diced pimentos.

Cover the bowl and refrigerate until ready to serve. Tightly covered, the pimento cheese will keep for up to 3 days in the refrigerator.

FRESH CHEESE

MAKES 1½ CUPS

1 quart whole milk

½ cup heavy cream

2½ tablespoons distilled white
   vinegar

¼ teaspoon kosher salt

⅛ teaspoon freshly ground white
   pepper

NOTE: You'll need to start this recipe a day ahead of time to allow the cheese to drain.

Line a fine-mesh sieve with a double layer of cheesecloth and place it over a bowl deep enough that the drained whey won't touch the bottom of the sieve.

Heat the milk and cream in a large nonreactive saucepan over medium heat, stirring frequently, until it registers 170°F on an instant-read thermometer. Stir in the vinegar, salt, and white pepper and keep the mixture at 170°F for 2 minutes. Curds should form. Pour the mixture into the sieve, place the bowl and sieve in the refrigerator, and refrigerate overnight.

The next day, transfer the cheese to a container, cover, and refrigerate until ready to use. Tightly covered, the cheese will keep for up to 3 days in the refrigerator.

Reserve the whey that drained into the bowl for cooking grits. Tightly covered, the whey will keep for up to 5 days in the refrigerator or up to 3 months in the freezer.

HERB ASH

MAKES ¼ CUP

4 ounces tender herbs, such as
   chives, washed and dried

½ teaspoon powdered sugar

½ teaspoon kosher salt

Herb ash will make a useful—and unusual—addition to your spice cabinet. It can give a quick charred flavor to anything you sprinkle it over. Try it on shrimp and grits or poached eggs.

Preheat the oven to 400°F. Line two rimmed baking sheets with parchment paper.

Lay the herbs out in a thin, even layer on the prepared baking sheets. Roast for about 20 minutes, until they are completely dried out and a deep, dark brown.

Remove the herbs from the oven and transfer to an absolutely dry blender. Blend on high until the herbs become a fine powder, about 1 minute. Transfer to an airtight container, stir in the sugar and salt, and cover the container. Tightly covered, the herb ash will keep for up to 1 month in a cool, dry place.

BBQ RUB

MAKES 2¼ CUPS

1 cup Bourbon Barrel Bourbon Smoked Paprika (see Resources, page 368)

½ cup packed light brown sugar

¼ cup kosher salt

3 tablespoons garlic powder

3 tablespoons onion powder

3 tablespoons freshly ground black pepper

1 tablespoon chili powder

Combine all the ingredients in a clean canning jar, screw the lid on tightly, and shake to mix well. Tightly sealed, the rub will keep for up to 1 month in a cool, dry place.

BLACKENING SEASONING

MAKES ABOUT 1 CUP

3 tablespoons plus ½ teaspoon dried thyme

3 tablespoons plus ½ teaspoon dried oregano

2 tablespoons plus 2 teaspoons Bourbon Barrel Bourbon Smoked Paprika (see Resources, page 368)

2 tablespoons freshly ground white pepper

2 tablespoons freshly ground black pepper

1 tablespoon onion powder

1 tablespoon garlic powder

1 tablespoon cayenne pepper

1 tablespoon Aleppo pepper (see Resources, page 369)

2¼ teaspoons kosher salt

This seasoning mix is a nod to Paul Prudhomme's famous blackening seasoning. Use it to add depth and kick to fried catfish (see page 106) or to season barbecue baked beans. It's also great for cooking up a pot of peel-and-eat shrimp.

Combine all the ingredients in a clean 1-pint canning jar, screw the lid on tightly, and shake to mix well. Tightly sealed, the blackening seasoning will keep in a cool, dry place for up to 1 month.

TURNIP CONDIMENT

MAKES 1½ CUPS

6 baby turnips (about 1½ inches in diameter), with their greens (about 8 ounces total)

1 cup apple cider vinegar

1 cup water

¼ cup sugar

½ teaspoon kosher salt

1½ teaspoons grated or minced garlic

3 tablespoons extra-virgin olive oil

1½ tablespoons grated lemon zest

1 tablespoon plus 2 teaspoons Turnip Ferment (page 271)

¼ teaspoon Surig 25% Vinegar (see Resources, page 368)

Serve this piquant condiment with Grilled Catfish with Hoppin' John (page 98), or spoon it over a dish of braised field peas.

NOTE: You'll need to start this recipe a day ahead of time to prep the turnips.

The day before you plan to serve the condiment, remove the greens from the turnips, transfer them to a container lined with a damp paper towel, cover, and refrigerate. Refrigerate one of the turnips. Peel the rest of the turnips, slice them into ⅛-inch-thick slices, and place in a nonreactive heat-proof container.

Combine the cider vinegar, water, sugar, and salt in a small nonreactive saucepan and bring to a boil over high heat, stirring to dissolve the sugar and salt. Pour the liquid over the sliced turnips and cool to room temperature, then cover and refrigerate overnight.

The next day, remove the stems from the turnip greens. Make stacks of the leaves, roll the stacks up into cylinders, and slice the cylinders into ribbons about ⅛ inch thick. Wash them in a large bowl of cold water, changing the water several times if they are sandy. Drain and dry the greens, finely chop, and put them in a bowl.

Remove the turnips from the pickling liquid (discard the liquid) and very finely dice them. Add to the bowl with the turnip greens. Peel the reserved raw turnip and grate it using a Microplane. Measure 2 tablespoons of the grated turnip and add to the bowl. Add the garlic, olive oil, lemon zest, turnip ferment, and Surig vinegar and stir to combine. Transfer to a container, cover, and refrigerate until ready to use. Tightly covered, the turnip condiment will keep for up to 1 day in the refrigerator; remove from the refrigerator 30 minutes before serving.

RAMP LEAF OIL

MAKES 1 CUP

6 ounces ramp leaves

1 cup grapeseed oil

This oil is good with Grilled Trout with Cornbread Puree (page 103). Or drizzle it over a scrambled egg sandwich for a decadent version of that favorite comfort food.

Place a coffee filter on top of a 1-quart canning jar, letting the center dip down into the jar to create a depression to hold the ramp leaves, and secure it with a rubber band.

Combine the ramp leaves and grapeseed oil in a blender and blend on high until the leaves and oil emulsify and then visibly separate, about 3 minutes. Transfer the mixture to a small nonreactive saucepan and heat over medium heat until the mixture registers 135°F on an instant-read thermometer, about 3 minutes.

Pour the mixture into the coffee filter, but do not press it down. Let stand until all the oil has drained through, about 1 hour.

Discard the solids and the filter. Cover the jar and refrigerate until ready to use. Tightly sealed, the oil will keep for up to 5 days in the refrigerator; bring to room temperature before using.

SPICY PEANUTS

MAKES 1 CUP

1 cup raw dried peanuts

2 teaspoons Oliver Farm Green Peanut Oil (see Resources, page 369)

2 teaspoons Espelette pepper

½ teaspoon kosher salt

Preheat the oven to 350°F.

Spread the peanuts in an even layer on a rimmed baking sheet and toast in the oven for about 20 minutes, until lightly browned and fragrant.

Transfer the peanuts to a bowl, add the green peanut oil, Espelette pepper, and salt, and toss to coat. Spread the peanuts out on the baking sheet and cool to room temperature.

Roughly chop the peanuts, transfer them to an airtight container, cover, and store until ready to use. Tightly covered, the peanuts will keep for up to 1 month at room temperature.

CITRUS CONDIMENT

MAKES ABOUT 1 CUP

¼ cup plus 1 tablespoon very finely diced orange zest (remove the zest in strips with a vegetable peeler and remove any white pith, then dice)

3 tablespoons very finely diced lemon zest (remove the zest in strips with a vegetable peeler and remove any white pith, then dice)

3 tablespoons very finely diced lime zest (remove the zest in strips with a vegetable peeler and remove any white pith, then dice)

⅔ cup fresh orange juice

¼ cup plus 2 tablespoons fresh lemon juice

¼ cup plus 2 tablespoons fresh lime juice

3 tablespoons mustard seeds

3 tablespoons sugar

1 tablespoon apple pectin

½ teaspoon citrus vinegar, preferably Jean-Marc Montegottero Calamansi Vinegar (see Resources, page 269)

¼ teaspoon Surig 25% Vinegar (see Resources, page 368)

Combine the citrus zests, citrus juices, and mustard seeds in a small nonreactive saucepan. Combine the sugar and pectin in a small bowl and stir them into the juice mixture. Bring to a simmer over medium heat, stirring frequently, then cook, stirring occasionally, until the mixture thickens and reduces by half, about 30 minutes.

Transfer to a container, stir in the vinegars, and cool to room temperature, then cover and refrigerate until ready to use. Tightly covered, the condiment will keep for up to 3 days in the refrigerator.

PRESERVED TOMATO CONDIMENT

MAKES ¾ CUP

1½ cups Preserved Tomatoes (page 278) or canned whole tomatoes, drained

2 teaspoons Rendered Fresh Beef Fat (page 342)

1 teaspoon coarse finishing salt, preferably J.Q. Dickinson's (see Resources, page 368)

½ teaspoon freshly ground black pepper

EQUIPMENT

Round 15-inch open-top fine-mesh wire grill basket

This condiment is the perfect accompaniment to a piece of grilled beef.

Prepare a hot fire in a charcoal grill (see page 96), removing the grill rack and distributing the hot coals on one side of the bottom of the grill. Place the grill rack at its normal height.

Lay the tomatoes in the grill basket in a single layer. Set the basket on the grill rack on the side opposite the coals. Grill the tomatoes, turning them occasionally, until they have lost most of their moisture but are not completely dry, about 40 minutes. Transfer the tomatoes to a cutting board and cool to room temperature.

Finely chop the tomatoes and transfer to a small container. Stir in the beef fat, finishing salt, and pepper. If not using immediately, cover and refrigerate until ready to use. Tightly covered, the condiment will keep for up to 2 days in the refrigerator. Remove from the refrigerator at least 30 minutes before serving.

PARSLEY SAUCE

MAKES ABOUT 2 CUPS

½ cup extra-virgin olive oil

¼ cup plus 2 tablespoons red wine vinegar

¼ cup very finely diced shallot

2 tablespoons minced garlic

2 tablespoons fresh lemon juice

2 teaspoons Aleppo pepper (see Resources, page 369)

2 teaspoons kosher salt

1 teaspoon freshly ground black pepper

1 cup finely chopped flat-leaf parsley

This pepper-spiked herb sauce is good on just about anything coming off the grill, particularly summer vegetables. Or use it as a dressing for a warm potato salad.

Combine the olive oil, vinegar, shallot, garlic, lemon juice, Aleppo pepper, salt, and black pepper in a container. *(The sauce can be prepared to this point up to 2 days ahead and stored, tightly covered, in the refrigerator.)*

Transfer the base to a small saucepan and warm over low heat. Stir in the parsley and serve immediately.

RESOURCES

CANNING SOURCES

Ball Corporation
freshpreserving.com/canning-101-getting-started
   .html

National Center for Home Food Preservation
nchfp.uga.edu/how/can_home.html

INGREDIENT AND EQUIPMENT SOURCES

Anson Mills
803-467-4122
info@ansonmills.com
ansonmills.com
Heritage grains, flours, Carolina Gold rice, Carolina
   Gold rice flour, beans, benne seeds, culinary lime,
   fine yellow cornmeal, Sea Island red peas

Benton's Smoky Mountain Country Hams
423-442-5003
bentonscountryhams2.com
Bacon (including scraps) and hams

Bigelow Tea
888-244-3564
bigelowtea.com
Charleston Tea Plantation American Classic Tea

Bob's Red Mill
800-349-2173
bobsredmill.com
Sorghum seeds and sorghum flour

Bourbon Barrel Foods
502-333-6103
info@bourbonbarrelfoods.com
bourbonbarrelfoods.com
Bourbon-barrel-aged Worcestershire sauce, bourbon-
   smoked paprika, bourbon-smoked black pepper,
   bourbon-smoked salt, Bluegrass soy sauce,
   bourbon vanilla sugar

Bulls Bay Saltworks
843-887-3007
bullsbaysaltworks.com
Charleston flake sea salt

Butcher & Packer Supply Co.
248-583-1250
butcher-packer.com
Corn syrup solids, dextrose, TCM, sodium
   erythorbate, Cure #2, phosphate, monosodium
   glutamate, summer sausage casings

Cajun Country Rice
800-738-7423
cajuncountryrice.com
Popcorn rice

Carolina Classics Catfish
252-746-2818
cccatfish.com
Catfish fillets

Charleston Seafood
888-609-FISH
charlestonseafood.com
Blue crab roe

Cortez Bottarga
wearebottarga.com
Mullet bottarga

Earthy Delights
855-328-8732
info@earthy.com
earthy.com
Pawpaws

Geechie Boy Mill
843-631-0077
geechieboymill.com
Jimmy Red cornmeal

The Hamery
615-893-9712
info@thehamery.com
thehamery.com
Bob Wood's country ham and ham scraps

Hammons Black Walnuts
888-429-6887
black-walnuts.com
Black walnuts

iGourmet.com
877-446-8763
cservice@igourmet.com
igourmet.com
Surig 25% vinegar and tomato vinegar

Jakes Brothers Country Meats
615-876-2911
Smoked pork sausage

J.Q. Dickinson Salt-Works
304-925-7918
info@jqdsalt.com
jqdsalt.com
Finishing salt

Keepwell Vinegar
info@keepwellvinegar.com
keepwellvinegar.com
Carolina Gold rice vinegar

Kelley's Katch Caviar
888-681-8565
americasfinest@kelleyskatch.com
kelleyskatch.com
Paddlefish caviar

Kenny's Farmhouse Cheese
888-571-4029
kristin@kennyscheese.com
kennyscheese.com
Norwood and Dry Fork Reserve cheeses

The Lee Bros. Boiled Peanuts Catalogue
843-720-8890
boiledpeanuts.com
Green peanuts and Duke's mayonnaise

Lindera Farms
703-967-1571
linderafarms@gmail.com
linderafarms.com
Vinegars (ramp, heirloom pepper, hickory, honey,
    magnolia, turmeric, and pawpaw)

Louisiana Dried Shrimp Company
504-382-0140
ldsshrimp@gmail.com
louisianadriedshrimp.com
Dried shrimp

Miyako Oriental Foods Inc.
626-962-9633
joearai@coldmountainmiso.com
coldmountainmiso.com
Cold Mountain dried rice koji

Modernist Pantry
888-578-3932
modernistpantry.com
Sheet gelatin

Muddy Pond Sorghum Mill
931-445-3509
info@muddypondsorghum.net
muddypondsorghum.com
Sorghum syrup

New England Cheese Making Supply Co.
413-397-2012
info@cheesemaking.com
cheesemaking.com
Yogurt starter culture, butter muslin

Northern Brewer
800-681-2739
brewmaster@northernbrewer.com
northernbrewer.com
Campden tablets

Oliver Farm Artisan Oils
229-406-0906
ifarmueat@hotmail.com
oliverfarm.com
Green peanut oil, benne oil, pecan oil, sunflower oil,
    okra seed oil

Rare Tea Cellar
773-661-9570
customerserv@rareteacellar.com
rareteacellar.com
Jean-Marc Montegottero calamansi vinegar

Red Clay Hot Sauce
sean@redclayhotsauce.com
redclayhotsauce.com
Red Clay Original hot sauce

Regalis Foods
718-361-8860
regalisfoods.com
Wild mushrooms

Sequatchie Cove Creamery
423-619-5867
info@sequatchiecovecheese.com
sequatchiecovecheese.com
Cumberland cheese

Southern Exposure Seed Exchange
540-894-9480
gardens@southernexposure.com
southernexposure.com
Greasy bean and Charleston Hots seeds

Sweet Grass Dairy
229-227-0752
sweetgrassdairy.com
Asher Blue cheese

Terra Spice Company
574-222-2462
info@terraspice.com
terraspice.com
Aleppo pepper, ascorbic acid, black cardamom pods,
    cayenne pepper sauce powder, fennel pollen,
    sumac, white and orange cheddar powders

WebstaurantStore
help@webstaurantstore.com
webstaurantstore.com
Foil crab tins

Weisenberger Mills
859-254-5282
sales@weisenberger.com
weisenberger.com
White cornmeal

White Lily
800-595-1380
whitelily.com
White Lily self-rising and all-purpose flours

ACKNOWLEDGMENTS

Thank you to this group of people who contributed in many ways, both large and small, to bring this book into reality.

Miles and Vanessa Adcox
Celeste Albers
Pete Ambrose
Arnold's Country Kitchen
Jessica Backhus
Brian Baxter
Bear Creek Farm
Allan Benton
Bill W.
David Black
Blackberry Farm
Adi Brock
Homer Brock
Josh Brock
Leo Brock
Renee Brock
Tyler Brown
Laura Lea Bryant
John Buck
Patty Bundy
Butter Pat Industries
Sue Chan
David Chang
Justin Cherry
Ashley Christensen
Yvonne Constancio
Katie Coss
Kristin Cunningham
Kate Davis
Chris and Ann Demant
Caitlin DeMichele
BJ Dennis
Lisa Donovan
Nathalie Dupree
John T. Edge
Peter Frank Edwards
Lolis Eric Elie
FatBack Collective
Raphael Geroni
Ed Gin
Zach Greenwald

Travis Grimes
Wes Grubbs
Amie Hartley-Leonard
Daniel Heinze
David Hughes
Husk
Jason Isbell and Amanda Shires
Michelle Ishay-Cohen
Matt Jamie
Samuel Jett
Greg Johnsman
Sibylle Kazeroid
Katy Keefe
Kudu Grills
Drew Kulsveen
Elliott Kyle
Jeremiah Langhorne
Hanh Le
Bella Lemos
Nate Leonard
Daniel Liberson
Ruthie Lindsey
Rob Looney
Ronni Lundy
Mark Marhefka
Ann and Scott Marshall
McCrady's
McCrady's Tavern
Allison McGeehon
Morgan McGlone
The Meadows
Travis Milton
Minero
Paul Mishkin
Audrey and Lewis Morgan
Angie Mosier
Missy and Tracey Mullins
Tre and Fallon Mullins
Bill Murray
Nancy Murray
Adam Musick

The Neighborhood Dining
  Group
Rory O'Connell
Chelsea O'Leary
Clay Oliver
John Christian Phifer
Nick Pihakis
Polished Pig Media
Jeff Poppen
Dennis Powell
Judy Pray
Jen Rainey
Colby Rasavong
Boo Ray
Ramona Reid
Amber Rinck
Glenn Roberts
Melany and Drew Robinson
Lia Ronnen
Ruby and Linda
Jeff Scott
Kim Severson
David Shields
Nina Simoneaux
John Sleasman
T. J. Smith
Southern Foodways Alliance
Jim Stein
Frank Stitt
Marion Sullivan
Judith Sutton
Lonny Sweet
Shawn Thackeray
Reed Turchi
The Van Winkles
Lucas Weir
Neka Wilson
Shelly Wilson
Quintin Wise
Mike Wolf
Bob Woods

INDEX

CONVERSION CHARTS

HERE ARE ROUNDED-OFF EQUIVALENTS BETWEEN THE METRIC SYSTEM AND THE TRADITIONAL SYSTEMS USED IN THE UNITED STATES TO MEASURE WEIGHT AND VOLUME.

WEIGHTS		VOLUME			OVEN TEMPERATURE			
US/UK	METRIC	AMERICAN	IMPERIAL	METRIC		°F	°C	GAS MARK
¼ oz	7 G	¼ TSP		1.25 ML	VERY COOL	250–275	130–140	½–1
½ oz	15 G	½ TSP		2.5 ML	COOL	300	148	2
1 oz	30 G	1 TSP		5 ML	WARM	325	163	3
2 oz	55 G	½ TBSP (1½ TSP)		7.5 ML	MEDIUM	350	177	4
3 oz	85 G	1 TBSP (3 TSP)		15 ML	MEDIUM HOT	375–400	190–204	5–6
4 oz	115 G	¼ CUP (4 TBSP)	2 FL OZ	60 ML	HOT	425	218	7
5 oz	140 G	⅓ CUP (5 TBSP)	2½ FL OZ	75 ML	VERY HOT	450–475	232–245	8–9
6 oz	170 G	½ CUP (8 TBSP)	4 FL OZ	125 ML				
7 oz	200 G	⅔ CUP (10 TBSP)	5 FL OZ	150 ML				
8 oz (½ LB)	225 G	¾ CUP (12 TBSP)	6 FL OZ	175 ML				
9 oz	255 G	1 CUP (16 TBSP)	8 FL OZ	250 ML				
10 oz	285 G	1¼ CUPS	10 FL OZ	300 ML				
11 oz	310 G	1½ CUPS	12 FL OZ	350 ML				
12 oz	340 G	1 PINT (2 CUPS)	16 FL OZ	500 ML				
13 oz	370 G	2½ CUPS	20 FL OZ (1 PINT)	625 ML				
14 oz	400 G	5 CUPS	40 FL OZ (1 QT)	1.25 L				
15 oz	425 G							
16 oz (1 LB)	450 G